Jewish Self-Determination
beyond Zionism

Jonathan Graubart

Jewish Self-Determination beyond Zionism

Lessons from Hannah Arendt and Other Pariahs

TEMPLE UNIVERSITY PRESS
Philadelphia • Rome • Tokyo

TEMPLE UNIVERSITY PRESS
Philadelphia, Pennsylvania 19122
tupress.temple.edu

Copyright © 2023 by Temple University—Of The Commonwealth System
 of Higher Education
All rights reserved
Published 2023

Library of Congress Cataloging-in-Publication Data

Names: Graubart, Jonathan, 1963– author.
Title: Jewish self-determination beyond Zionism : lessons from Hannah
 Arendt and other pariahs / Jonathan Graubart.
Description: Philadelphia : Temple University Press, 2023. | Includes
 bibliographical references and index. | Summary: "Seeks to develop a new
 Jewish vision of dissent by reconceiving Jewish self-determination to
 feature social justice, inclusiveness, internationalism, and
 reconciliation with Palestinians, synthesizing and adapting the ideas of
 Martin Buber and Hannah Arendt and putting them in dialogue with a range
 of contemporary Jewish and Palestinian critical perspectives"— Provided
 by publisher.
Identifiers: LCCN 2022040379 (print) | LCCN 2022040380 (ebook) | ISBN
 9781439923573 (cloth) | ISBN 9781439923580 (paperback) | ISBN
 9781439923597 (pdf)
Subjects: LCSH: Zionism—Philosophy. | Jewish nationalism—Philosophy. |
 Arab-Israeli conflict—Peace.
Classification: LCC DS149 .G646 2023 (print) | LCC DS149 (ebook) | DDC
 320.54095694—dc23/eng/20221018
LC record available at https://lccn.loc.gov/2022040379
LC ebook record available at https://lccn.loc.gov/2022040380

♾ The paper used in this publication meets the requirements of the
American National Standard for Information Sciences—Permanence
of Paper for Printed Library Materials, ANSI Z39.48-1992

Printed in the United States of America

9 8 7 6 5 4 3 2 1

Contents

	Preface and Acknowledgments	vii
	Introduction	1
1	The Need for a Reformation of Jewish Self-Determination	11
2	Bringing Humanism to Politics: Martin Buber on Zionism	23
3	Hannah Arendt's Pariah Zionist Challenge	49
4	Missing Every Opportunity for Peace and Reconciliation	74
5	Toward an Updated Critical Jewish Vision on Zionism: Engaging Humanist Zionism with Contemporary Critical Jewish Voices	96
6	Lessons from Edward Said and Ella Shohat on Reconciliation and Coexistence	122
	Conclusion: How to Further an Ambitious New Vision	147
	Notes	163
	Index	197

Preface and Acknowledgments

Within Israel and most mainstream American Jewish organizations, to declare oneself an anti-Zionist has become the supreme internal transgression, worse than conversion, intermarriage, or making common cause with the evangelical Christian right. Indeed, the preeminent American watchdog of American antisemitism, the Anti-Defamation League (ADL), gets most animated by expressions of anti-Zionism. In a major 2022 speech on the status of antisemitism in the United States, its CEO, Jonathan Greenblatt, targeted leftist anti-Zionist groups, notwithstanding that the ADL's own survey identified white supremacists and other nonleft individuals as the primary perpetrators.[1] "Let me clarify this for you as clearly as I can," he proclaimed and repeated, "antizionism *is* antisemitism."[2] Greenblatt singled out Jewish Voice for Peace (JVP) as one of three groups that "epitomize the Radical Left, the photo inverse of the Extreme Right." He vowed that the ADL would not allow JVP to use its "Judaism as a shield" from his group's wrath.

To justify his equation of anti-Zionism with white supremacy, Greenblatt characterized it as an "ideology rooted in rage," which displays a "willful denial of even a superficial history of Judaism and the vast history of the Jewish people." Yet it is the dismissive attitude of the ADL and most mainstream Jewish organizations toward anti-Zionism that betrays a superficial rendering of Judaism and Jewish politics. Up to 1948, there was a long and ideologically diverse history of both anti-Zionism and, as this book features, internal Zionist opposition to a hegemonic Jewish nation-state. In recent decades, the lion's share of critical Jewish opposition to Israeli policies and the tenets of Zionism has been on the left. Sadly, Greenblatt's effort at an ex cathedra rendering of Jewish history writes off a rich tradition of ethical dissent. Rather than abusing its Jewish identity, as Greenblatt charges, JVP is carrying out an admirable legacy of grounding its rejection of Jewish nationalist hegemony and its solidarity with Palestinians in Jewish values and history. Since my young adulthood in the late 1980s, I have been part of this legacy, including being a cofounder of JVP's San Diego chapter in 2013.

Yet unlike some of my fellow Jewish dissenters, I am unwilling to reject all aspects of Zionism. To the annoyance of several JVP colleagues, I was one of a small minority of members who voted no on the group's referendum to declare itself anti-Zionist. Much as I respect the anti-Zionist perspective and recoil at equations of it with antisemitism, I do not want to lose sight of the complex legacy of Zionism. Granted, the dominant Zionist wing demanded Jewish supremacy in Palestine and carried out policies that displaced and subordinated the indigenous Palestinian Arab population. Moreover, contemporary Zionism has become equated with support for a hegemonic Jewish nation-state over at least most of the territory constituting Israel-Palestine. Nevertheless, the umbrella ideology of Zionism historically attracted many Jews who had no thought of Jewish supremacy or conquest but were excited about building a new Jewish community. Some, such as a young Noam Chomsky, hoped for a new type of egalitarian socialist community that would be part of a global transformation. Indeed, there was a small but influential pre-1948 Zionist movement that expressly opposed the hegemonic aims of the mainstream and campaigned for a just and egalitarian coexistence with Palestinians. The hegemonic Zionists prevailed, but the spirit of an alternative self-determination continues to inspire Jewish dissenters to the present. Perhaps a new term will have to be coined given the negative baggage Zionism has accumulated. But even if such a term gains momentum, it will be important to link this new vision to a venerable political legacy.

This book marks my effort to advance an ethical vision of Jewish self-determination in a way that reckons with the grave injustices inflicted by Zionist politics for more than a century. I have contemplated this theme ever since I first joined the ranks of Jewish dissenters on Israel-Palestine in response to the first intifada in the late 1980s. Over the next decade, three towering Jewish dissenters most shaped my evolving ethical vision. The first was Noam Chomsky. While still a mainstream American Zionist in college, I knew of him only as a "self-hating" Jew who, for all his brilliance, had become a vicious critic of Israel. As my views shifted, I moved to the dark side and scoured used book stores in the San Francisco Bay Area for Chomsky books. His *Fateful Triangle*, published shortly after Israel's 1982 invasion of Lebanon, opened my eyes not just to the brutality of that war but also to a long record of Israeli aggression and intransigency, to the imperialist nature of the U.S.-Israeli relationship, and to the normative complicity of leading American Jewish pundits and intellectuals. I was more moved, however, by his earlier *Peace in the Middle East?*, which offered personal reflections on his youthful hopes for Zionism and ideas for reviving the emancipatory socialist binational dimensions of Zionism in the post-1967 era. Having been alerted to this alternative antihegemonic binational Zionist history, I found an edited collection of letters and short essays by the American rabbi Judah Magnes, who moved to Palestine, cofounded Hebrew University, and tirelessly advocated for a binational, egalitarian framework.[3] I cheered on his valiant efforts to prevent an all-out clash with Palestinians and grieved for his ultimate failure to prevent the 1948 war or enable the return of the hundreds of thousands of displaced Palestinians.

The last of my seminal Jewish influences was Hannah Arendt. I happened to find an old copy of *Eichmann in Jerusalem* on a family bookshelf containing an assortment of books my father had purchased decades ago. The book contains a number of fascinating and provocative insights, but what most impressed me was Arendt's demolition of the official Zionist rendering of Eichmann's trial. While Israel's iconic prime minister David Ben-Gurion—whom Arendt dubbed the "stage master" directing the prosecutor's case—celebrated the trial as proof that only a Jewish state could bring justice for Jewish victims, she lamented that such a propagandistic narrative impeded the search for either understanding how the Holocaust could happen or developing an effective system of global justice to deal with future crimes against humanity. I was subsequently excited to learn that Arendt had been both a brilliant critic of the pathologies of mainstream Zionism and a visionary advocate for a type of Zionism that broke from the nation-state model and introduced a new federalist system of coexistence between distinct national groups. Hence, when I embarked on this research project in 2016, I began by devouring her series of essays from the 1940s on Zionism. Above all others, I am most indebted normatively and intellectually to Arendt's interjections. As I ritualistically inform my students when assigning one of her works, she is the nonfamily figure with whom I would most want to meet in a séance. Admittedly, I would be very nervous to learn what the spectral Arendt would think of this project.

In thinking about acknowledgments, I was tempted to follow the lead of Rita Moreno, who in 1962 decided she would not thank anyone if she were to win the Oscar for her role as Anita in *West Side Story*. But as Moreno later regretted this stance, I changed my mind. To be sure, there is no one, outside of reviewers and editors for Temple University Press, who has read through the entire manuscript. But I have had a few colleagues and former students review specific chapters or offer much-needed encouragement. Of my colleagues in the San Diego State University (SDSU) Political Science Department, I am especially grateful to two of my closest lifetime friends, Latha Varadarajan and Farid Abdel-Nour. Although I am formally Latha's senior colleague by a few years, she served as my mentor for learning how to break from the conventional mode of international relations professor and integrate radical political engagement and broader intellectual concerns into my teaching and research. Over the years, we have been close allies in challenging liberal internationalist pieties and the increasing corporatization and commodification of education at SDSU and other universities. She also serves as my closest friend and confidante when I want to kvetch about faculty and administrators at SDSU. Although neither Israel-Palestine nor Jewish ethics count among her intellectual or normative passions, she has generously indulged my interests. In our regular Saturday-morning walks, she greets me with "Shabbat shalom," which I believe are her only two Hebrew words (to be fair, her language skills overall well exceed mine). After I received a round of early rejections from publishers and indulged in a bout of despair, Latha assured me that my project would find a well-respected press and, as is her wont, insisted that I treat her to a fancy meal when her prediction came true.

Farid is my one close friend who shares both my intellectual and political passions in Israel-Palestine and in questions of Jewish and Palestinian identity. He is a kindred spirit who holds a broadly similar perspective through his close engagement of the Palestinian historical experience. Farid has been my most valuable guide for clarifying and sharpening my arguments in this book. More generally, he has inspired me over the years to step back from heated debate and foster a focused discussion on the normative and empirical issues at stake with regard to Israel-Palestine. Although we have attended a number of political rallies on the subject, our most productive collaboration has been organizing a series of teach-ins during periods of heightened aggression. Of equal importance is Farid's friendship and enthusiastic support for both this project and past scholarly projects.

Of my former students, Stav Geffner ranks as my most valued interlocutor despite being my junior by three decades. As a Jewish Israeli American, she too has had to struggle with conflicting sentiments toward Israel and Zionism. Indicative of her creativity and astute intellectual judgment, Stav persuaded me to devote my 2016 peace studies lecture series to the topic of Jewish dissenters in Israel, where I brought in Amira Hass, Peter Beinart, Lia Tarachansky, Avnery Gvaryahu, and Yuval Evri. I am also grateful to Stephanie Banh, Rachel Beck, Osama Alkhawaja, and Mustafa Alemi for their comments.

The latter three were active in the SDSU chapter of Students for Justice in Palestine and very interested in learning of alternative Jewish perspectives.

Finally, I wish to thank my close friend Adam Aron, whom I met through the San Diego JVP chapter and who later inspired me to extend my passions to the urgent cause of combating the climate crisis, and my brother, Rabbi Philip Graubart, who courageously invited me to discuss my project in his mainstream Conservative synagogue, Beth El in San Diego, notwithstanding multiple objections from members of his shul to my critical stance on Zionism.

Jewish Self-Determination
beyond Zionism

Introduction

> The romantic Zionist ideal, to which Jewish liberals—and I was one, once—subscribed for so many decades, has been tarnished by the reality of modern Israel. The attacks on freedom of speech and human rights organizations in Israel, the land-grabbing settler movement, a growing strain of anti-Arab and anti-immigrant racism, extremist politics, and a powerful, intolerant religious right—this mixture has pushed liberal Zionism to the brink.
>
> —Antony Lerman, "The End of Liberal Zionism: Israel's Move to the Right Challenges Diaspora Jews"[1]

In December 2018, Israel's prime minister, Benjamin Netanyahu, welcomed Italy's interior minister and leader of the far-right nationalist League Party, Matteo Salvini, as a "great friend of Israel."[2] Netanyahu and other top Israeli politicians have courted other troubling political figures, such as former U.S. president Trump, Hungary's prime minister Viktor Orbán, and other leaders of anti-immigrant and antisemitic parties in central and eastern Europe.[3] At home, Israel pursues its own extremist nationalism. On the eve of the 2015 elections, Netanyahu warned that "Arab voters are coming out in droves."[4] The most dramatic display of this defiant nationalist stance is the Knesset's enactment in 2018 of the Jewish nation-state law as a basic law—the equivalent of a constitutional amendment—that declares "the right to exercise national self-determination" in Israel as "unique to the Jewish people." The Knesset's action prompted the human rights group B'Tselem to conduct an overall analysis of Israel. It found Israel to be an "apartheid regime" that "uses laws, practices, and organized violence to cement the supremacy of one group over another."[5] The recently departed Israeli historian of fascism Zeev Sternhell offered a similarly bleak assessment:

> We are at the height of an erosion process of the liberal values in which our society is based. Those who regard liberal values as a danger to the nation, the homeland and the Jewish state are the ones currently in

power. They are striving to delegitimize the left and anyone who does not hold the view that conquering the land and settling it through the use of force are the fundamental foundations of Zion.[6]

Sternhell's anguish reflects a common liberal Zionist perception that Israel's intolerant nationalism of recent years marks a sharp departure from Zionism's liberal foundation. Most liberal Zionist critics continue to take pride in Israel's establishment and to support a Jewish nation-state. For them, Zionism's moral decline took root only in the post-1967 era, particularly with the rise to power in the late 1970s of Israel's hard-line Likud Party, which greatly expanded the state's settlements and colonization of the occupied territories. Only then, so the argument goes, did Israel transition from being a genuine (if flawed) liberal democracy to an occupier of another people increasingly prone to illiberal impulses. Regrettably, add American liberal Zionist critics, the American Jewish establishment has enabled this descent through its continued defense of Israeli policies. Accordingly, liberal Zionists target Israel's occupation as the root injustice to be extirpated. They call for a two-state resolution, whereby Israel retains an overwhelming Jewish majority while the new state of Palestine satisfies Palestinian self-determination aspirations. Under this solution, they hope that Israel will once again harmonize its Jewish and liberal democratic ideals.

Jewish anti-Zionists, by contrast, renounce the entire Zionist historical project as settler-colonial in which European Jewish settlers, backed by the dominant global powers, wrested control of Palestine and displaced the bulk of the indigenous population. They regard the post-1967 occupation as a continuation of settler colonialism. Rather than seek a transformed version, Jewish anti-Zionists, such as the U.S.-based Jewish Voice for Peace, "unequivocally oppose Zionism because it is counter to" the ideals of equality and freedom.[7] Many also condemn Zionism's moral degradation of the Jewish people. For example, the theologian Mark Ellis characterizes the prevailing nature of U.S. Judaism as a "Constantinian Judaism" devoted to defense of the Israeli state.[8] The anti-Zionist path forward is a democratic single state and full implementation of the right to return for Palestinian refugees and their descendants.

This book identifies much of value in both the liberal Zionist and Jewish anti-Zionist perspectives but finds neither satisfying for diagnosing the evolution of the Zionist project, advancing an alternative vision of Jewish self-determination, or prescribing a program of reckoning and reconciliation. At heart, each is hobbled by the post-1948 constriction in Zionist discourse. Prior to Israel's establishment, the spectrum of Zionist positions extended to those who supported Jewish self-determination but opposed a hegemonic Jewish state.

Subsequently, commitment to a Jewish nation-state and belief that Israel's establishment outweighed the moral costs of the Nakba—the permanent displacement of most Palestinians—have become litmus tests. Thus, liberal Zionists rarely challenge the major decisions taken by Israel's founders and often perform moral gymnastics to distinguish the Nakba from Israel's post-1967 depredations. Similarly, they remain committed to retaining Israel's identity as a Jewish state, stress the demographic separation of Jews and Arabs into two states, and oppose any large-scale return of descendants of Palestinian refugees to Israel. By taking these positions, liberal Zionists avoid coming to terms with the moral tensions between the values of a Jewish state and those of a liberal democratic one. Conversely, because of their opposition to a Jewish nation-state and repudiation of the Nakba, Jewish anti-Zionists typically deny any appealing values and institutions in Zionism, past or present. To avoid giving legitimacy to Zionism, most refrain from positing an alternative program of Jewish self-determination in the territory consisting of Israel-Palestine.

Encouragingly, two formerly conventional liberal Zionists, Peter Beinart and Omri Boehm, have recently come out in favor of a non-statist variant of Zionism.[9] Both endorse a binational single state that encompasses autonomous cultural and political institutions for Jews and Arabs within a unified state. This binational arrangement, they argue, preserves what had prior to the late 1930s been the goal of the leading Zionist figures, including David Ben-Gurion: "A thriving Jewish community with the autonomy to run its own affairs."[10] By recovering and adapting the purportedly original intent of the Zionist founders, conclude Beinart and Boehm, a new and just vison can take shape.

Beinart and Boehm's interjections are much welcome for decoupling Zionism from a hegemonic Jewish state. This book, too, advances a non-statist vision of Jewish self-determination to be realized in a binational political arrangement. Where we primarily differ is in our interpretation of Zionism's foundations. As elaborated in subsequent chapters, even if Ben-Gurion and other Zionist leaders did not originally propose an avowedly Jewish nation-state, their end goal was Jewish domination of Palestine, including an overwhelming Jewish majority. Thus, Palestine's Arabs were slated to be a drastically reduced minority who would enjoy collective rights once they conceded the inevitability of the Zionist project. I thus posit the need for a far-reaching reckoning of Zionism's foundations. Only then will it be possible to assess what went wrong with the Zionist project and achieve a just reconciliation.

This book incorporates a non-statist vision of Jewish self-determination within a critical framework that scrutinizes the foundational shortcomings of the Zionist project and features a just and collaborative coexistence of Israeli Jews and Palestinian Arabs. For guidance, I retrieve the ideas of the first significant dissenting Zionist movement on the left. From the outset of the British Mandate, these dissenters welcomed the fostering of a revived Jewish community in Palestine but energetically opposed the separatist and hegemonic policies of the pre-state Zionist leadership. They implored the Zionist community to take concrete steps to bring about a just and collaborative coexistence. Because their leading intellectual mentor was Martin Buber, who articulated a "Hebrew humanism," I identify this dissenting framework as *Humanist Zionism*. This book engages the Humanist Zionist vision with a range of post-1967 critical Jewish perspectives, as well as that of Edward Said, to provide an updated critical Jewish vision attuned to contemporary dynamics. Inspired by both Humanist Zionists and Jewish anti-Zionists, this book's vision confronts the Zionist movement's foundational sins and demands a full reckoning with the Palestinians. Unlike most anti-Zionists, however, I aim to recover the appealing social justice and spiritual dynamics that inspired many Jews to emigrate to Palestine in the pre-state years. Like liberal Zionism, this book's vision welcomes Jewish attachment to Israel-Palestine, but it rejects hegemonic nationalism and accords Palestinians an equal claim to the same territory. Similar to Beinart and Boehm, I regard an updated binational program as the best path forward.

Since the turn of the century, which saw the outbreak of the second intifada and the onset of a virtually uninterrupted grim situation, there has been a marked renewal of interest in the pre-state dissenting Zionists.[11] Jacqueline Rose explains the cause of the surge. One is "struck," she observes, "with an overwhelming sense of a moment missed, of voices silenced.... Today we are all still suffering the loss of their critical, insightful vision."[12] This book enlists these silenced voices as a foundation for a contemporary dissenting Jewish perspective, which challenges the fundamental premises of Zionism and reconceives Jewish self-determination to require a just and interactive coexistence among Jews and Palestinians.

The Enduring Value of Humanist Zionism as Advanced by Martin Buber and Hannah Arendt

The dissenting Humanist Zionist movement emerged at the Twelfth Zionist Congress in 1921, shortly after the establishment of the Jewish Yishuv in British-Mandate Palestine.[13] Its main institutional voices were Brit Shalom in the 1920s–1930s and Ihud in the 1940s.[14] The Humanist Zionists looked to Palestine as a base for invigorating Jewish life globally, reviving Hebrew as a spoken language, and developing community institutions and practices informed by the best of Jewish and outside values and traditions. In contrast to the mainstream Zionist movement, which preferred to negotiate with Great Britain and other outside powers, the Humanist Zionists were anti-imperialist and urged an accommodation with the indigenous Arabs. They opposed a hegemonic Jewish state because it would displace Palestinians and elevate realpolitik and state interests over Jewish renewal and social justice. Their alternative was a binational political arrangement, which featured autonomous development for each community, collective equality, and shared spaces of governance and community interactions.[15]

Although never having a large following, the Humanist Zionists attracted much attention and exerted considerable influence by virtue of the attractiveness of their political program and the prominence of their members. They made up the only Zionist movement that prioritized outreach to the Palestinian Arabs, decried the leadership's insensitivity to the impact of its policies on Palestinians, and outlined a program for just coexistence and extensive interaction rather than separate development.[16] Their supporters included Gershom Scholem, the preeminent authority on Jewish mysticism; Henrietta Szold, the founder of the Hadassah Women's Zionist Organization of America; and, from a distance, Albert Einstein. The two most resolute advocates were Judah Magnes and Martin Buber. Magnes was a charismatic rabbi, community leader, and social justice activist in the American Jewish community who moved to Palestine and became the first chancellor of Hebrew University.[17] He maintained close connections with leading U.S. Jewish philanthropists and enjoyed easy access to U.S. and British diplomats. Buber was a renowned German scholar of Judaism whose range extended to comparative theology, philosophy, psychology, education, and political theory.[18] To the frustration of David Ben-Gurion and the rest of the Zionist leadership, Ihud's binational proposals attracted considerable international interest, including from the 1946 Anglo-American Committee of Inquiry task force. The latter praised Ihud and agreed that partitioning Palestine into separate states "would result in civil strife such as might threaten the peace of the world."[19]

Regrettably, the Humanist Zionist program lost out politically, and the Jewish nation-state of Israel was established with the UN's approval. It may be tempting to follow Israeli historian Benny Morris's lead and dismiss the pre-state dissenting Zionists as utopians with only modest support among Jews and very little from Palestinians.[20] But such an attitude fixates on the fate of the pre-state binational proposals and misses the cogency and depth of the underlying Humanist Zionist vision. Whatever the political feasibility in the 1940s of the binational program, the Humanist Zionists were remarkably prescient on the enduring moral costs of forging a Jewish nation-state over the fervent objections of the indigenous Palestinians. A more judicious Benny Morris might have acknowledged that the UN's approval in 1947 of partition was not a practical plan for attaining a peaceful resolution, much less a just one. Indeed, the partition resolution triggered war and the ensuing permanent displacement of the vast majority of the Palestinians. The Jewish people gained a state, but as Hannah Arendt later lamented, this "solution" "merely produced a new category of refugees, the Arabs."[21] Moreover, as also anticipated by the Humanist Zionists, the Jewish state became both militarist and committed to diminishing the Palestinian footprint, both of which have compromised liberal democratic principles and enabled perpetual conflict, regional isolation, and a dependence on outside powers.

To capture the heart of Humanist Zionism, I focus on its two most insightful thinkers, Martin Buber and Hannah Arendt. Buber was the movement's leading intellectual voice and lived in Palestine/Israel from 1938 to his death in 1965.[22] He articulated a vision of Hebrew humanism, grounded in a set of Jewish and universal ethics, which emphasized Jewish renewal, justice, and an interactive coexistence with Palestinians.[23] He welcomed the movement of Jews to Palestine as fulfilling a covenant with God to settle in the land of ancient Israel in pursuit of Hebrew humanism. Importantly, Buber decried the priority that mainstream Zionists gave to a Jewish nation-state because it "regard[ed] Israel as a nation like unto other nations and recognize[d] no task for Israel save that of preserving and asserting itself."[24] He saw this fixation as undermining the desired end goal of Zionism.

Buber identified a just accommodation with the Palestinians as integral to Hebrew humanism. "A regenerated Jewish people in Palestine," he affirmed, "has not only to aim at living peacefully together with the Arab people, but also at a comprehensive cooperation with it in opening and developing the country."[25] He appreciated the difficulties of this task and acknowledged that tension could not be avoided altogether. As the recent arrivals, the Jews were obligated to take the initiative by getting to know the Palestinians—their culture, religion, historical experiences, political goals, and, above all, attachment to the land—and adjust accordingly. Buber implored the Jewish community to distinguish between what was necessary for self-determination and rehabilitation and what amounted to a will to dominate. The latter, he warned, transformed manageable tension into a zero-sum political conflict.[26] Throughout his life, Buber demanded that the Jewish community in pre-1948 Palestine and post-1948 Israel reckon with the harms it inflicted on the Palestinian community, including the Nakba. He offered a framework for redress and reconciliation based on equality, empathy, and mutual respect.

Unlike Buber, Arendt was only briefly active in Zionist politics—starting in the early 1940s and ending shortly after Israel's establishment—and never showed interest in moving to Palestine-Israel. Instead, she pioneered the role of the critical diaspora Jewish Zionist, who brought important new dimensions to Humanist Zionism. Her commentary on Zionism has attracted more academic and popular interest than those of all other Humanist Zionists, including Buber.[27] Most feature her trenchant critiques of Zionism. Meanwhile, since writing *Eichmann in Jerusalem* in the early 1960s, Arendt has been a persona non grata for mainstream Zionists.[28] Yet she never became anti-Zionist. She took pride in Palestine's pre-state Yishuv for developing a new Jewish cultural center and socially just institutions, such as the kibbutzim. Arendt saw the potential of Zionism to advance Jewish emancipation and contribute to global struggles for a more egalitarian, democratic, and peaceful world. To fulfill this promise, Zionists would need to reject a nation-state and collaborate with Palestine's Arabs on an alternative program.

Arendt's greatest contributions to Humanist Zionism are summoning a sophisticated historical context for the European Jewish experience, assessing the dangers of statist nationalism and imperialism, articulating a federalist alternative to nation-states, and diagnosing root pathologies in mainstream Zionism. She linked the onset of Zionism to the evolution in Europe of nationalism, the nation-state system, imperialism, modern antisemitism, and internal political and social dynamics in Europe's Jewish communities. Although Arendt credited Zionists for giving Jews agency, she diagnosed the prevailing wing as suffering from two underlying maladies. First, it subscribed to a belief in an eternal antisemitism unaffected by broader historical developments or the choices made by Jewish communities.[29] Consequently, mainstream Zionists regarded all outsiders as suspect and adopted a persecution complex. What followed was the second malady of a "tribal" nationalism, which rejects collaboration with the outside world as futile given unrelenting antisemitism.

This book synthesizes the collective insights of Buber and Arendt into a composite Humanist Zionism and engages them with a range of post-1967 Jewish dissenters and with Edward Said to advance a transformed critical Jewish vision attuned to contemporary realities. On the one hand, this new vision sharply diagnoses mainstream Zionism's foundational shortcomings, which continue to afflict both Israeli society and mainstream Zionist organizations in the United States and elsewhere. These shortcomings include a creed that assumes an eternal antisemitism and an insular nationalism perpetually suspicious of the outside. On the other hand, this book's vision advances a distinct Jewish self-determination committed to cultural enrichment and emancipation, internationalism, and the fostering of new political, social, and economic channels for attaining genuine reconciliation between Israelis and Palestinians.

Plan for the Book

The next chapter elaborates on the urgency of breaking from Zionism as currently understood and developing a Jewish-based critical perspective, which includes a transformed vision of Jewish self-determination oriented toward a just coexistence with Palestinians. It begins by reviewing the grim status of actually existing Zionism, as reflected in Israeli society and in mainstream American Jewish organizations. The chapter then assesses the recent efforts by Beinart and Boehm to confront the status quo by advancing a new Jewish critical framework aimed at rescuing liberal Zionism and bringing about a just resolution. Each, I argue, integrates a sharp critique of actually existing Zionism and the reigning peace orthodoxy with an innovative and compelling alternative set of ideas. Yet the chapter identifies a major shortcoming in that each embraces the supposed original ideals of Zionism. Relying on a recent study by Dmitry Shumsky of leading Zionist pioneers, Beinart and Boehm claim that their new anti-statist, binational Zionism revives Zionism's foundational ideas prior to the late 1930s.[30] Although this claim is rhetorically seductive, I show that they read too much into Shumsky's findings and gloss over the decidedly hegemonic and anti-Palestinian dimensions of the prevailing Zionist project from its outset. The chapter argues, by contrast, that any worthwhile reconceptualization of Jewish self-determination needs to confront and repudiate the foundational program. Accordingly, I close by making the case for recovering the voices of the original anti-statist Zionist dissenters, the Humanist Zionists.

The next three chapters bring out the richness and continued value of the Humanist Zionist synthesis of Buber and Arendt in anchoring a comprehensive critical Jewish perspective. Chapter 2 features Buber's evolving approach toward Zionism. It begins by situating his ideas within the broader challenge that Brit Shalom and later Ihud launched against the Zionist mainstream from the early 1920s to 1948. The chapter then reviews Buber's efforts between 1949 and 1965 to adapt his vision to the new reality of a Jewish nation-state. I establish three enduring aspects to Buber's Zionism. First, contrary to the charges leveled by some critics of romantic idealism and naivete, he consistently grounded his vision in a nuanced political assessment of what was attainable in the historical setting at hand. Second, Buber offered a compelling alternative Zionism. Finally, he provided an empirically informed guide for advancing Jewish-Palestinian reconciliation.

Chapter 3 turns to the iconoclastic outsider Hannah Arendt. It first identifies central themes from Arendt's examination of the modern European Jewish experience, drawing from *The Origins of Totalitarianism*, whose preparation partially overlapped with her Zionist essays. I focus on her critique of the destructive forces unleashed by nationalism and imperialism, for which the Jewish question became central, and of the dysfunctions within Europe's Jewish communities. The chapter next situates Arendt's approach toward Zionism within the lessons she derived from the European experience. While she saw the potential of Zionism to inaugurate an emancipatory and globally engaged Jewish politics, she feared that the prevailing Zionist politics retained an insularity wedded to traditional great-power politics, which would bring disaster to Jews and Arabs. I then review how Arendt modified her Zionism following Israel's establishment. She remained highly critical of Israel's insular nationalism but accepted the new reality of Israel as a state closely attached to the Jewish people. Crucially, she continued to attach the long-term health of Israel and the Jewish people to a more just and cohesive global order rather than to a powerful Jewish state.

Chapter 4 follows up on the warnings of Arendt and other Humanist Zionists of the long-term costs of founding a Jewish state based on military conquest and ethnic predominance. It examines three pivotal historical periods. The first is Israel's initial decade, in which it institutionalized a hegemonic Jewish nationalism and a hard-line stance toward Palestinians and its neighboring states. The second is the dozen years following the 1967 war, which saw the crystallization of Israel's occupation, of a two-state global consensus—rejected by Israel—and of the U.S.-Israeli special relationship. The third is the decade from 1991 through 2001. It began with tantalizing prospects for Israeli-Palestinian peace and ended in the second intifada and the harsh Israeli crackdown. Collectively, the chapter demonstrates the enduring cogency of Humanist Zionism in diagnosing what to expect of a state wedded to both insular nationalism and a belief in the eternal hostility of outsiders, especially its most immediate adversaries. In each era, Israeli leaders failed to take advantage of promising opportunities to either mitigate conflict with Palestinians and neighboring Arab states or minimize injustices inflicted on Palestinians living in both Israel and the occupied territories.

Chapter 5 engages Humanist Zionism with a range of post-1967 critical Jewish perspectives. These include the initial reflections from Noam Chomsky and Uri Avnery and more recent interventions from leading liberal Zionist and anti-Zionist Jewish dissenters. The chapter's primary aim is to mine insights from contemporary critical approaches to develop a new critical Jewish vision anchored in the Humanist Zionist framework but free of its gaps and shortcomings and attuned to post-1967 developments.

Chapter 6 addresses a major shortcoming of Buber and Arendt. Both slighted or disparaged the experiences of Palestinians and Middle East–origin Jews, the Mizrahim. Although Buber and, to a lesser extent, Arendt sought much greater outreach and sensitivity to Palestinians, the partnership they advanced came with a whiff of condescension and paternalism. Neither identified affirmative contributions of Palestinians other than Buber's praise for their connections to the land. All the more disappointing was their neglect of the experiences of the Jews who had lived for centuries in majority-Arab communities across the greater Middle East. To redress the Eurocentrism of Buber and Arendt, I summon the respective pioneers of critical Palestinian and critical Mizrahi scholarship, Edward Said and Ella Shohat. Like the Humanist Zionists, Said and Shohat have decried conventional nationalism, articulated a non-nationalist self-determination, challenged internal orthodoxies, and advocated for a binational shared future. Yet each brings in a very different orientation by emphasizing the harms inflicted on Zionism's victims and the ways this subjugation has shaped the collective perceptions and identities of Jews and Palestinians. Reading Said and Shohat together with Buber and Arendt allows me to further refine a transformed critical Jewish vision and develop a program of reconciliation attentive to the intersecting experiences of European-origin Jews, Palestinians, and Mizrahim.

The final chapter addresses how to advance the book's long-term goals. It features a close engagement of the two most polarizing issues among the Jewish left as well as Palestinians and the broader left. One is whether it is necessary to categorically renounce Zionism in order to develop a just vision of coexistence. The second is whether, as demanded not only by anti-Zionists but also by a new crop of reconstructed liberal Zionists such as Peter Beinart and Ian Lustick, to abandon all two-state advocacy. On the first issue, I call for a middle ground that neither renounces Zionism nor retains it as part of a shorthand label for this book's vision. On the second issue, I propose a creative and pragmatic advocacy that links the global consensus version of a two-state resolution to a more ambitious and comprehensive binational arrangement for all of Israel-Palestine. Such a program would repudiate the emaciated two-state version that emerged in U.S.-led talks following the 1993 Oslo accord and update the antiestablishment two-state program introduced by Jewish peace activists in the late 1960s and 1970s, which aimed to resist Israel's occupation and subjugation of Palestinian, strengthen Jewish dissent, and foster Jewish-Palestinian solidarity. The end goal is not detached nation-states but an egalitarian and integrated binational polity across Israel-Palestine.

1

The Need for a Reformation of Jewish Self-Determination

Partisans of an assertive Zionist nationalism can take comfort that Israel is a military juggernaut in the region, economically prosperous with a thriving high-tech industry, and home to a rich and diverse Jewish culture. It has even improved its official standing in the region by attaining, with the implicit acquiescence of Saudi Arabia, full diplomatic relations with the United Arab Emirates and Bahrain in 2020. For those subscribing to a very different vision, however, Buber's rejoinder in 1949 still applies: "We have full independence, a state and all that appertains to it, but where is the nation in that state? And where is the nation's spirit."[1] Judged in terms of the moral values Buber espoused—to be reviewed next chapter—the Zionist project has reached a new low. Israeli society is entrenched in a culture of belligerency and chauvinism, which is both incapable of terminating its extensive domination of Palestinians and resistant to domestic dissent and global appeals to human rights and humanitarianism. Fortunately, the grave crisis has also sparked a new wave of dissent in Jewish communities along with a greater openness to challenging once-sacred tenets of Zionism. If such Jewish dissent were to gain sufficient numbers and cohesion—which, for now, is still a long way off—it could enable a fundamental break with the status quo. The time is thus ripe for developing alternative, Jewish-informed critical perspectives.

To show the urgency of breaking from the status quo, this chapter begins with a review of the crisis afflicting Israeli society and the leading U.S. Jewish organizations. It then assesses the ambitious efforts of Peter Beinart and Omri Boehm to develop a new critical Jewish approach. Both deserve much credit for reviving a non-statist form of Jewish self-determination and for breaking from the prevailing liberal-Zionist-supported orthodoxy on how to resolve the conflict. The problem lies in their reclaiming of the supposed original ideals of the Zionist founders. In so doing, they obscure the long-standing hegemonic and disruptive roots of the prevailing Zionist project. It is thus imperative to confront the founders, not embrace them. To appreciate the foundational failings of Zionism and reconceive of Jewish self-determination, there is no better starting point than that of the original pre-state Zionist dissenters.

The Gloomy State of Actually Existing Zionism

Israel's moral stain is most evident in its doubling down on its colonization of the occupied territories and accompanying subjugation. Since the beginning of Benjamin Netanyahu's second tenure as prime minister in 2009, Israel has virtually dropped all pretense of treating East Jerusalem, the West Bank, and the Gaza Strip as territories under temporary occupation. Rather, as B'Tselem, Human Rights Watch, and Amnesty International have documented, Israel's control of the occupied territories is not self-contained but embedded within a broader policy of maintaining Jewish domination across all of the land comprising the original Palestinian Mandate.[2] Because this policy is combined with systematic oppression and inhumane acts in the occupied territories, Human Rights Watch and Amnesty International have both concluded that Israel perpetrates apartheid and persecution, both of which are crimes against humanity.[3] Israel has so far refrained from formal annexation. Instead, it asserts various degrees of control, ranging from complete sovereignty to indirect control and isolation of the Palestinian population. Israel's major means of control are the fragmentation of the Palestinian population (through restrictions on their mobility and residency), the expansion of settlements and accompanying infrastructure, the establishment of militarized buffer zones, the maintenance of an elaborate legal and administrative structure that embeds the settlements within Israel's system of governance and relegates Palestinians to military rule, the systematic denial of permits for new Palestinian housing or economic activity, and the disproportionate suppression of civil disobedience and resistance.

Of all the occupied territories, Israel has been most resolute from the outset in asserting de facto complete sovereignty over East Jerusalem. In June 1967 it attached East Jerusalem and twenty-eight surrounding villages to the municipality of Jerusalem.[4] In so doing, Israel laid the legal foundation for extending its domestic law throughout while maintaining distinct legal regimes for Jews and most Palestinians. What has changed in recent years is an acceleration of efforts to Judaize the area. Israel's separation barrier cuts through East

Jerusalem, separating thousands of Palestinians from the rest of the city.[5] From 2009 through 2020, Israel demolished nearly fifteen hundred Palestinian structures, which displaced over twenty-five hundred individuals.[6] A private settlement organization and the Jewish National Fund have recently secured eviction orders against dozens of Palestinian families in East Jerusalem neighborhoods on the basis that their homes belonged to Jewish families prior to 1948.[7] Following a protest over planned evictions in the Sheikh Jarrah neighborhood in May 2021, Israel locked down the area to prevent the entry of Palestinians from the outside but gave free access to right-wing Jewish activists.[8] This convergence of events triggered the eleven-day Israeli offensive.

In the West Bank, Israel has collapsed the distinction between the territory and Israel proper for all Jewish residents while aggravating the fragmentation of the Palestinian population. It asserts complete sovereignty over Area C, which comprises 60 percent of the West Bank, and has an extensive system of civilian settlements on land confiscated from Palestinians, housing over four hundred thousand Jews.[9] While Israel provides a range of subsidies and tax breaks for Jews relocating to Area C, it rejects almost all Palestinian applications for building permits and has demolished over five hundred structures, leaving more than six thousand Palestinians displaced.[10] Throughout the West Bank, Palestinians confront nearly six hundred road blocks and checkpoints, as well as a separation barrier that cuts off many Palestinians from their farmland and from each other.

Palestinians face the direst circumstances in the Gaza Strip. Although Israel removed its settlements and military bases in 2005, it retains control over the area's air, land, territorial waters, and critical infrastructure, including electricity. It also enforces a no-entry buffer zone on the Gaza side of the border. Israel's domination features de-development and isolation. It bans Gazans from traveling to the West Bank or elsewhere and severely restricts the import and export of any goods deemed to have what the state defines as "dual use" potential, meaning of military value.[11] Resistance is brutally suppressed. Israeli Defense Force (IDF) soldiers regularly shoot Gazans who approach the buffer zone, and in response to mostly nonviolent protests near the border fences in 2018 and 2019, they shot at "unarmed protesters, children and disabled persons, and at health workers and journalists performing their duties, knowing who they [we]re."[12] Israel's deadliest actions have been major offensives in 2008–2009, 2012, 2014, and 2021, which have killed over two thousand civilians and destroyed thousands of homes, several hospitals, and Gaza's only power plant.[13]

Although Israel maintains significant liberal democratic features within its globally recognized boundaries and recognizes most Palestinian residents as citizens, it practices de jure and de facto discrimination in such matters as resources provided, policing and criminal justice, access to land and housing, and cultural rights and recognition. Since 2004, the state has accelerated its drive to increase the Jewish character of Israel proper, especially in the Galilee and Negev. It launched a major subsidy and infrastructure program to stimulate Jewish settlement, and in 2011 it enacted a law to facilitate Jewish-only areas by permitting local admission committees to reject residency to those "not suitable for the social life of the community."[14] To make more land available in the Negev for Jewish settlement, the state demolished more than ten thousand Bedouin structures between 2013 and 2019.[15] More generally, the Knesset has since 2003 enacted and renewed temporary legislation that bars the granting of citizenship or long-term legal status to Palestinians from the occupied territories who marry Israeli citizens or permanent residents. In justifying the 2005 renewal, then–finance minister Netanyahu stated, "Instead of making it easier for Palestinians who want to get citizenship, we should make the process much more difficult."[16] Because of internal political feuding between Netanyahu and the new governing coalition that took power in 2021, the Knesset failed at first to gain the requisite votes to renew this legislation. The various right-wing parties, however, renewed it in 2022 and added a section that declares the law's aim to be protecting the country's Jewish majority.[17]

Most disturbing, and what fuels all the recent actions discussed earlier, is the overall shift in Israeli politics and society to a more intolerant and chauvinistic orientation. During the 2014 Gaza offensive, right-wing gangs marched to the chant of "Death to Arabs, death to leftists" and carried out beatings of Israeli Jewish protesters and Palestinian citizens.[18] Thousands of right-wing nationalists issued similar chants at a Jerusalem Flag March following the 2021 Gaza offensive.[19] The general public attitude is not much better. Consider the following:

- 71 percent agree that Israeli human rights groups harm the state.[20]
- 62 percent agree that all means are permissible in the fight against terrorism.[21]
- 48 percent agree that "Arabs should be expelled or transferred from Israel."[22]

Even establishment figures, such as the deputy military chief in 2016 and a former defense minister, warn of a descent into extremism.[23]

Israel's politicians have mirrored public attitudes. The Knesset has passed bills that reduce state funding to institutions that commemorate the Nakba, impose specific procedural burdens on human rights groups, and allow officials to ban visitors who have advocated boycotts.[24] In 2019, the government denied U.S. congresswomen Ilhan Omar and Rashida Tlaib permission to enter.[25] The state's most symbolically defiant act was enacting the Jewish Nation-State Law in 2018, which declares "the right to exercise national self-determination" in Israel as "unique to the Jewish people" and "the development of Jewish settlement as a national value."[26]

Notwithstanding that Netanyahu and his Likud Party have temporarily been removed from power following the 2021 elections, Israel's voting patterns remain hard line. In the past election, the only two liberal Zionist parties who raise any substantive criticisms of the occupation won only 13 seats collectively out of 120.[27] The new prime minister, Naftali Bennett, is a former leader of the Israeli settlement movement with views to the right of Likud. Among the policy positions of the new coalition government are support for Judaizing the Negev and Galilee, complete control over Area C, and a further clampdown on building Palestinian structures in Area C.[28] His government also took the deliberately provocative step of designating six well-regarded Palestinian human rights groups as "terrorist" organizations.[29]

To be sure, the world's still-largest Jewish community in the United States holds far more liberal political and social views in general and on Israel-Palestine in particular.[30] Nevertheless, its establishment organizations, such as the American Israel Public Affairs Committee (AIPAC), the Anti-Defamation League (ADL), the American Jewish Committee, Hillel, and the Zionist Organization of America, maintain an aggressive defense of Israel. While their missions and ideological positions vary, they converge on the following:

- Promoting Israel's overall image in the United States.
- Defending major Israeli actions, including its large-scale military attacks on Gaza.
- Championing the close U.S.-Israeli strategic relationship, including extensive U.S. aid.
- Delegitimizing forceful critics of Israeli policies and actions, including dissenting Jewish voices. In 2020, AIPAC went so far as to launch Facebook ads comparing Ilhan Omar and other members of Congress to Hamas and charging them with "pushing anti-Semitism and anti-Israel policies down the throats of the American people."[31]

As criticism of Israel has taken off in recent years, the major U.S. Jewish organizations have turned more aggressively to the antisemitic label to tar critics of Israel. During Israel's 2021 offensive, the ADL released statements of solidarity with Israel and opposition to "terrorists," and it magnified the antisemitic elements—some real, some speculative—of the protests against Israeli war crimes.[32] The focal point for this weaponizing of the charge of antisemitism is the prodding of state legislatures, the federal government, and universities to adopt a new definition, which encompasses anti-Zionism and forceful criticisms of Israel. Entitled "The Working Definition of Antisemitism" and adopted in 2016 by the International Holocaust Remembrance Alliance (IHRA), the document attaches a list of "contemporary examples of antisemitism," which includes the following:

- "Denying the Jewish people the right to self-determination, e.g., by claiming that the existence of a State of Israel is a racist endeavor."
- "Applying double standards by requiring of it a behavior not expected or demanded of any other democratic nation."[33]

To the consternation of not just critics of Israel but also scholars and civil libertarians, partisans of the IHRA definition have enjoyed considerable success. Most notably, President Donald Trump signed an executive order in 2019 that empowers the Department of Education to apply the IHRA definition as a guide to finding violations of Title VI of the 1964 Civil Rights Act.[34] To date, President Joseph Biden has not rescinded this order.

Guided by this politically loaded understanding of antisemitism, establishment U.S. Jewish groups have focused their wrath on Boycott, Divestment, Sanctions (BDS) campaigns. While hard-right Jewish groups, such as the Canary Mission, have been active on this front, the ADL has been the most influential. Consistent with its characterization of "anti-Zionism and extreme criticism of Israel" as antisemitism, the group labels BDS's three goals of an end to occupation, full equality for Israel's Palestinian citizens, and right of return for Palestinian refugees as antisemitism.[35] Speaking to the UN in 2016 at a forum for Israel partisans sponsored by the official Israeli delegation, ADL director Jonathan Greenblatt proclaimed BDS an "irrational hatred of the Jewish people" no different from the early boycotts in Nazi Germany, demanded that "university presidents and administrators use their influence . . . to articulate . . . how evil . . . BDS really is," and honored "those who use naming and shaming" of BDS supporters.[36]

The politicization of the charge of antisemitism by the ADL and other establishment U.S. Jewish groups is not simply political opportunism but comports with a genuine worldview of antisemitism diagnosed by Arendt. One part is the eternal antisemitism syndrome, which regards anti-Zionism and strong criticisms of Israel as not a "new" antisemitism in substance but just a new means of carrying out an irrational and latent hatred. Holding this fixation, the only reliable salvation is a strong Jewish nation-state. Hence, what unites most mainstream U.S. Jewish groups, notwithstanding significant splits on other issues, is a prioritization of Constantinian Judaism, meaning aggressive defense of Israel. Given this entrenched intransigence in Israel and the U.S. Jewish establishment, Jewish dissenters have a formidable task ahead of them.

Rescuing Zionism by Returning to Its Foundations?

As the above review indicates, it is urgent to break completely from the Zionist establishment and to disavow the U.S.-mediated peace process, which has in practice facilitated a deepening of Israeli colonization and deterioration in living standards for most Palestinians.[37] In the past few years, two well-known liberal Zionist thinkers, Peter Beinart and Omri Boehm, have offered new directions for Zionism intended to retrieve the supposedly more tolerant and just origins of Zionism. Both sketch provocative and innovative arguments that merit closer engagement both for their promise and for their limitations.

In July 2020, the most well-known American liberal Zionist public intellectual, Peter Beinart, wrote an essay in *Jewish Currents* and an opinion piece in the *New York Times*, which created a ruckus in the American Jewish community and beyond.[38] He announced his break from the standard liberal Zionist framework in favor of a non-statist Zionism to be realized in a single and fully egalitarian, binational federation. Later that year, the Israeli liberal Zionist philosophy professor Omri Boehm published a book for wide release, *Haifa Republic*, which articulated a broadly similar vision. Both seek to transform rather than renounce liberal Zionism. Each argument features four premises. One, Israeli colonization has rendered the two-state solution impossible. Two, Israel is on the path to moral catastrophe. Three, a transformed Zionist approach is desperately needed to avert this catastrophe. Four, this transformed approach should be based on the original aims of the Zionist pioneers.

On the death of the two-state solution, to which I return in the concluding chapter, both play up the number of settlements and placement deep into the West Bank, the collapse of any legal or administrative distinction between the settlements and Israel proper, and the entrenched political support. Tragically, lament Beinart and Boehm, most liberal Zionists deny this reality and still insist on a resolution of two separate nation-states. Not only is this prescription no longer possible, they observe, it lacks the normative heft required to rally a mass opposition. For Beinart, the focus on national independence represents a bygone model that no longer inspires sustained movements.[39] Boehm cuts more to the bone by taking apart the historic contradiction in the liberal Zionist call for a "Jewish and democratic" state. The pledge in Israel's Declaration of Independence to uphold the equality of Israel's Arab citizens "has always depended on a conditional relation," in which the realization of Arab rights does not threaten the state's overarching Jewish status.[40] As its Arab citizens are not about to support Israel's distinct Jewish character, they will always represent a "potentially subversive" element.[41]

The way forward for Beinart and Boehm is a transformed liberal Zionism in which the liberalism is not compromised by a form of Jewish self-determination that privileges the state's Jewish character. Such a vision demands a new platform that features a united, egalitarian state in all of what is now Israel proper and the occupied territories. Importantly, Beinart and Boehm remain attached to both the liberalism and Zionism dimensions. Hence, Beinart distances himself from Palestinian liberal one-staters, such as Omar Barghouti or Yousef Munayyer, who favor a presumed postapartheid South Africa model of equality and individual rights for all with no formal accommodation of distinct national identities.[42] Unlike South Africa, counters Beinart, Israel-Palestine is intrinsically binational. More fundamentally, he and Boehm are invested in maintaining a robust Jewish society in the land of Israel-Palestine. Accordingly, both endorse a binational system that accords substantial autonomy to each group. Beinart points to a few models for guidance, while Boehm sketches an eleven-point program that he calls the "Haifa Republic."[43] Boehm adds that such a binational program can instill in Israeli Jews and Palestinians a mentality of "cohabitation" and joint politics, which will "reinvigorate Israeli politics."[44]

Up to this point, having reviewed the first three shared premises of Beinart and Boehm, there is much to appreciate in their transformed liberal Zionism. Both integrate an uncompromising critique of the really existing Zionist project—far more cutting and extensive than the standard liberal Zionist one—with an alternative vision of Jewish self-determination and reconciliation. Beinart and Boehm, however, falter on their shared fourth premise of appealing to the supposed original intent of the Zionist pioneers.

Their motives for appealing to the foundational Zionist thinkers are understandable given the radical break each proposes. Having long shared the view that a Jewish state is an existential necessity, Beinart appreciates that the "belief that Jews in the land of Israel risk genocide without a Jewish state is central to what it means to be a Zionist today."[45] Hence, he devotes the final part of his essay to reassuring mainstream Jews that Zionism can thrive without a Jewish state. Relying on historian Dmitry Shumsky's study of prominent Zionist pioneers, Beinart argues that for several decades, modern Zionism simply entailed an autonomous Jewish community space in the ancient Jewish land, not a Jewish nation-state.[46] It took the enormity of the Nazi Holocaust for Zionists to shift their demand to a Jewish nation-state. Although this shift may have been understandable under the immediate circumstances—Beinart never repudiates the original establishment of the state of Israel—it spawned a dangerous mentality among the mainstream Israeli Jewish community of converting Palestinians from a people with its own aspirations to a reincarnated Nazi race. By recovering the original non-statist Zionist vision, he concludes, Israelis can not only humanize Palestinians and welcome them as equals but also free all Jews "from the Holocaust's grip."[47]

For all his respect for the founders, Beinart recognizes that they were not "particularly concerned with Palestinian rights."[48] Boehm includes no such qualification. "Contrary to common misconceptions," he asserts, his egalitarian binational vision "represents a type of politics that was a matter of consensus for many long years among Zionism's founders."[49] Indeed, relying on a hasty reading of Shumsky, Boehm collapses the differences between Jabotinsky—the founder of the militant Zionist nationalism represented now by the Likud Party—and Brit Shalom on the basis that both sought some version of a binational state.[50] The mainstream Zionist shift only came about, he argues, with the Peel Commission's 1937 report recommending both partition and "compulsory transfer" of Arabs. "Almost instantly," Ben-Gurion and others turned to demanding exclusive Jewish sovereignty over at least a significant portion of Palestine.[51] The onset of the full horrors of the Holocaust a few years later, continues Boehm, further entrenched the new Zionist mindset, including a willingness to carry out the Nakba. Israelis, he concludes, must confront this ominous historical turn in the late 1930s and abandon the enduring Zionist mindset it launched. To do so, he assures us, Zionists need only "return to the civilized, liberal politics of the original Zionists" rather than turn to the anti-Zionist left or peripheral pre-state Jewish dissenters.[52]

One can see the appeal of grounding this dramatic challenge to contemporary Zionism in the ideas of a group of founders still widely venerated in Israel and among U.S. and other outside Zionist Jewish communities. Moreover, Boehm and Beinart are correct that the Zionist movement did not originally emphasize a full-fledged Jewish nation-state for Palestine. The problem lies in their elevation of form over substance. To see why, it is useful to review the essential findings of the text on which both rely, Dmitry Shumsky's *Beyond the Nation-State*.

The book chronicles the evolving approach of five of the most influential early Zionist figures, including Theodore Herzl, Ze'ev Jabotinsky, and Ben-Gurion. It documents how all were substantially influenced by an overlapping set of beliefs espoused by central and eastern European ethno-nationalist movements during the late nineteenth and early twentieth centuries regarding the realization of national self-determination within multinational empires. These movements called not for the breakup of the multinational regimes into separate nations but for a "complex integration of the various collective identities of different cultural, ethnic, and territorial groups."[53] Under such a reconstituted multinational system, explains Shumsky, distinct ethno-national groups would enjoy collective rights throughout a less hierarchical multinational federation and more extensive territorial autonomy in areas understood to be their historical homeland and where they constituted a majority. The idea was to accommodate collective rights and national self-determination for all under a range of demographic residential patterns.

Notwithstanding considerable ideological and tactical divides, Shumsky identifies a set of shared core premises held by the Zionist pioneers, up to the late 1930s, which were adapted from the central-eastern European setting. Jews would migrate to Palestine in sufficient numbers to comprise a majority, where they would practice territorial autonomy within a larger multinational federation, be it the Ottoman Empire or, after World War I, some new entity. Even the militant Revisionist Jabotinsky, adds Shumsky, took for granted that Palestine's Arabs would retain substantial autonomy to govern their own affairs. Shumsky ends his study by tracing the circumstances—the Peel Commission Report and the Holocaust—that prompted Ben-Gurion and others to abandon this multinational autonomy vision. The release of the Biltmore Program in 1942, which demanded a Jewish commonwealth in Palestine with no reference to Arabs, effectively codified the shift.[54] Thereafter, observes Shumsky, Zionism has become equated with the demand for a homogeneous Jewish nation-state.

Although Shumsky's study offers valuable and fresh insights into the foundations and evolution of mainstream Zionist thought, it does not support the much bolder claim from Boehm and, to a lesser extent, Beinart. The Zionist pioneers may not have demanded an exclusive Jewish nation-state, but they did not embody a "civilized, liberal politics" worthy of reviving.[55] With the exception of Ahad Ha'am, the leading Zionist figures in Shumsky's study (and the mainstream movement more generally) sought Jewish predominance in Palestine and solicited the help of imperialist powers. Consider, first of all, that the founders aimed from the outset to transform Palestine from a territory with an overwhelming Arab majority to one with a decided Jewish majority. This goal meant encouraging substantial immigration of primarily European Jews to Palestine and Jewish-only settlements that would disrupt Arab living patterns. Notably, the King-Crane Commission, a post–World War I U.S.-appointed task force charged with discerning popular attitudes in the Middle

East, was informed by a Zionist delegation that it "looked forward to a practically complete dispossession of the present non-Jewish inhabitants of Palestine" and subsequently concluded "that the Zionist program could be carried out . . . [only] by force of arms."[56] Ben-Gurion agreed, stating in 1919, "We want Palestine to be ours as a nation. The Arabs want it to be theirs—as a nation— . . . I don't know what Arab would agree to Palestine belonging to the Jews."[57] Echoing this sentiment a few years later, Jabotinsky remarked, "If you wish to colonize a land in which people are already living, you must find a garrison for the land, or find a benefactor who will provide a garrison on your behalf."[58]

For all his tactical differences with Jabotinsky on how aggressive a stance to assume, Ben-Gurion and the Zionist leadership followed Jabotinsky's approach of courting a powerful benefactor throughout the British Mandate years. Starting with the Balfour Declaration of 1917, the Zionist movement successfully lobbied the British overseers for highly preferential treatment in the administration of Palestine. Under the Balfour Declaration and subsequent League of Nations Mandate for Palestine, Great Britain authorized the creation of political, administrative, and economic institutions to establish a "Jewish National Home."[59] The Mandate included the creation of a quasi-governmental Jewish Agency to govern Jewish affairs and no comparable body for the 90-plus percent Arab population. It also encouraged Jewish immigration and land purchases. Taking advantage of this imperialist arrangement, which immediately gave the Jewish community a decided political advantage over the Arabs, the former established a separate state-in-the-making, which steadily displaced Arab peasants and paved the path for eventual predominance in numbers and power.

In sum, long before the Biltmore declaration or even the Peel Commission's report, the Zionist movement had declared and implemented a set of policies aimed to bring about Jewish predominance and diminish the status of the majority indigenous population. Hence, the leadership's formal shift to demanding a Jewish nation-state did not require much of a substantive change in attitude toward Palestine's Arabs. The latter were still expected to yield to the demands of the much stronger Jewish community. Indeed, contrary to Shumsky's interpretation, Ben-Gurion's claim that the Biltmore Program did not constitute a substantive policy shift is defensible.[60] The leadership's primary concern was Jewish predominance, not a shared space with Palestinians. With what Shumsky identifies as the "onset of the era of the nation-state," the Zionists readily adapted their essential aims to the new global reality.[61]

Conclusion: Look to the Original Dissenters, Not the Founders

The faith of Boehm and Beinart in the judgment of the Zionist founders is misplaced. Far from promoting an egalitarian coexistence, they inaugurated an ideology of Jewish hegemony, courting of imperialist powers, and subordination of the indigenous Arab community. Any project, then, that seeks a Jewish-based transformation on Jewish self-determination and coexistence will need to confront the original Zionism program rather than summon it as a benchmark. Fortunately, as discussed in this book's introduction, there is a noteworthy Zionist movement from the pre-state era that forthrightly condemned the prevailing Zionist approach: what I have labeled the Humanist Zionists. Suggesting, as Boehm does, that even Jabotinsky and Buber shared the same basic binational approach and differed only on tactics is a profound misreading of the actual political divide. As reviewed in the next chapter, their binational program rested on a diametrically opposed set of premises regarding the desired Jewish relationship with Palestinians. For this reason, not just the Revisionists but also the mainstream Zionists regularly denounced the Humanist Zionists as disloyal or misguided. Regrettably, Boehm and Beinart have followed a standard pattern of relegating the Humanist Zionist dissenters to a periphery. Yet to embark on the type of far-reaching reformation rightly desired by Beinart and Boehm, it is essential to recover their voices and seek appropriate lessons on how to proceed. The next chapter begins this task.

2

Bringing Humanism to Politics

Martin Buber on Zionism

The single biggest reason for the outsized influence of Humanist Zionism in the pre-state years was the moral and intellectual stature of Martin Buber. At the onset of the British Mandate over Palestine, Buber was a leading scholar of Jewish and comparative theology and a range of other disciplines. He was also a prominent moral voice and social justice advocate.[1] It was natural, then, for the first wave of anti-statist Zionist dissenters to turn to Buber as their leading mentor. Committed to a range of intellectual and normative pursuits, he served mostly as a source of ideas rather than as a direct protagonist during the 1920s and early 1930s. Nevertheless, Buber quickly became the outstanding normative voice for Humanist Zionism.

This chapter pieces together Buber's core tenets on Zionism, showing how his vision and proposed programs evolved in response to the shifting political dynamics in Palestine-Israel from the early 1920s to his death in 1965. His first prominent interjection occurred at the 1921 Zionist Congress. Buber refined his views over the next decade as mentor to the first organized Humanist Zionist movement, Brit Shalom. He then became a direct protagonist upon moving to Palestine in 1938. For the next decade, he collaborated with Judah Magnes and the Ihud movement—the successor to Brit Shalom—in pursuit of reconciliation with Palestinians and the establishment of a binational, federalist program. In Buber's final years, he adapted his vision to the new reality of a Jewish nation-state and sketched a new path for a just coexistence.

This chapter establishes that the Humanist Zionist movement, under Buber's mentorship, waged a fundamental challenge to the prevailing Zionist vision. It repudiated both the insensitivity to Palestinians and the narrow focus on Jewish sovereignty for its own sake. The Humanist Zionist binational program dramatically diverged from the mainstream Zionist leadership's nominal acknowledgment of two nations residing in Palestine. An essential component of Buber's Humanist Zionism was close collaboration with Palestine's Arabs, as opposed to a separate and contentious coexistence. In the course of this chapter, I establish three enduring aspects to Buber's Zionism. First, contrary to the charges of romantic idealism and naivete leveled by some critics, he consistently grounded his vision in a nuanced political assessment of what was attainable in the historical setting at hand. It was because of the changed political reality post-1948, for example, that he gave up on a single binational state and emphasized equality between Jews and Arabs, an international resolution of the Palestinian refugee situation, and a long-term plan for a regional federation. Second, Buber offered a comprehensive alternative Zionism to guide Jews committed to social justice and self-determination. He incorporated and integrated religious and secular Jewish experiences with social justice values from the contemporary outside world. Finally, Buber provided a conceptual and practical program for advancing Jewish-Palestinian reconciliation, which features a full reckoning from Israel's Jews of the injustices they inflicted, a demanding dialogue between Jews and Palestinians, and realization that not all injustices can be undone.

The Birth of the Humanist Zionist Dissent

In 1921, the Twelfth Zionist Congress met in Karlsbad, Czechoslovakia. Given its timing, this forum launched a decades-long central debate on the goals and policies of Zionism. The Karlsbad Congress was the first one since 1913.[2] The interim saw the outbreak of World War I, followed by the creation of eleven new nation-states in central, eastern, and southern Europe, combined with minority treaties to protect non-national residents.[3] Most importantly, Great Britain had taken control of Palestine and issued the Balfour Declaration in 1917, which called for the "establishment in Palestine of a national home for the Jewish people" and relegated the overwhelming Arab majority to the status of "existing non-Jewish community" whose "civil and religious rights would not be prejudiced."[4] The declaration became part of the League of Nations–ratified Mandate for Palestine.[5]

Balfour and the ensuing mandate emboldened the prevailing Zionist wings, whose primary long-term goal was Jewish predominance in Palestine.[6] With the Mandate's endorsement, the leadership established extensive governing institutions in Palestine.[7] It was careful not to openly advocate a Jewish state because of the small number of Jews in Palestine at the time and British sensitivity to antagonizing Arabs throughout the Middle East.[8] But the Yishuv established an infrastructure that would transition into a state upon British withdrawal. Thus, it acquired land for exclusive Jewish use, facilitated mass migration, and developed separately from the Arab community.[9] Aware that its goals were incompatible with those of Palestine's Arabs, the Zionist leadership mostly bypassed negotiations with them. It hoped that through increased numbers, economic development, and outside support, it could eventually secure acquiescence from the Palestinians.[10]

Alarmed by the post-Balfour direction of Zionism, a coalition of dissenters formed a new group named Hitachdut (Union). It consisted of HaPoel HaTzair (Young Worker), led by labor Zionist A. D. Gordon, and a religiously oriented socialist Zionist youth group from central Europe inspired by Buber.[11] These dissenters favored the revival of a Jewish community in its ancient land based on Jewish religious, ethical, and cultural traditions.[12] They opposed a Jewish state because it would subsume this underlying goal.[13] Shaken by World War I and its aftermath, these dissenters opposed imperialism and conventional nationalism.[14] They urged the Yishuv to develop just relations with the Arabs in Palestine and beyond.

Hitachdut chose Buber as its spokesperson at the 1921 Zionist Congress because of the members' high regard for his writings on the Hasidim and on Jewish spiritual traditions more broadly.[15] Buber was then considerably reworking his approach toward nationalism in general and Zionism in particular. He too was disturbed by the wave of chauvinistic nationalism that engulfed Europe, which prompted him to seek a decentralized, federalist alternative to the nation-state model.[16] Buber modified his already spiritualist Zionist vision to align with a multinational, anti-imperialist federalism. At the congress, he charged the leaders with being consumed by the insular, power-driven nationalism prevalent in Europe.[17] If this tendency persisted, he warned, Zionism would become an unappealing ideology with no distinct identity or underlying spirit. Buber implored the delegates to strive for a vision that revived the Jewish people's "peculiar character," meaning its history and ethical teachings. In furtherance of this appeal, he introduced a resolution calling for "a just alliance with the Arab peoples" so that all of Palestine would "flourish economically and culturally."[18]

Although the congress passed a modified resolution bearing the same name of Buber's proposal—"Resolution on the Arab Question"—its content eviscerated the heart of the original.[19] While the resolution supported an "honorable entente," it denounced the enmity and violence of Palestine's Arabs and removed Buber's language on rejecting "domineering nationalism" and forming a "deep and enduring solidarity."[20] Moreover, no concrete plan was included to develop trust with the majority-Arab population. Despite Hitachdut's defeat, the Twelfth Congress energized the Humanist Zionist opposition and consecrated Buber's status as its preeminent intellectual and moral voice.[21]

Brit Shalom's Intervention into Zionist Politics

In 1925, Brit Shalom picked up Hitachdut's mantle to form the first formal organization advocating Humanist Zionism. Consisting of central and eastern European intellectuals, it sought to integrate the Zionist community into the community of Eastern nations and foster harmonious relations between the Jews and Arabs of Palestine.[22] Brit Shalom was loosely divided between a moderate wing, which favored cooperation with Arabs for pragmatic reasons—the Arabs being the overwhelming majority—and a more radical ideological wing, heavily influenced by Buber, which sought a new political order free of imperialism and conventional nationalism.[23] Reflecting the initial predominance of the moderate wing, Brit Shalom originally defined itself as simply a study group, which aimed to foster bonds and cross-national knowledge between the Jews and Arabs. As it became more politically assertive and radical in its approach, it assumed a far more contentious role.

In both its moderate and radical phases, Brit Shalom exerted an influence and notoriety well disproportionate to its small membership. Helping raise the group's profile initially was the compatibility of its approach with the political interests of both British Mandate officials and the Yishuv leadership. British policy was to balance Jewish and Arab interests so that Jewish development did not impede Arab development.[24] It tried to form a common legislative council but demanded that the Arabs accept the terms of the Mandate, which favored a Jewish homeland.[25] Several British Jewish administrators in Palestine, including the son of Herbert Samuel, the first high commissioner, openly supported Brit Shalom.[26] The Zionist leadership, in turn, was friendly to Brit Shalom because it perceived the need to exhibit a favorable stance on Arab development in Palestine. Having no leverage at that time to demand a Jewish state, the Zionist movement sought to accommodate the British. It officially supported autonomous development for both communities based on the principles of parity and nondomination.[27] Most notably, Chaim Weizmann, the longtime president of the World Zionist Organization—the supreme governing body—donated money to Brit Shalom and repeatedly voiced support for the group's stance toward Palestine's Arabs.[28] Even the more hard-line David Ben-Gurion formally supported national development for both peoples and considered it "essential to establish just relations between Jews and Arabs."[29]

Nevertheless, there were marked tendencies, which imposed limits to what the dominant Zionist wing would tolerate. Ben-Gurion never wavered from a policy of separate development from the Arab community and mass migration, which would enable an eventual Jewish majority and Jewish state.[30] Although the labor Zionist movement occasionally issued statements in favor of worker cooperation, it included no plans for fostering such relations, while its policy of "Hebrew labor" (the exclusive employment of Jewish workers) precluded solidarity.[31] As tensions between Jews and Arabs intensified later in the decade, Brit Shalom became much less tolerated. One exacerbating factor was the surging popularity of the militaristic-nationalist Revisionist movement led by Jabotinsky. It demanded a Jewish state on all of Palestine (including what is now Jordan) and adopted aggressive tactics to advance this goal.[32] Placed on the defensive, the Yishuv leadership adopted a more forceful line. Matters came to a head in August 1929 when a violent dispute broke out over control of the area in Jerusalem containing the Western Wall and al-Aksa Mosque. The violence spread to other parts of Palestine, including the killings of sixty orthodox Jews in Hebron.[33] In this tense climate, the Zionist press and leading figures attacked Brit Shalom for its conciliatory stance.[34] Even Weizmann complained to a Brit Shalom member, "I was distressed to see that you press us for actions, in fact for negotiations with the Arabs, and for declarations now, when, in my opinion, such a step at present would be fatal . . . the Arab mind is not ripe at all for any negotiations."[35]

As the mood polarized, Brit Shalom took a more aggressive stance as well, with the radical wing becoming dominant by 1929.[36] It proposed a binational political system for Palestine and developed a detailed program for furthering a shared political and social space with the Arab community. This included support of the 1922 British proposal for a common legislative council, a commitment to upgrade the Arab standard of living, a Jewish-Arab workers' union, and an educational program for both communities, whereby each studied the language, history, and culture of the other.[37] To break down Arab distrust, some members called for abandoning the Zionist commitment to a Jewish majority.[38] Eventually, the combination of the backlash from the Zionist mainstream and the alarm at the Nazis taking power in Germany proved too daunting for Brit Shalom. As its membership declined, the group effectively disbanded by 1933.[39]

Nevertheless, in its relatively short duration, Brit Shalom exerted a considerable influence on Zionist politics, which persisted after its breakup. As discussed below, the essential vision was revived several years later with the rise of Ihud and political sympathizers. Moreover, Brit Shalom prompted Buber to elaborate on his Humanist Zionism. Through much of the 1920s, he had been simply a distant supporter and general influence, immersed in other intellectual pursuits, including the publication of his most well-known work, *I and Thou*. But with Brit Shalom under attack and in search of direct guidance, the members appealed to the person they most admired to take an active role on the group's behalf. Buber made a brief presentation at the Sixteenth Zionist Congress in August 1929 and followed this up with extended comments on how to develop a Humanist Zionism sensitive to Palestinian concerns.[40] I turn now to reviewing his central premises on Zionism.

Linking Jewish Particularism to Humanist Socialism: Hebrew Humanism

Buber's support for and understanding of Zionism was grounded first of all in a religious foundation. Fundamental to the Hebrew Bible, he argued, was God's "instruction to establish a 'holy' national community in the promised land."[41] Zionism is thus a "unique category extending far beyond the frontier of national problems and touching the domain of the universally human, the cosmic and even of Being itself."[42] Inspired by the Jewish mysticism of Rabbi Abraham Isaac Kook of Hebron, Buber believed that only through a return to cultivating the holy land could Jews regain their holiness and unity.[43] It is from this religious basis that Buber justified and expanded on the modern Zionist project. The religious sources instructed the Jewish people to "strive for nothing less than the concrete transformation of our life as a whole," act on behalf of ultimate truths, and desire "justice . . . in each and everything we undertake."[44] Buber's Zionism was thus a distinct Jewish nationalism, devoted to the most essential Jewish values but also serving humanity at large.[45] For the Jewish people, the pursuit of internal and external redemption was mutually dependent and reinforcing.

The religious spiritual teachings reinforced Buber's fervent opposition to the conventional European nationalist (and imperialist-friendly) version favored by most Zionist leaders. In addition to his secular reasons for rejecting the prevailing Zionism, Buber was appalled by the absence of a spiritual dimension. It was hence imperative "to erect an authoritative . . . opposition" lest "the soul of the movement . . . be corrupted, maybe for ever."[46] The only desirable Zionism, maintained Buber, rejects "that Jewish nationalism which regards Israel as a nation like unto other nations and recognizes no task for Israel save that of reserving and asserting itself."[47] Accordingly, he took strong issue with Theodore Herzl, the most influential Zionist of the late nineteenth and early twentieth centuries. Herzl's vision of a Jewish state in which Jews could escape antisemitism, complained Buber, denuded Zionism of anything distinctly Jewish and indeed rested on a hope that a Jewish state would level "national peculiarities" out of existence.[48] Revealingly, observed Buber, Herzl had been open to establishing the Jewish state outside of Palestine, severing Zion from its promised land, and changed his mind only in concession to the emotional status Palestine held for the majority of Jews.[49]

True to his expansive intellectual pursuits and quest to adapt Judaism's "timeless" truths to the "special conditions, tasks, and possibilities" of contemporary times, Buber liberally incorporated insights from nonreligious, humanist resources for guidance.[50] He labeled this amalgam of broader humanist values and specific Jewish ones as "Hebrew humanism." Among his most important secular resources was the cultural Zionism formulated by Ahad Ha'am.[51] Ha'am sought not a Jewish state but a living Jewish community in its ancient homeland, which would create a distinct and contemporary national consciousness true to the people's unique cultural and historical experiences.[52] He hoped the Jewish community in Palestine would be a spiritual center for inspiring Jewish life globally.[53] Even though it lacked an explicit religious sensibility, Buber welcomed the call to Jewish communal life in the holy land as a crucial dimension for reviving and updating the core spiritual values of the Jewish Bible.

To give greater shape to the moral content of Zionism, Buber turned to the decentralized, community-based socialist framework, inspired by the writings of his close friend Gustav Landauer.[54] He praised the underlying goal, as phrased by Landauer, of "a common spirit in freedom," because it paralleled Judaism's call for a transformation in the human spirit and in social organization.[55] Rather than taking over the state and the means of production, community-based socialists advocated for a new social order rooted in egalitarian, close-knit communities. Such communities would not be isolated villages conducting abstract utopian experiments but would be actively engaged with other communities in a global struggle for justice.[56] Cooperation and cross-community bonds would be facilitated by federalist political arrangements. Buber's goal for the Jewish homeland was a "religious socialism," which integrates community-based socialism with the Jewish religious spirit.[57] He thus admired the religious-socialist Zionism of the nineteenth-century forerunner of socialist Zionism, Moses Hess—a friend to Karl Marx—who proposed a society of common landownership and a "Mosaic" legal code guided by "socialistic principles."[58]

Moving from abstract visionary to observer of concrete forms of social organization taking place, Buber saw great hope in Palestine's kibbutzim, the collectively run agricultural communities committed to equality and participatory governance. The kibbutzim, he observed, were neither isolated from the society at large nor simply an instrumental solution for cultivating the land under the material and political challenges faced by the Yishuv. The individual "kvuza" operated under an inherent logic of federation whereby to pool resources and permit more diversity, collectives entered into larger associations guided by the principles of solidarity and mutual help.[59] For Buber, the kibbutz model accommodated a range of distinct "cultures" and methods of collective living. It thus demonstrated how to put decentralized socialism into practice. Moreover, the kibbutzim were exerting a transformational influence on both kibbutz members and the Yishuv at large.[60] "More than anywhere else in the world," observed Buber, the kibbutzim had furthered a "concrete social transformation, not of institutions and organizations, but of interpersonal relations."[61] Hence, the kibbutzim offered a glimpse into a "new kind of society . . . more important than the vast [and centralized] Russian experiment."[62]

Consistent with his antiparochial outlook, Buber did not let his enthusiasm for kibbutzim blind him to a fundamental shortcoming, their lack of outreach to Palestine's Arabs.[63] Despite their exciting new approach for humanity, he faulted the kibbutzim for excluding the Arabs. "No contradiction could be greater than for us to build a true communal life within our own community, while at the same time excluding the other inhabitants of the country from participation, even though the lives and hopes, like ours, are dependent upon the future of the country."[64] Buber deemed it imperative to break from a Zionism that "dare[d] to disengage Judaism from its connection with the world and . . . sanction[ed] a group-egoism which disclaim[ed] responsibility."[65] Such parochialism engendered a chauvinistic superiority and contradicted the Jewish spirit of "national universalism," whereby Jewish redemption is part of a broader mission to restore and liberate humanity.[66] To get there, Buber insisted that the Jewish community in Palestine find a common spirit in humanity with the territory's Arabs.

Minimizing Injustice: The Ethical and Pragmatic Demand for Coexistence

Although Buber's support for binationalism and coexistence is often recognized in Zionist histories, the nuances are typically brushed out, leaving a romanticized caricature that is comfortably dismissed. This section corrects the record by revealing a morally complex and politically attuned framework. What is least appreciated is that Buber's moral imperative to seek coexistence was driven by an underlying pragmatic recognition that the Jews could not claim exclusive attachment to the ancient Jewish homeland. The "coexistence of another people in the same country," remarked Buber, made the challenge of Zionism considerably more difficult both in the practical sense of setting up a new Jewish community and in the ethical sense of being true to Judaism's highest moral values.[67] He quickly realized that no pristine resolution was possible. Establishing a Jewish community in Palestine would inevitably produce conflict and injustice for Palestine's Arabs. For Buber, it was unacceptable to either abandon the Zionist project or act in a manner that undermined self-determination for the indigenous Arabs or diminished their attachment to Palestine. Hence, he developed an innovative approach that would minimize—not eliminate—the conflict and injustice, generate cross-national bonds, and provide the wherewithal for both peoples to develop their distinct national communities.

Buber formulated this approach in reaction to the 1929 massacres, which had put to rest all illusions that Jewish development in Palestine could proceed without fierce resistance. In pointed contrast to the mix of despair and indignation at Palestinian violence expressed by many Zionists, his message was to engage in self-scrutiny and empathy. Buber urged the Jewish community to appreciate the disruptive impact of Zionist settlement in Palestine. Given that Jews were immigrating into Palestine "in increasing numbers, year by year," the community needed to take stock of how Palestinians regarded this situation.[68] For them, the very project of Zionism would reasonably be viewed as an injustice. Moreover, the Yishuv compounded the injustice in its manner of settlement. Economically, the practices of land acquisition (which often displaced Palestinian tenants), Hebrew labor, and separate development furthered a collective pattern of disregarding the interests and desires of the Palestinians.[69] Politically, the leadership insulted the Arab inhabitants by issuing various unilateral proclamations for Jewish sovereignty and by negotiating with Great Britain and other outside powers rather than with the local community leaders. In so doing, the Yishuv "received the stamp of the agent of imperialism."[70]

But unlike Brit Shalom member and Buber disciple Hans Kohn, who concluded after the 1929 violence that Humanist Zionism would never be possible, Buber remained resolute in support of Jewish settlement in Palestine.[71] Indeed, he took great issue with Mohandas Gandhi for declaring his opposition to a national home for Jews in Palestine.[72] In an anguished letter, Buber repeated the religious-spiritual justifications reviewed above while adding two points directed to Gandhi's anti-Zionist stance. To the comment that Jews "should make that country their home where they are born," Buber answered that the long-term prosperity of the Jewish people was "indissolubly bound up" with the ingathering in Palestine.[73] It was only by having this home soil that dispersal became bearable and purposeful. To Gandhi's argument that Palestine belonged solely to the Arabs, Buber replied, "We cannot renounce the Jewish claim; something even higher than the life of our people is bound up with the Land, namely the work which is the divine mission."[74] He denied that Arabs had an exclusive claim to Palestine, noting that their claim rested in part on a historical conquest.[75] Buber's point was that there are no moral absolutes in this setting, making it necessary to respect multiple claims.

Just as he avoided moral absolutes, Buber refused to retreat to a zero-sum political realism. The idea of a tragic conflict whereby Jews had no choice but to displace Arabs was shared by a number of leading Zionists. The Revisionist Jabotinsky bluntly expressed this idea while demanding a Jewish majority and Jewish sovereignty over all of Palestine. "If we were Arabs," he proclaimed, "we would not agree to this either. And the Arabs are good Zionists too, like us. The country is full of Arab memories. I do not believe that it is possible to bridge the gap between us and the Arabs by words, gifts, and bribery."[76] Jabotinsky concluded that an "iron wall" of overwhelming force was necessary to compel acquiescence.[77] After the 1929 violence, Brit Shalom cofounder Arthur Ruppin effectively agreed:

> It is true that in the whole question of our relations with the Arabs we have not in the past tried to find a formula which would satisfy not only the vital interests of the Jews but also the vital interests of the Arabs. Nevertheless, I think that today no such formula can be found. . . . What we can obtain (from the Arabs) we do not need, and what we need we shall not be able to obtain. What the Arabs are willing to give us is at most minority rights for the Jews in the Arab state.[78]

Buber did not deny an intrinsic tension between Arab and Jewish claims to Palestine. Rather, he rejected the argument that an all-out clash was inevitable in which only one would prevail. As he wrote Gandhi, "No objective decision can be made as to which is" more just. It "must be possible," he continued, "to find some form of agreement . . . for we love this land and we believe in its future, and, seeing that such love and such faith are surely present also on the other side, a union in the common service of the Land must be within the range of the possible."[79] To carry out this most difficult mission, goodwill was needed from both communities with the "support of well-meaning persons of all nations."[80] This did not mean avoiding any injustice, cautioned Buber, because it is an inevitable feature of human life and certainly unavoidable in Palestine. But the commitment to humanity begins "the moment we say to ourselves: we will do not more injustice to others than we are forced to do in order to exist."[81]

From this insight, Buber developed a far-reaching path forward. The most fundamental challenge, he reasoned, was for both sides to transform their understanding of the conflict from one of tragedy to one of ordinary conflict. The tragic understanding follows an insular nationalist mindset. It converts a genuine but manageable conflict into an absolute clash in which each side is expected to strive for domination.[82] He identified this conflict inflation as a "political 'surplus' conflict." It was therefore essential to break free of the political surplus mindset and return to the normal "domain of life itself" where conflicts are to be expected but where "solutions are found."[83] Such solutions can take the form of conventional compromises where each side narrows its demands. All the more productive is to treat the conflict as an opportunity to reach a "positive, synthetic, creative compromise" that engenders new affirmative "life circumstances" of solidarity.[84] Therein lies the path for advancing a new common spirit of humanity.

With a sincere commitment to overcoming differences, continued Buber, Jews and Arabs could escape the domain of political surplus and take stock of "what [was] really needed by each of the two peoples."[85] Both were in need of "a strong and developed autonomy," which would enable the flourishing of self-governance, spiritual-cultural values, and economic vitality. With regard to determining what was required to fulfill these needs, a spirit of mutual cooperation was essential to provide for periodic joint reexaminations "in an atmosphere of mutual trust."[86] Under a cooperative framework, both sides would be able to appreciate that demands for an exclusive nation-state "[fell] into the category of political 'surplus,' of the desire to achieve more than what is truly needed."[87]

To advance this transformed understanding, Buber called on the Jews to assume the initiative because they were the recent migrants initiating the disruption to Palestine. The first step was a thorough reckoning of Zionist intrusions, missteps, and injustices. Concurrently, he urged Zionists to develop genuine empathy. This entailed understanding the Arabs not as obstacles to Zionism but as three-dimensional human beings with their own religious, cultural, and historical experiences. Buber implored Jews to learn Arabic, become informed on Islam, and engage in cultural exchanges.[88] With greater cross-national understanding, both peoples would be able to find bases for furthering substantive coexistence. He identified two foundational points of convergence. First, the Jews and Arabs have common historical, linguistic, and cultural roots. Both trace their roots to Abraham, have closely related languages, and share many cultural traits, "especially if one considers the ways of the Oriental Jews who have made their permanent home in Palestine for many generations."[89]

Such linkages facilitated the "blossoming of spiritual and philosophical creativity among the Jews" during the "Spanish-Arabic" period of exile.[90] A second foundational bond is a shared love for the land of Palestine, which could be developed to instill "a great joint undertaking to make the land bring forth its fruit."[91]

From a reckoning and empathy, Buber believed that the Jewish community would find the path for making amends. Crucial in this regard was for the Yishuv to reverse its policy of separate development. Writing in 1929, he noted with regret, "We have not settled Palestine together with the Arabs but alongside them."[92] Consequently, the two communities had fallen into a mindset of conflict. If the Jews failed to advance a "together with" settlement, they "[would] never realize the aims of Zionism."[93] Buber had in mind an autonomous development committed to regular outreach and collaboration. For full Jewish renewal, the Jewish community "ha[d] not only to aim at living peacefully together with the Arab people, but also at a comprehensive cooperation with it in opening and developing the country."[94] Economically, the Yishuv should be "developing a practical community of interest" that "everywhere and at all times" took the Arab people into account.[95] Doing so would mean thoroughly involving the Arabs in building up the land, including the collaboration of Arab and Jewish labor.[96]

In supporting labor collaboration, Buber was taking on the Yishuv's Hebrew labor policy supported by the dominant wing of socialist Zionists under Ben-Gurion. These labor Zionists, complained Buber, were happy to issue abstract assurances of long-term class solidarity of interests with the Arab fellahin.[97] But in reality, such proclamations served as an alibi to justify exclusion under the view that the Arab community lacked the requisite class consciousness to break free of the landholding, reactionary effendis. Although Buber hoped Palestinian Arabs would develop in a community-based socialist direction, he insisted on a relationship of mutual respect. Rather than wait for a new, progressive Arab society to take shape, the Yishuv must engage with the existing community to create a Palestine of common benefit for all. Buber also cautioned his community not to succumb to the chauvinistic nationalist mentality of elevating one's own nation and disparaging others.[98] The Jews, he rejoined, had their own effendis in terms of elite capitalist interests. Moreover, the Arabs had their principled figures committed to genuine national unity and liberation. The challenge was to focus on a common humanity: "I do not know of any political activity more harmful than regarding one's ally or opponent as if he were cast in one fixed mold. . . . Only when we pay attention to the fact that human nature is much the same all over the world will [we] be able to come to grips with reality."[99]

Along with shared economic development, Buber held it essential to find a cooperative political approach in the development of Palestine. Ever since the lobbying for the Balfour Declaration, he complained, Zionist leaders had been pursuing an "international" approach rather than an "intranational" one.[100] The former gave "tribute . . . to the traditional colonial policy" of obtaining the blessing and protection of great powers while bypassing the local population. This international policy, argued Buber, was morally wrong and politically short-sighted. Morally, it not only disregarded and antagonized Palestine's Arabs but reaffirmed an imperial order, which treated the non-European world as spoils for the world's great powers. Pragmatically, the Zionist leadership's pro-imperial stance set the Jewish community up for a painful long-term reckoning. For one thing, he contended, the imperial order was becoming undone, making any arrangement based on it unstable. For another thing, the support of Great Britain or other outside powers was grounded in ephemeral strategic interests rather than genuine solidarity. Hence, calculations could readily change, leaving the Jewish entity isolated in "vast, hostile surroundings."[101] Buber urged the leadership to give precedence to the intranational principle, which meant gaining the approval of the Arabs of Palestine and the surrounding region. With a firm local foundation in place for sustained coexistence, the parties would then gain international approval in a process much more likely to enable peaceful relations in the Middle East.[102] With an elaborate framework in place, informed by ongoing events, Buber was well-positioned to become a direct political protagonist upon his move to Palestine.

Buber in Palestine, 1938–1948

After five courageous years in Nazi Germany, where he rallied the morale of the Jewish community, Buber emigrated to Palestine in 1938.[103] For the next ten years, he joined Judah Magnes as the preeminent advocates for a binational, humanist alternative to partition and statehood. In this decade, the Humanist Zionist vision gained new strength, helped by the qualified support of left-labor Zionist parties and individuals from a range of other Zionist camps. The period also saw an upsurge in violence and a hardening of attitudes among both the Jewish and Palestinian communities. Neither Buber nor Magnes could plausibly be accused of being removed from reality. Both were witnesses to the daily violence from Jews and Arabs and knowledgeable of the political and social dynamics in both communities. Thus, they developed their proposal for a single binational state embedded within a regional federation not as an abstract blueprint but as a serious proposal to avoid violence. This section situates the joint advocacy of Buber and Magnes within the major political developments of this period. Although their efforts ultimately failed, they merit serious attention because they pointed to a potentially viable compromise had there been greater resolve and long-term reflection from all parties.

The Setting upon Buber's Arrival

Buber arrived in a Palestine engulfed in violent conflict. The Arab Revolt, which had begun in April 1936, was still going strong. One major precipitating factor was the fallout from the consolidation of the Nazi regime in Germany. Although neither the war nor the death camps had begun, the strength of the Nazi Party combined with the upsurge in chauvinistic nationalism and antisemitism in eastern and central Europe, especially in Poland, had heightened the urgency of the Jewish problem. More and more Jews came to regard the establishment of a Jewish state in Palestine as urgent. After all, as the British Peel Commission noted, the United States had become far less open following legislation in 1924 that imposed "drastic restrictions" on immigration.[104] Hence, Jewish immigration to Palestine surged in 1933 along with financial support. The Yishuv leadership increased its resolve to demand a Jewish state as the ultimate goal, now more confident of gaining a Jewish majority in the not-too-distant future.[105]

Palestine's Arab community viewed these developments with great alarm. The revolt began with a general strike combined with acts of violence primarily aimed at British targets but extending to Jewish ones.[106] Hoping to quell the violence, the British established the Peel Commission in 1937 to investigate the causes of the revolt and give recommendations for a long-term shift in policy. It found that the Arab Revolt was driven by a combination of a growing nationalism and a fear of increased Zionist development, immigration, and land acquisition.[107] The commission also determined that the national claims of both communities could not be reconciled in a single state. It further determined that British control could not be maintained for much longer given the increasingly polarized atmosphere. The commission recommended an end to the Mandate, save for the holy areas of Jerusalem and Bethlehem and a connecting corridor. It called for partitioning the rest of Palestine into a Jewish state and an Arab state (to be attached to Transjordan) based roughly on where the two communities were concentrated. To facilitate greater homogeneity, the commission proposed land exchanges and population transfers guided by the model of compulsory transfer implemented by Greece and Turkey in the early 1920s.[108]

Although the British government accepted the Peel Commission's recommendations, the Arab leadership strongly rejected them, while the Zionist leadership expressed a qualified openness. Ben-Gurion supported partition but believed that the commission gave the Jewish state too little land. He was happy, however, that the commission had proposed the idea of population transfer.[109] The British soon abandoned the plan. After a brief lull, the violence resumed, including attacks on the Jewish community. While the Yishuv leadership adopted a policy of havlagah (restraint), support for both violent retaliations and preemptive attacks was growing, leading to the formation of the Revisionist Irgun Party in 1939.[110] Buber's first political intervention as a Palestinian resident was to condemn the growing resort to violent reprisals. Such actions, he decried, were not self-defense but the killing of innocents, which broke faith with the "tenets of Judaism and of humanity" and would "bar the way to peace" with Palestine's Arabs.[111] Buber called on the Jewish people to "suffer in sympathy not only with our own wounded and bereaved, but the wounded and bereaved" Arabs.[112] He then embarked on his most vigorous period of direct activism in support of an alternative vision.

Collaboration with Judah Magnes

Buber's political activism in Palestine was most inspired by the tireless advocate of Jewish-Arab comity Judah Magnes.[113] Magnes rose to prominence as an American Reform Jewish rabbi at a prestigious synagogue and then as a community leader who cofounded the American Jewish Committee and Kehillah, an umbrella Jewish organization in New York City for uniting the local Jewish communities.[114] To the discomfort of other American Jewish community leaders, Magnes was a fervent advocate for social justice and an outspoken opponent of the U.S. entry into World War I. Following his emigration to Palestine in 1922, he continued to combine general public service with social justice advocacy. For his organizational skills, wide contacts, and support from American Jewish philanthropists, Magnes was selected as the first chancellor and president of Hebrew University, which opened in the mid-1920s. To the frustration of Zionist leaders, such as Chaim Weizmann, who wanted Hebrew University closely aligned to the official Zionist movement, Magnes became a high-profile proponent for an independent Zionism centered on Jewish-Arab coexistence.[115]

Although the United States lacked a comparable alternative Zionist movement to that in central Europe at the time, Magnes developed a vision similar in fundamentals to that of Buber. To begin with, he became a fierce opponent of imperialism and of conventional nationalism in response to the militarism and censorship that swept up the United States during its entry into World War I.[116] Magnes proceeded to revise his views on Jewish ethics and Zionism.

Sympathetic to the egalitarian, anti-war position of his Quaker collaborators, he formulated an analogous view of Judaism, which attached Jewish religious tenets to humanist values.[117] Magnes eventually characterized himself as a "radical liberal" who was "opposed economically to the dominance of the motive of private profit" and supportive of pluralism and pacifism.[118] He supported a Jewish homeland in the ancient holy land as a spiritual center for putting Jewish ethics into practice and "strengthening the Jewish people."[119] The homeland would further "human solidarity and understanding" in a land open to Jews and Arabs "where nationalism is but the basis of internationalism."[120] Magnes opposed the Balfour Declaration as a legitimization of imperialism that bestowed "political favoritism" on the Jews and undermined comity in the region.[121]

Like Buber, Magnes made Jewish-Arab coexistence a fundamental test for an ethical Zionism. In denouncing the Balfour Declaration, he implored Jews in Palestine to stay clear of imperialist actors and to cooperate with the Arabs.[122] Magnes proposed practical collaboration in shared goals. He endorsed a joint legislative assembly whereby a lower chamber would be selected by popular vote and an upper chamber would provide parity for the Jews, Arabs, and Brits.[123] Such steps, reasoned Magnes, would provide a political education in compromise and cooperation.[124] He eventually incorporated Buber's ideas on genuine dialogue from *I and Thou* to elaborate further on this theme.[125] For much of the 1920s and 1930s, Magnes campaigned energetically for coexistence and reached out to prominent Palestinians.[126] Although he did not join advocacy groups, so as to not compromise his position as president of Hebrew University, he worked informally with Brit Shalom members and made the group and other independent Zionists welcome to the university.[127]

By the time of Buber's emigration to Palestine, Magnes was more alarmed than ever at the deteriorating situation, the increased militancy in the Yishuv, and the Peel Commission's legitimization of partition.[128] He thus stepped up his activism, eliciting support from independent Zionists and non-Zionist Jews in the United States. Having known Buber for over ten years and long admired his work, Magnes reached out to him for help in reviving a Zionist movement committed to Arab-Jewish coexistence in an undivided Palestine.[129] In 1939, they formed a discussion group with several other Hebrew University professors called Ha-Ol (the Yoke) that focused on Jewish ethical obligations regarding relations with Palestine's Arabs and on social and political matters more generally. The group soon disbanded, but Buber and Magnes entered into a period of intense political collaboration in support of binationalism. The highlight of such activity was the establishment of Ihud (Union).

Ihud and the Failed Last Stand to Forestall Partition and War

Ihud emerged as an offshoot of a broad coalition named the League for Jewish-Arab Rapprochement (LJAR). LJAR formed in 1939 as a forum for bringing together a range of individuals and groups who supported binationalism.[130] These included capitalist Zionists and minority factions of most Zionist parties, but the two most important strands were the Humanist Zionists, allied with Buber and Magnes, and the left wing of Marxist-socialist Zionists.[131] Leading the latter was Hashomer Hatzair (the Young Guard), which had a sizable following.[132] It had been formally committed to binationalism since 1929. Although the group shared the anti-capitalist, anti-imperialist view of Humanist Zionists—though not the decentralized socialism—it had marked ideological and policy differences, which had foreclosed an alliance with Brit Shalom. To begin with, Hashomer Hatzair rejected the idea of a Jewish spiritual center.[133] Its end goal was a binational socialist society, not a Jewish homeland. Moreover, Hashomer Hatzair opposed Brit Shalom's cooperative stance toward the existing Arab national movement on the Marxist grounds that the movement was "reactionary."[134] It insisted on a Jewish majority to provide the requisite "progressive" forces for attaining a socialist society. Until 1936, the group lacked a concrete program of outreach to the Arab community.[135] After the Arab Revolt broke out, Hashomer Hatzair reassessed its stance and resolved to carry out extensive outreach and assistance to the Arab community. Accordingly, it became receptive to coalition work with non-Marxist Zionist groups, allowing individual members to join LJAR in 1939.

Hashomer Hatzair's receptivity further increased following the official proclamation at the Zionist conference in New York's Biltmore Hotel in May 1942 for a Jewish state. It joined LJAR as a group, and the coalition issued an oppositional program in June 1942 that signaled its resolve to advocate forcefully for binationalism.[136] Concurrently, LJAR asked Magnes to assemble a separate bloc of intellectuals, affiliated with the coalition, that would further refine the binational vision. Ihud formed in August 1942, led by an executive committee of Buber, Magnes, and four others, including Hadassah founder Henrietta Szold.[137] Its initial program called for a cooperative union of the Jewish and Arab communities "in all branches of life—social, economic, cultural, political, thus making for the revival of the whole Semitic World."[138] This binational state would be part of a broader regional federation that guaranteed the national rights of all people within it and supported the "struggle throughout the world for a New Order in international relations" based on justice and equality. Although Magnes recruited members from a wide spectrum of Zionist affiliations, Ihud was shaped in practice by the Humanist Zionists.[139] Given Magnes's exceptional energy and skills at outreach and Buber's intellectual and moral esteem, they became the primary focal points. Buber's role was grand theoretician.

The heart of Buber's vision has been set forth above. But one distinct element concerns Jewish immigration, a central cause of unrest since the Arab Revolt. Before moving to Palestine, he had supported migration to the maximum absorptive capacity of the land. But his firsthand experience in a Palestine under violent turmoil inspired a reevaluation.[140] To the objections of not only the mainstream Zionist parties but also Hashomer Hatzair, Buber and Magnes supported a compromise in which a Jewish majority was not required and limitations—at least beyond parity—would be mutually determined by the Jewish and Arab communities. Buber situated this compromise within his distinction between essential needs and political surplus. Specifically, he took on a 1944 speech by Ben-Gurion that demanded the migration of not "many" Jews but an amount that would make Jews a "majority."[141] Such a stance, objected Buber, elevated the political striving for domination over the genuine needs of a Jewish homeland. What Jews genuinely needed was sufficient land and population to create a dynamic community. This goal was captured by "many" because it was "a concept rooted in life's essential realities." The call for a "majority" by contrast was a declaration of a zero-sum conflict given the common association in contemporary international relations of the term with the power to "determine the fate of the minority."[142] For an enduring modus vivendi to take shape, concluded Buber, Palestine's Arabs and Jews must escape a mindset of domination and seek the thriving of many in both communities.

What gave Ihud outsized influence was the international respect Buber and Magnes enjoyed and the group's conscientious effort to reach a compromise.[143] Leading U.S. State Department officials lauded Magnes as an "outstanding" Jewish leader in Palestine who offered a rare voice of moderation on behalf of a peaceful solution.[144] To be sure, they understood that Magnes represented a minority Zionist view. But they encouraged Magnes's involvement because of his potential to sway the opinion of many American Jews "who favor[ed] additional homes for the Jews in Palestine, but who d[id] not favor extreme Zionist positions of the Jewish Agency."[145] As late as May 1948, Secretary of State George Marshall met Magnes and arranged for him to meet President Truman in hopes of dissuading the president from supporting partition.[146] Given their lack of faith in the Zionist leadership and general support for dissent and pluralism, Magnes and Buber took full advantage of their access. In response to leadership demands to refrain from publicly expressing opposing positions, Ihud declared that "every Zionist group has the right of entering into direct contact with Jews and non-Jews for the purpose of clarifying the situation and of exchanging views."[147] Buber individually decried the efforts to silence or impugn Ihud and other opposing Zionist perspectives for reasons of supposed "national interests."[148] Such censoriousness, he warned, silenced much-needed debate and crippled the quest to reach an informed consensus. It was, in fact, the presumed "Traitor," argued Buber, who represented the best hope of preventing the "unprecedented catastrophe" that would arise from the Biltmore Program.[149]

Ihud reached its peak of international influence in connection with the U.S.-British task force established in late 1945. Before the Anglo-American Committee of Inquiry, Magnes and Buber were given ample time to set forth their Zionist vision and program for reaching a resolution.[150] They proposed the immediate entry of one hundred thousand Jewish displaced persons from Europe, an immigration policy based on parity, land reform, increased assistance to the Arab community, a phased transition to binational governance that included separate national councils and joint governing bodies, institutions for fostering dialogue and cross-cultural education, and replacement of the Mandate with a bounded trusteeship to enable an orderly transition to independence. The committee reacted enthusiastically, with one member remarking, "How wonderful it has been to hear this afternoon a counsel of conciliation put forward."[151] The ensuing report largely agreed with Ihud's call for binationalism, calling for a trusteeship that would implement the principles of nondomination, equality of rights, and self-governance in which the state would serve "the rights and interests of Moslems, Jews and Christians alike."[152] The report also shared Ihud's view that partition was not a recipe for peaceful compromise but an invitation to "civil strife such as might threaten the peace of the world."[153]

Unfortunately for Buber and Magnes, neither the committee's report nor a subsequent autonomy plan, which proposed a trusteeship of autonomous Jewish and Arab provinces under British coordination and left the possibility open for a binational state, gained U.S. or British support.[154] What dissuaded both governments was a combination of strong opposition from the Arab and Jewish leadership in Palestine, objections from influential American Jewish groups, and the unwillingness to devote the necessary resources for maintaining a trusteeship.[155] The British turned the matter over to the United Nations, which set up the UN Special Committee on Palestine (UNSCOP) in 1947. Although Magnes and other binationalists gained an audience with UNSCOP, they failed to impress the committee. UNSCOP recommended a partition plan that allotted 55 percent of Palestine to the Jewish state—in which there would be a large Arab minority—and 40 percent to the Arab state, and established a separate international status for Jerusalem.[156] In a nod to the idea of federation, the plan called for a full economic union of the two states and free transit between the two. In November 1947, the UN approved the plan.

As expected, the Palestinian leadership and neighboring Arab states rejected partition. There followed the 1948 war, the permanent displacement of over seven hundred thousand Palestinians, and the creation of Israel as a Jewish nation-state, which took over 78 percent of Palestine, including West Jerusalem. Of the remaining 22 percent, Jordan acquired the West Bank and East Jerusalem, while Egypt took over the Gaza Strip. Although many Jews in Israel and outside celebrated the creation of a Jewish state, the moral catastrophe that Buber and Magnes strove to avert had come to fruition. Most Palestinians became refugees, while the war left an enduring legacy of bitterness and hostility. There was hence little realistic hope in realizing the UN partition's call for an economic union and free transit. Rather, the part of Palestine now constituting Israel was completely severed from the rest of Palestine.

With the new turn of events, both Buber and Magnes accepted that their binational plan was dead. Marking a symbolic termination was the death of Judah Magnes in October 1948. Fittingly, he died in the midst of a desperate political effort in New York to rally U.S. support for a federation between Israel and a state of Palestine and for redress of the Palestinian refugee problem. Buber was now the lone towering voice for Humanist Zionism.

Adapting Humanist Zionism to the New Reality: Buber in Israel, 1949–1965

Following the establishment of the state of Israel, Buber's period of robust political activism ended. Both the reality of a separate state accepted by the UN as a member state and Magnes's death dampened his enthusiasm. Nevertheless, he remained an outstanding moral figure and advocate for Jewish-Arab reconciliation up to his death in 1965. Buber also retained his Humanist Zionist conviction. This section examines his interjections in this period to see how he adapted his vision to a changed context where a Jewish nation-state was an accomplished fact, most Palestinians had been forcibly displaced, a large influx of Jews had migrated to the state, and the remaining Palestinian residents in Israel were mostly under martial law. No longer seeing a single binational state as viable, Buber focused on the enduring challenge of advancing Humanist Zionism, including a just modus vivendi with the Palestinians, in a postwar setting in which most Israeli Jews were committed to their own state and largely uninterested in sharing it with Palestinians.

Inspiring Buber to update his vision was his alarm at the mood of triumphalism that swept up Israel after the military victory and UN recognition. Many mainstream Zionists seized on the 1948 events as validation of what they perceived to be the misguided and naive nature of Buber's humanist alternative. Future foreign minister and UN ambassador Abba Eban offered a polite rejoinder in an August 1948 article for the American Jewish periodical *Commentary*:

> In a just world, those who gathered around Magnes might, on the merit of their more specialized and conscientious interest, have deserved to be the architects of Arab-Jewish agreement. But the world is more realistic than just. The doctrine of "accomplished fact" has been entirely vindicated against that of "prior consent."[157]

More aggressive were the taunting comments to Buber from a Jerusalem shop owner: "An utter political rout like the one your circle suffered is no common thing. It looks as if you'll have to face the facts and resign yourself to total silence."[158] Rather than stay silent, Buber set forth an updated direction in a 1949 speech entitled "Should the Ichud Accept the Doctrine of History?"

He began by challenging the might-makes-right stance, which presumed that political defeat signified lack of merit or viability. What mattered was "whether the cause we fought for is a good one" and whether it could still be pursued "with perhaps a change in course according to the changed situation."[159] The underlying goal, reminded Buber, was "national rehabilitation," which had been impeded by resorting to military conquest:[160] "We have full independence, a state and all that appertains to it, but where is the nation in the state? And where is the nation's spirit?"[161] The Humanist Zionist cause, he concluded, remained compelling, particularly the prioritization of a just coexistence with the Palestinian Arabs. Accordingly, Buber implored his fellow Humanist Zionists to reflect on why the binational campaign—which was a means for advancing the underlying cause—had failed and how to move forward.

He located the primary fault in the blindness that had struck the three protagonists in Palestine: the Jews, the Arabs, and the Brits. The Jewish leadership had demanded far more than was needed for a homeland, the Arab leadership had rejected any overtures, and the British colonial officials had repelled refugees from Europe and lacked sensitivity to either community: "Out of the unconscious and harmful cooperation of these three forms of blindness . . . rose the tide of History, which washed away all the possibilities of realizing our program."[162] Fortunately, continued Buber, such blindness was not a fixed feature of human relations. After all, each community had conciliatory movements, as seen not only in Brit Shalom and Ihud but also in the recommendations of the Anglo-American Committee and in the November 1946 accord between LJAR and Falastin al-Jedida (the New Palestine), which called for binationalism.[163] It was vital, maintained Buber, to confront these blind spots and recall the missed opportunities in order to do better the next time rather than fall back on a simplistic historical determinism. The "might of battalions is only decisive temporarily, whereas the power of a creative accord among nations is the only one which lasts for generations."[164]

Buber accepted that there was no returning to the pre-state binational program. He called for finding a "new juncture of the true path."[165] Doing so, he conceded, would be a great challenge demanding "serious self-examination" and a "resolve to live a life of truth." Buber pursued these themes in several other presentations in 1949. In a lead article for a new Hebrew journal devoted to Arab-Jewish rapprochement, he urged a commitment "for the existence of justice in each and everything we undertake, both in our relations with individuals and in our relations with other communities."[166] In a public forum that Ben-Gurion convened with leading intellectuals, Buber proposed that the state launch an ambitious, community-based, and interactive educational system to instill in all residents, especially the many new migrants, a passion for Jewish renewal and the values of Hebrew humanism.[167]

For the next decade and a half, Buber gave frequent interviews and speeches where he reiterated his vision and gave it specific political content. His starting point concerned the Palestinian refugees. Buber challenged Ben-Gurion to demonstrate that the state could act with genuine morality, as opposed to "raison d'état," by committing to resolve the refugee crisis.[168] Consistent with his view that morality and politics needed to temper each other, he did not call for a purist solution that allowed back all refugees to their original homes. Rather, Israel had to be sensitive to both the refugees and the many new Jewish migrants to Israel who would be especially affected by a mass return.[169] The challenge was to remove the "political surplus" by taking all viable steps to minimize the injustice and facilitate a productive way forward. Thus, Israel should accept responsibility and agree to a settlement program informed by a sincere assessment of the state's absorptive capacity. Equally important was to work with the global community to enable all interested parties to provide input and support for reaching a just and comprehensive resolution. Israel would therefore contribute to a new international model for addressing refugee crises, which, in turn, would point the way to a global transformation whereby the pursuit of peace and cooperation replaced "a world of conflict and disunity."[170]

Buber also devoted considerable attention to the status of Israel's Palestinian residents, who then made up roughly 15 percent of the population. Notwithstanding that Israel's Declaration of Independence promised full equality to its non-Jewish citizens, the reality, as I discuss in Chapter 4, was far different.[171] Under an elastic interpretation of security, Israel imposed martial law on its Palestinian residents. This system in combination with specific legislative acts led to expropriating Palestinian lands, cordoning off Palestinians to segregated areas to make room for Jewish immigrants, and establishing strict control over Palestinian lives.[172] Buber protested the expropriation as a "grave injustice."[173] More generally, he insisted on full equality for Israel's Palestinians. Buber took issue with Ben-Gurion's remark that Israel's discriminatory treatment was justified by the hostility that Palestinians and other Arabs exhibit toward Israel because Ben-Gurion was absolving Israel of responsibility.[174] He reminded the Jewish community that it had repeatedly chosen coercive measures, such as expropriation, rather than take conciliatory steps. Moreover, Israel's Palestinian minority "hear[d], day in and day out, that the ruling nation hate[d] it."[175] Buber recognized genuine security concerns given the overall hostile relationship between Israel and the surrounding Arab states. But justice required taking the maximum steps feasible to bring about full equality, including the termination of martial law. Israel, he lamented, had consistently failed the great moral test of reaching out to the Arab population. To move in a genuinely humanist direction, he implored Israel to break this pattern and do everything in its power to bring about a spirit of true cooperation.[176]

Buber's long-term goal was to embed Israeli-Palestinian relations within a federation for all states in the region. This federation would be structured to prevent any one nationality from dominating another and to facilitate peaceful cooperation across the multiple communities in the region.[177] Under such a federation, which would guarantee robust self-determination for all nationalities, Jews and Arabs in Israel would feel secure to take ambitious efforts for reconciliation. He realized that this federation would not emerge soon given Israeli-Arab hostility and intra-Arab conflict. But there remained the prospects of global transformations that would permit a breakthrough. Hence, Israelis were obliged to "prepare the ground" for such a modus vivendi. After all, concluded Buber, "there can be no peace between Jews and Arabs that is only a cessation of war; there can only be a peace of genuine cooperation."[178]

Conclusion

As he approached death, Buber no doubt realized that Israel had done little to prepare the ground for a just reconciliation other than taking steps to lift the formal martial rule over its Palestinian citizens.[179] It was perhaps of some comfort that he was accorded great respect by Israel's leading figures. Ben-

Gurion attended an eightieth birthday celebration held at Hebrew University in 1958 and paid tribute again following Buber's death in 1965.[180] The pallbearers at his funeral included Prime Minister Levi Eshkol and President Zalman Shazar.[181] These personal honors, however, did not usher in a humanist transformation of Zionism. Two years later, Israel took a fateful turn for the worse when it launched a successful invasion that gained it control of the rest of the Palestine Mandate along with the Sinai and Golan Heights. Later, this book assesses the impact and moral implications of Israel's long occupation. Suffice it to note for now that Israel's fifty-plus years of occupation have hardly been conducive to facilitating a just coexistence. Yet this deterioration makes it all the more urgent to revive Buber's alternative Zionism rather than relegate it to the dustbin of history. In this spirit, I close with some reflections on the three especially valuable insights listed in this chapter's introduction: adapting the underlying vision to the contemporary political and social context, grounding Jewish self-determination in both Jewish and universal values and experiences, and demanding a far-reaching reconciliation that comes to terms with past injustices and accepts a shared future.

Consider, first, Buber's sensitivity to the setting in Palestine when advancing his binational program in the decade before the 1948 war. It is tempting in retrospect to dismiss the proposal because neither community on the whole wished to share sovereignty of Palestine. Buber, however, was well aware of this lack of support. But unlike most partition supporters, he confronted the practical implications of pursuing the main alternatives to binationalism. One was a single state dominated by one people in which the other people were granted collective minority rights. The more morally defensible version was a Palestinian Arab state because Arabs had long been the overwhelming majority.[182] It was clear, however, that few Jews (including the Humanist Zionists) would have trusted this arrangement, given the negative record of minority rights in Europe and a surging Arab nationalism that rendered non-Arab residents suspect.[183] Conversely, the other main alternative, the UN partition plan, was manifestly unfavorable to Palestinians. Besides leaving their state with less territory and no viable seaport, the partition consigned several hundred thousand Palestinians to live as a minority in a Jewish state, whose leadership saw a "demographic" threat and had considered various plans of forced transfer.[184] Notably, as reviewed above, the Anglo-American Committee of Inquiry and other outside observers concluded that a partition plan would bring war. It is, of course, impossible to know whether an adequately supported long-term plan for fostering a binational political arrangement would have succeeded but it was the one plan seriously designed to avoid war and displacement.

After Israel's establishment, Buber adapted his program for realizing Humanist Zionism's ideals. He acknowledged that a single binational state was no longer feasible while being one of the few prominent Jewish voices to stress the urgency of finding a path for just coexistence. The status quo, cautioned Buber, entailed an insular Jewish nation-state, mass displacement of Palestinians, and Israel's perpetual subjugation of Palestinians. Hence, he denounced Israel's complacency and arrogance, which relied on Israeli might and great power support and devalued reconciliation. After all, notwithstanding the great demographic changes, Jews and Palestinians—be they in Israel, the West Bank, Gaza, East Jerusalem, or in exile elsewhere—retained deep and enduring attachment to the same land. Ignoring this permanent reality, observed Buber, was not just morally unacceptable but politically dangerous in the long run, because Israel would be isolated in the region and the object of constant hostility.

Fifty-plus years later, the fundamental realities and challenges Buber identified endure. Israel-Palestine remains a site for which two peoples have intense nationalist aspirations. Although the physical and de facto barriers between Jewish and Palestinian communities have heightened, the territory remains in practice binational but highly unequal. As Ran Greenstein observes, Israel-Palestine has become a "patchwork quilt of mono-ethnic and bi-ethnic regions, separated by political intent rather than by natural or geographical logic."[185] Buber correctly understood the long-term necessity of finding a creative but viable set of statewide and regional institutions for enabling a more just and ultimately more secure living arrangement.

A second crucial lesson from Buber is the importance of linking a hard-hitting critique of prevailing Zionist policies and plea for reconciliation to an articulation of an alternative Jewish self-determination. More than all other pre-state dissenting Zionists, Buber labored to assemble a Zionism informed by a complementary mix of the most inspiring Jewish and contemporary outside teachings. He provided a guiding vision for his fellow Humanist Zionists that could resonate with other sympathetic observant and secular Jews. Of course, contemporary Jewish dissenters will not incorporate the same sources Buber invoked and, as discussed in later chapters, will need to integrate Mizrahi experiences and values. But what should be retained is basing an alternative vision of Jewish self-determination in a mix of Jewish and universal values and practices, where the health of the Jewish community is measured not by the strength of the Jewish nation-state but by its commitment to self-scrutiny, justice, and ethical relations toward others.

Finally, Buber's insights on how to attain a genuine reconciliation between Jews and Palestinians hold up well as a frame of reference even after a century of conflict, displacement, and subjugation. Especially valuable is his overarching goal, to transform the relationship from an irreconcilable "political surplus" conflict to a manageable conflict, where satisfying solutions can be found. Buber appreciated as far back as 1929 that the onus falls on the Jewish community to take the first step, which is to recognize the negative consequences the Zionist settlement had on the existing Palestinian population and the subsequent injustices perpetrated by Zionists. Encouragingly, as reviewed in later chapters, a growing number of Israeli and diaspora Jewish individuals and groups have engaged in such a moral reckoning by honestly confronting the Nakba and other past injustices and by documenting and denouncing ongoing war crimes and human rights violations. Regrettably, however, such self-scrutiny has faced a growing backlash, as reflected in hostile comments by top government officials, recent Knesset legislation, and negative public attitudes toward human rights and protest groups. It is thus crucial to boost the political momentum toward an expansive public reckoning. Failure to do so, warned Buber, will give Palestinians no reason to trust Israelis and make substantive dialogue impossible.

In terms of advancing a productive dialogue, Buber provided useful general guidelines. These featured intense cross-cultural education and exchanges, a candid account of grievances, empathy for the other's sufferings and affirmative national aspirations, and an acceptance that no ideal resolution is attainable. Some tensions will always be present, Buber warned, and not all past injustices can be rectified. But what can be attained with requisite goodwill on both sides is a much fairer resolution that minimizes tensions and past injustices inflicted on the Palestinians and enables both communities to realize the heart of their national aspirations.

Chapters 5 and 6 draw from Mark Ellis, Edward Said, and Ella Shohat to provide specific guidance on carrying out a candid and expansive dialogue between European-based Jews, Mizrahim, and Palestinians. Ultimately, Buber's great enduring lesson concerns the imperative of probing self-scrutiny of past and present actions to retrieve a just Zionism. Herein lies the most persuasive explanation for the slighting of Buber's Zionism by most Zionist histories. What they recoiled from was not so much a perceived romanticism but Buber's unflinching demands. It is up to contemporary dissenting Jews to restore Buber's status.

3

Hannah Arendt's Pariah Zionist Challenge

> Herzl's picture of the Jewish people as surrounded and forced together by a world of enemies has in our day conquered the Zionist movement and become the common sentiment of the Jewish masses. Our failure to be surprised at this development . . . makes it more dangerous. If we actually are faced with open or concealed enemies on every side, if the whole world is ultimately against us, then we are lost.
>
> —HANNAH ARENDT, "The Jewish State—Fifty Years After: Where Have Herzl's Politics Led?"[1]

Unlike Buber, Arendt was not a Zionist political activist, apart from a few years when she associated with Ihud. She approached Zionism in the manner of what she would call a "conscious pariah."[2] Through a series of essays written for American Jewish publications in the 1940s, Arendt identified with Zionism while subjecting its leading figures and groups to searing scrutiny. Her attachment to Humanist Zionism was less intense than that of Buber, Magnes, and other activists in Brit Shalom-Ihud. Arendt did not regard settling in historic Israel as essential for Jewish spiritual development and never considered moving there. She is best understood as the first outstanding diaspora Zionist dissenter. Arendt combined a penetrating identification of Zionism's pathologies and promises, a sophisticated reading of Jewish and European history, and a comprehensive situating of Zionist politics within global political dynamics.

Although both Buber and Arendt, as worldly German Jews, were intellectually marked by the continental European experience, Arendt's identification went considerably further. She rebuked the mainstream Zionist movement for situating "the center of the Jewish people's existence outside the pale of European peoples."[3] Her attraction to and frustration with Zionism were influenced by the trauma of being a German Jew, poised for a leading academic career in philosophy just as the Nazis came to power. She was especially shaken by the broader social transformation whereby even "friends" "got in line" with the new order.[4] Arendt collaborated with Zionist friends in political resistance, which forced her to flee to Paris in 1933 without travel papers.[5] There, she worked for a Zionist group that helped refugee Jewish children relocate to Palestine. Arendt became a Zionist then because she deemed it necessary to defend oneself as a Jew, and the Zionist movement was the only one doing so.[6] When the war broke out, France confined her to an internment camp for German nationals where, as a Jew, she could not enlist German protection.[7] Later, Arendt recalled that "contemporary history has created a new kind of human being—the kind that are put in concentration camps by their foes and in internment camps by their friends."[8] Upon settling in the United States, she set out to understand the modern Jewish experience in Europe, especially the evolution of antisemitism, up to it becoming the focal point for the Nazi ideology.

Arendt had little patience for two popular explanations. One was the scapegoat thesis whereby Jews were chosen to be "the hidden authors of all evil" because they were powerless.[9] Two was the doctrine of "eternal antisemitism," which regards Jew-hating and Jew-killing as the normal state of affairs "to which history gives only more or less opportunity."[10] Both explanations slighted historical developments and politics and denied agency to Jews. As a result, they "[cut] off Jewish history from European history" and "made superfluous a political understanding of the part Jewish plutocracy played within the framework of national states, and its effects on the life of the Jewish people."[11] Arendt instead situated modern antisemitism in a historical trajectory that began with the rise of the nation-state and continued with the turn to imperialism and subsequent post–World War I breakdown of the European order. Concurrently, she assessed "certain aspects of Jewish history and specifically Jewish functions during the last centuries."[12]

Arendt's analysis led her to develop a distinct approach toward Zionism that favored a joint commitment to Jewish and global emancipation and interrogated the movement's prevailing premises and policies. She valued Zionism for its potential to contribute to a much-needed political awakening whereby Jews actively engaged in the political and social affairs of Europe and the world beyond. To her regret, the prevailing movement distorted this political renaissance by its embrace of a nation-state system and corresponding hierarchical global order. More troubling, the movement subscribed to the eternal antisemitism mentality, which led Zionists to reject substantive coexistence with Palestinians or affirmative engagement with the outside world. Arendt articulated an alternative Zionism rooted in a new model of multinational federalism.

This chapter first identifies central themes from Arendt's examination of the modern European Jewish experience, drawing primarily from *Origins of Totalitarianism*, whose preparation partially overlapped with her Zionist essays. I focus on her critique of the destructive forces unleashed by nationalism and imperialism, for which the Jewish question became central, and of the dysfunctions within Europe's Jewish communities. The chapter next situates Arendt's approach toward Zionism within the lessons she derived from the European experience. While she saw the potential of Zionism to inaugurate an emancipatory and globally engaged Jewish politics, she feared that the movement's insularity and courting of great powers would bring disaster to Jews and Arabs. I then review how Arendt modified her Zionism after Israel's establishment. She remained critical of Israel's insular nationalism but accepted the new reality of Israel as a state attached to the Jewish people.

Arendt's lasting value for developing an updated critical Jewish vision centers on three recurring themes. One is rejecting the homogeneous nation-state model as the framework for Zionism. Although the nation-state system has proved more resilient than Arendt expected, it remains incapable of providing sustained peace in territories such as Israel-Palestine where two or more distinct national groups retain deep attachment. Her work therefore points to the imperative of delinking Jewish nationalism from Israel's state project. The second theme is diagnosing the foundational and still-enduring pathologies of subscribing to a view of eternal antisemitism and a corresponding tribal nationalism. The third is attaching the long-term health of Israel and the Jewish people to a more just and cohesive global order.

Lessons from the Modern Jewish Experience in Europe

Arendt developed the foundation of her critical approach toward Zionism in the course of chronicling the European Jewish experience in her monumental work *Origins of Totalitarianism*. One sees the basis for her fierce opposition to mainstream Zionism, which aimed to join a Jewish nation-state to a nation-state political order and rely on the great powers for its security. Arendt exposed the failings of Europe's nation-state system, its toxic nationalisms, and its system-destroying imperialist politics. Similarly, her harsh assessment of the European Jewish communities paralleled her later attacks on the Zionist leadership. These were misperceptions of the nature and causes of modern antisemitism, the courting of the powerful, and indifference to broader European developments. Guided by this critique, Arendt urged an internal and external transformation of the Jewish people, to which Zionism could contribute.

The Jewish Peoples' Interaction with the Modern Nation-State and Nationalism

Arendt's review of the modern Jewish experience in Europe featured the following dynamics. One was the popular association between Jews and the state ruling structure and the corresponding separation of Jews from European societies. This perception paved the way for a modern political antisemitism. The second was the dysfunctional patterns of Jewish life, marked by internal hierarchies and aloofness from the broader community. The third was the added dangers introduced by the rise of two distinct strands of nationalism, one embedded within the nation-state and the other a tribal nationalism whose ambitions were not confined to a single state.

Arendt placed the start of proto-modern states in the seventeenth and eighteenth centuries. Such states underwent a qualitative expansion in the power and reach of monarchies, including the development of an independent and prominent state economic sector. The monarchy asserted itself as representative of the state as a whole, supreme to all sectors of society. Under this development, the "court Jews," who provided finance for feudal lords across Europe, became far more significant. Initially, they were the only ones willing to finance the state's expansion, thereby linking their prospects to the state's success.[13] Over time, the Jewish notables, benefiting from inter-European connections, extended their services to other crucial state functions, such as supplying weapons to armies, building an administrative infrastructure, and facilitating diplomacy.[14] Monarchies welcomed working with Jewish notables because the latter stayed out of interstate and internal political struggles. Notwithstanding that the notables made up only a tiny segment of the Jewish community, they were widely perceived as representing the Jews. Accordingly, "each class of society which came into a conflict with the state as such became antisemitic because the only social group which seemed to represent the state were the Jews."[15]

Crucially, maintained Arendt, the Jewish communities adopted a mode of organization and stance toward the outside world that proved to be progressively self-defeating. Internally, their communities developed sharp divisions in status and wealth.[16] At the top was a small group of notables, made up of the financiers, who dealt regularly with high state officials, enjoyed many privileges, and assumed a leadership role. Next was a middle sector who assisted in a number of state functions, especially war making. Last, and most numerous, were the poor masses who lacked rights or privileges. The Jewish communities abstained from participation in the political and social issues of their states. Instead, they prioritized alliances with the ruling authorities, having "drawn the conclusion that authority, and especially high authority, was favorable to them and that lower officials, and especially the common people, were dangerous."[17] Thus, added Arendt, a "perfect harmony of interests was established between the powerful Jews and the state" whereby the former gained privileges and control of the Jewish communities while the state maintained its overall segregation of and discrimination against Jews.[18] Most disadvantaged by this arrangement were the Jewish masses, who suffered the brunt of state discrimination and societal antisemitism.

To explain the evolution of antisemitism in Europe, Arendt began with the flourishing of two variants of nationalism in the late eighteenth and nineteenth centuries. One was rooted in the modern nation-state, which inspired the French Revolution and thrived in western and northern Europe. Such nationalism paralleled the rise of the bourgeoisie, the expansion of capitalism, and popular sovereignty. Nationalism meant a sense of belonging based on a number of characteristics, including a common historical narrative and culture, and attachment to a territory.[19] Functionally, nationalism enabled a cohesion to compensate for the intensifying class differences. Although such nationalism—linked to ideas of equality and human rights—carried an appealing element, Arendt diagnosed features that could produce great division and violence. To begin with, the state remained a powerful, coercive voice, whose reach was expanding. Meanwhile, the notion of a nation-state conveyed a gap between residents who were nationals, which came to assume a "pseudomystical aura," and others.[20] Consequently, the state was "partly transformed from an instrument of law [for all] into an instrument of the nation."[21] Because the nation was upheld as the absolute authority, the mere grafting of a declaration of the "Rights of Man" offered little restraint, especially with regard to non-nationals. Most vulnerable were the Jews, the quintessential non-nationals of Europe.

Ironically, argued Arendt, even the features of human rights, democracy, and equality had an equivocal impact on the Jewish condition. On the positive side, the issue of making Jews equal citizens had become linked among liberals, especially in Germany, with the broader struggle for human liberation and progress.[22] Regrettably, internal hierarchies hindered Jews from taking part as a people in this struggle. The Jewish notables preferred maintaining their special privileges for services rendered to the state to "shar[ing] their 'equality' with poorer brethren [from eastern Europe] whom they did not recognize as equals."[23] As a result, concluded Arendt, Jews lost the political support of many liberals, who charged the former with prioritizing their own privileges over broader societal liberation.

An even more ominous development, continued Arendt, for Jews and for Europe in general, was the rise of "tribal nationalism" in the late nineteenth century among oppressed and dispersed nationalities residing in the multinational empires of Austria-Hungary and Russia and in the Balkans.[24] There, the requisite factors for a nation-state—a shared identity among a relatively stable population and clear borders—had never been present. Tribal nationalists saw their people as "surrounded by a 'world of enemies,'" claimed to be "unique" and "incompatible" with others, and "denie[d] theoretically the very possibility of a common mankind."[25] The most dangerous tribal nationalism was that which crystallized into pan-movements among Germans and Slavs. They "combined some kind of national home country . . . with a large, dispersed irredenta, Germans and Slavs abroad."[26]

This tribal nationalism, Arendt stressed, both exacerbated the prevailing form of antisemitism and introduced a more toxic variant. Some tribal nationalists, especially those divided across several regimes, such as the Poles, assumed a virulent form of standard modern antisemitism. They associated the large Jewish minority with not just "an oppressive state machine but of a foreign oppressor."[27] German tribal nationalists in Austria-Hungary felt a similar sentiment. The pan-movements, however, added a new ideological element whereby "hatred for the Jews was . . . severed from all actual experience concerning the Jewish people . . . and followed only the peculiar logic of an ideology."[28] The ideology was a claim to being chosen, which depended not on a common territory or state but on the enduring presence of a unique people. The Jews, as a highly visible, distinct group without a home state and with its own claim to being chosen, served as a perfect foil. Consequently, "the pan-movements' claim to chosenness could clash seriously only with the Jewish claim."[29] Even worse, added Arendt, the Jews appeared to be faring better, which created the "superstitious apprehension that it actually might be the Jews . . . whom God had chosen."[30]

Notwithstanding these dangerous trends, the overall Jewish status in Europe remained reasonably stable through the late nineteenth century. Keeping the worst antisemitic impulses in check, reasoned Arendt, was the prevailing commitment to European comity. Governments valued Jewish notables as an "inter-European, non-national element in a world of growing or existing nations," who could secure allies in war and negotiate peace treaties.[31] Once, however, the crisis in capitalism emerged, leading to the great expansion in imperialism, support for inter-European peace dramatically diminished.

Imperialism and Its Corrosive Impact on Europe, the Globe, and the Jews

Following the standard understanding, Arendt dated the onset of the classic imperialist era to the 1880s with the Scramble for Africa. She defined imperialism as an ideology whereby "expansion [i]s a permanent and supreme aim of politics."[32] Unlike standard accounts, Arendt gave considerable attention not just to the capitalist-driven overseas imperialism but to the even more destructive continental imperialism practiced by the pan-movements. Collectively, the two variants laid wreck to the nation-state order and European comity and made antisemitism the most potent rallying cry.

Arendt explained the surge in overseas imperialism according to the following factors. Similar to Lenin and Hobson, the leading Marxist and liberal critics of imperialism, she identified the need for new channels of capitalist expansion and exploitation in response to "the overproduction of capital and the emergence of 'superfluous' money ... which could no longer find productive investment within the national borders."[33] A corresponding factor was the political confidence of the bourgeoisie, who had supplanted Jewish notables as the primary financiers of state activity. It aimed "to use the state and its instruments of violence for its own economic interests."[34] A further prod for imperialism was to provide opportunities for a growing labor force made idle by capitalism's crisis. Besides profit-driven motives, Arendt saw more republic-oriented actors, including civil servants, as looking to conquest and control as a means of summoning a common purpose. They hoped that the overseas expansion would heal domestic class conflicts and provide a nonthreatening outlet for a growing sector of the population dislocated by capitalism. In sum, imperialism rested on a mob–capital–civil sector alliance.[35]

For all of its seductive appeal to the nation-state, imperialism inevitably became a "remedy ... worse than the evil."[36] At heart, concluded Arendt, was a fundamental contradiction between the logic of a nation-state and that of imperialism. The former rests on a defined border and consent of its base population, while imperialism demands a vast, continuing expansion. As Napoleon's experience proved, conquest awakens the conquered people's national sentiment for independence and can be contained only by tyrannical means. For such tyranny to be successful, it will need to "[destroy] first of all the national institutions of its own people."[37]

For the peak era of overseas imperialism, the destructive impact was only partial, explained Arendt, but still highly corrosive. Under British imperialism, for example, a colonial administration operated separately from the home government and developed a distinct mindset of racial superiority and a "white man's burden." The colonial regime came to resent periodic constraints from the home government on its repressive methods.[38] Notwithstanding its formal subordination to a liberal British state, it perpetrated shocking acts of mass brutality and even contemplated "administrative massacres."[39] Enabling such actions were a racism that could override all Western moral standards and the availability of a mob, meaning a "mass of people . . . free of all principles and so large numerically that they surpassed the ability of state and society to take care of them."[40]

Also alarming was the destructive impact of imperialism on European and global stability. Arendt agreed with Hobson's description of imperialism as "a perversion of nationalism 'in which nations . . . transform the wholesome stimulative rivalry of various national types into the cut-throat struggle of competing empires.'"[41] Because the international community lacked constraining institutions, she saw "a competition between fully armed business concerns—'empires'—[which would end in] victory for one and death for the others."[42]

Arendt acknowledged some checks on the overseas imperialist policies and practices carried out by nation-states. The saving grace was that the mostly liberal domestic regimes, delimited by state borders, remained intact: "National institutions resisted throughout the brutality and megalomania of imperialist aspirations, and bourgeois attempts to use the state and its instruments of violence for its own economic purposes were always only half successful."[43] Great Britain, for example, perpetrated atrocities but became less cruel after World War I, while "a minimum of human rights was always safeguarded."[44] Continental imperialism, by contrast, had no internal constraints. Its underlying idea was for central and eastern European nations to forge a path for expansion within Europe, given that most overseas colonial territories had been claimed. But this expansionist drive was not simply instrumental. Rather, the promulgators were the Pan-Germans and Pan-Slavs, who sought conquest not for capitalist exploitation but to fulfill a mission of tribal nationalism. The architects of continental imperialism were not the bourgeoisie but the mob, led "by a certain brand of intellectuals."[45]

Unlike overseas imperialism, there was no transition from racist thinking into full-fledged racial superiority and barbarism. Racism of the sort that denied any common humanity was integral from the outset with no gap between the home territory and the conquered lands. With the dominance of tribal nationalism, antisemitism became the focal rallying point for continental conquest. Besides being seen as the leading challengers to the mantle of chosenness, the Jews were the "minority par excellence" across Europe and "a symbol for all of Europe's unresolved national questions."[46]

The Jewish situation enjoyed a brief respite with the end of World War I. Pan-German continental imperialism had been defeated in war, while the Bolshevik Revolution disrupted Pan-Slavic expansion. This peace, however, was brittle. The conditions had become ripe for complete destruction, as discussed below.

The Collapse of Europe and the Decimation of Its Jews

The Great War itself, Arendt argued, "exploded the European comity of nations beyond repair."[47] The war brought the breakup of several multinational empires, civil wars, mass migration, economic chaos, and a legacy of bitterness, while imperialism remained intact. Nevertheless, she convincingly demonstrated that the policies instituted by the victor states markedly aggravated the crisis and hastened the destruction of the European order. The gravest misstep was turning to the nation-state solution to address the political turmoil in central, eastern, and southern Europe. Doing so unleashed the full cruelty latent in the nation-state system of political organization. Moreover, added Arendt, the attachment of a series of minority treaties simply reinforced nationalist tensions. Consequently, the next world war involved the full barbarity of human nature.

As part of the post–World War I settlement, the delegates agreed to nine new nation-states in the area formerly controlled by either Austria-Hungary, Russia, or Germany.[48] Each new state was required to enter into a minority treaty with the League of Nations, ostensibly to ensure basic rights for recognized minorities. Arendt perceptively identified two disastrous shortcomings to the nation-state approach. First, even in western and northern Europe, the nation-state structure could no longer cope with the new setting. Mass migration of the stateless to established states prompted a sharp differentiation between nationals and other residents. France, for example, abandoned a universal rule-of-law approach and implemented repressive measures toward non-nationals free of legal constraints.[49]

Second, argued Arendt, the new states "lacked the very conditions for the rise of nation-states: homogeneity of population and rootedness in the soil."[50] These new states combined multiple peoples in single states, designated a dominant nation as "state people," and created a separate group of "minorities" who would require special handling and international protection. Arendt vividly exposed the grave shortcomings of the minority treaties. To begin with, they did not cover minorities lacking significant numbers in multiple succession states; nor did they apply to the established states. More to the point, even where the minority treaties applied, they conveyed the message "that only nationals could be full citizens, only people of the same national origin could enjoy the full protection of legal institutions."[51] When combined with the resentment of the dominant nation for having to sign the minority treaty, a pattern emerged of government oppression, with little restraint from the League of Nations, and minorities reacting with discontent and a yearning for national liberation.

With the substantial discrepancy across Europe between the state's residents and the favored nationality, the dark side of the nation-state model fully emerged. Arendt located the most important step as the turn to mass denationalization, whereby governments withdrew their connection to a subset of the state's residents. In this situation, lamented Arendt, the hollowness of the Rights of Man revealed itself: "The moment human beings lacked their own government and had to fall back upon their minimum rights, no authority was left to protect them."[52] Such a state of affairs, she added, endangered the very idea of a civilization with a cohesive political life because it was confronted with a situation where "millions of people" were forced into "conditions which, despite all appearances, [we]re the conditions of savages."[53]

As European comity disappeared by the 1930s, the Jewish situation moved from precarious to disastrous. Most ominously, a proto-genocidal antisemitism took shape among the Pan-Germans, anchored in Germany's governing Nazi Party. As the most visible non-nationals across Europe, the Jews became a unifying target of resentment. Hitler's first step was to denationalize the Jews. The new nation-states soon followed suit, eager to be rid of their non-nationals. They started with the Jews as "the only nationality that actually had no other protection than a minority system which . . . had become a mockery."[54] With the onset of World War II, the once unthinkable became possible.

Hopes for Transforming European Jewish Politics through Solidarity

Before considering Arendt's hopes for Zionism, it is instructive to review several essays from the early 1940s that advanced a new Jewish politics for a postwar Europe. She hoped that Europe's complete collapse would spark a fundamental change in outlook. Toward this end, she summoned an alternative Jewish tradition of "conscious pariahs." Pariahs embraced a Jewish and outcast identity, exhibited a bold spirit and creativity, and lived in a manner that demanded "an admission of Jews as *Jews* to the rank of humanity."[55] Arendt singled out the French Jewish literary critic and anarchist agitator Bernard Lazare as the exemplary conscious pariah. He was keenly aware of a "double slavery" in which the Jewish people were "threatened not only by the antisemites from without but also by . . . its own 'benefactors' from within."[56] Arendt admired Lazare's stance toward the wave of antisemitism that engulfed France during the Dreyfus affair. Unlike his contemporary Theodore Herzl, Lazare insisted that the Jewish striving for emancipation demanded the simultaneous opposition to internal and external oppression. Hence, Jewish liberation had to be attached to wider justice. Lazare sought a "real comrade-in-arms, whom he hoped to find among all the oppressed groups of contemporary Europe."[57]

Inspired by Lazare, Arendt regarded the early 1940s as a ripe time for a true collaboration: "For the first time, Jewish history is not separate but tied up with that of all other nations" because the "outlawing of the Jewish people in Europe had been followed closely by the outlawing of most European nations."[58] Arendt hoped the masses of European stateless would form a vanguard for a new European order that decisively broke from the failed nation-state system. "Our only chance," she concluded, "indeed the only chance for all small peoples—lies in a new European federal system."[59] Soon thereafter, Arendt extended her scope beyond Europe's future and applied her vision of a new Jewish politics of liberation to the Zionist setting.

Promises and Perils of Zionism

Arendt's Zionism was marked by a sharp polarity. On the favorable end, she saw great potential for contributing to a Jewish political awakening. Arendt regarded the Zionist movement as the first distinctly Jewish ideology "in which they have taken seriously a hostility that would place them in the center of world events."[60] Moreover, Arendt saw promising new forms of community life taking shape in Palestine's Yishuv, which she hoped could contribute to a broader postwar global transformation. Conversely, Arendt was bitterly disappointed with how Zionist politics played out. One grave failing was the movement's embrace of the nation-state model and imperialist global order, which had devastated Jews and Europe and dismissed the welfare of most of the world's population. Equally disheartening was Zionism's absorption of a variant of tribal nationalism, which regarded all non-Jews as suspect.

The Seeds of a Jewish Renewal in Palestine

Arendt admired what she regarded as two important non-nationalist developments in Palestine's Jewish community. The first was building a "Jewish cultural center [that] would inspire the spiritual development of all Jews in other countries, but would not need ethnic homogeneity and national sovereignty."[61] Arendt singled out the founding of Hebrew University for nurturing the long-standing Jewish commitment to learning and for being a repository to enrich the study of Jewish thought in dialogue with the broader world of scholarship. She was not surprised that Hebrew University under the leadership of Judah Magnes became the focal point for movements active in Jewish-Arab understanding and reconciliation.[62]

The second appealing Zionist trend was implementing social justice through the "workers' cooperatives, social and health services, and free and equal education."[63] They sought "to build a new type of society in which there would be no exploitation of man by man."[64] Like Buber, Arendt was especially impressed by the kibbutzim for advancing "an age-old Jewish dream of a society based on justice, formed in complete equality [and] indifferent to all profit motives."[65] She regarded them as "perhaps the most promising of all social experiments made in the twentieth century" because they offered "hope for solutions that may one day become acceptable and applicable for the large mass of men everywhere whose dignity and humanity are today so seriously threatened by the standard of a competitive and acquisitive society."[66]

What Was Ruining the Zionist Appeal?

To Arendt's regret, the great achievements of the eastern European socialist Zionist pioneers lacked "any appreciable political influence"; hence, a "political history of Zionism could easily pass over the genuine national revolutionary movement which sprang from the Jewish masses."[67] These pioneers were content with their own communities and ceded broader politics to the victorious "Herzlian tradition" of statist Zionism. Accordingly, Arendt devoted the bulk of her Zionist writings to attacks on this tradition, often singling out Herzl's writings. She regarded this tradition as a subset of the nationalism among minority groups in central and eastern Europe in the nineteenth century, which held that national survival depended on a fully sovereign nation-state.[68] With this goal paramount, the leading Zionists pursued an "outmoded and outright reactionary political [line]" of courting great powers to support a nation-state.[69] The result, complained Arendt, was a nationalism that "trust[ed] in nothing but the rude force of the nation" and, even worse, "depend[ed] upon the force of a foreign nation."[70]

Further exasperating for Arendt was mainstream Zionism's grounding in the "Central European ideology of nationalism and tribal thinking."[71] Such tribal nationalism "never bothered much about sovereignty of the people" in the French Revolution's tradition but aspired to "autarchical existence."[72] She did not suggest that Zionist tribal nationalism was as expansive or destructive as the German variant. But, consistent with Herzl's understanding of a nation "held together by a common enemy," the mainstream Zionists believed they were surrounded by enemies.[73] Adding particular toxicity to Zionist tribal nationalism, added Arendt, was its fixation on an eternal antisemitism, which had "conquered the Zionist movement and become the common sentiment of the Jewish masses."[74] In Herzl's reality, there were "eternally established nation-states arrayed compactly against the Jews on one side, and on the other side the Jews themselves, in dispersion and eternally persecuted."[75] Nothing else mattered, including "class structure, . . . political parties or movements, . . . countries or . . . periods of history."

Arendt laid out the highly dysfunctional consequences of such an undifferentiated and stark divide of reality. One was a grave misapprehension of political dynamics in Europe and worldwide. The Zionists' courting of Britain's imperial ambitions in the interwar years, for example, took place in the face of "sheer ignorance" of the evolving, destructive nature of imperialism.[76] A most perverse consequence was the stance Herzlian Zionism adopted toward antisemitism. Rather than confront it, Zionists accepted antisemitism as an unchanging reality to be exploited for propaganda purposes. To Arendt's alarm, Zionists actually welcomed antisemitism as a cohesive rallying point. As a Zionist emissary in the early twentieth century, Herzl solicited support from antisemitic governments by appealing to their presumed desire to rid their states of Jews.[77] He deemed antisemites to "be our most reliable friends, the antisemitic countries our allies."[78]

Concomitant with seeking to enlist antisemitism for its cause, Zionists wrote off Jewish life in the diaspora. After all, reasoned Arendt, standard Zionism held that the only sustainable future for Jews was to escape to their own state. Hauntingly, Zionists seemed unaffected by the reality that Palestine could absorb only a minority of the world's Jews. She derided their attitude as follows: "We shall be the only surviving Jews in the end; all that matters is our survival; let charity take care of the pressing needs of the masses; . . . we are interested in the future of a nation, not in the fate of individuals."[79] Rather than providing a spark for Judaism worldwide, as envisioned by cultural Zionists, mainstream Zionists saw a future Israel as marking the death knell for diaspora Judaism.

A related consequence of the Zionist fixation on eternal antisemitism was a lack of interest in European Jewish developments, including their engagement with the outside community. European Jews were reduced to passive victims of reflexive gentile tormentors. Such a stance "[cut] off Jewish history from European history" and did not allow for any Jewish influence on the shaping of European developments.[80] With all Jews lumped together as victims, Zionism removed Europe's class of Jewish notables from judgment. Instead, Zionists established a narrative that "we are in the same boat," which greatly distorted reality and precluded much-needed internal change. This absolving of Europe's Jewish plutocrats, interjected Arendt, proved convenient with the formation of the Zionist Jewish Agency in 1929. From that point on, Zionist groups actively courted these Jews for donations and refrained from all criticisms.[81]

For Arendt, the Herzlian eternal antisemitism syndrome's most unhealthy trait was the foreclosing of substantive engagement with other peoples: "Herzl's picture of the Jewish people as surrounded and forced together by a world of enemies has in our day conquered the Zionist movement and become the common sentiment of the Jewish masses. Our failure to be surprised at this development . . . makes it more dangerous. If we actually are faced with open or concealed enemies on every side, if the whole world is ultimately against us, then we are lost."[82] Under the view that all gentiles were predisposed to hate Jews, Herzl and his followers "saw the destinies of the Jews as completely without connection with the destinies of other nations."[83] Far from seeking allies with other oppressed groups, lamented Arendt, the Herzlian logic dictated realpolitik alliances with the oppressor. Thus, Herzl offered Zionist assistance to the Ottoman Empire in suppressing Arab national resistance in exchange for Ottoman support of increased Zionist settlement. Notably, Herzl was unmoved by protesting cables from other oppressed nationalities who pointed out the regime's recurring massacres of Armenians.[84] Following Herzl's example, observed Arendt, the Zionist Organization in the 1930s bypassed the global boycott against German goods by negotiating a deal with the Nazis that brought Jewish migrants to Palestine in exchange for the latter bringing in German goods for sale.[85]

In sum, Arendt berated the Zionist movement for updating the failings of Europe's Jewish communities instead of acting as a vanguard for a new, emancipatory Jewish politics. Mainstream Zionists chose separation over engagement with the outside world. Similarly, just as Europe's Jewish notables bypassed the public and worked closely with governments, the Zionist leadership courted great powers as allies, not other oppressed groups. Summarizing her overall dismay, Arendt reflected on the "spectacle of a national movement, that start[ed] out with such an idealistic élan, sold out at the very first moment to the powers that be; that felt no solidarity with other oppressed peoples . . . [and] that endeavored even in the morning-dream of freedom and justice to compromise with the most evil forces of our time by taking advantage of imperialistic interests."[86]

The Costs of Zionism's Pathologies on Jewish-Arab Relations

Although less attentive than Buber to Jewish-Palestinian relations, Arendt shared his perspective that a just modus vivendi with Palestine's Arabs was the ultimate moral and political test of Zionism. Her original contribution was to situate Zionism's failings within the afflictions of the dominant Herzlian wing, which consisted of the insistence on an exclusive Jewish nation-state, indifference to Palestine's Arabs, and a foreign policy geared toward the courting of imperialist forces.

Arendt compared the Zionist plan of creating a Jewish nation-state in an area with an overwhelming Arab population to the calamitous post–World War I establishment of a series of nation-states in central and southern Europe in a multinational and fractious area. To settle the land, the Zionists regarded it sufficient to secure the blessing of Great Britain, forgetting "that the Arabs, not the English, were the permanent reality in Near Eastern policies."[87] Similarly, the Zionists' pointing to ancient attachments and oppression in Europe as their justification for a hegemonic nation-state rested on a "closed framework of one's own people and history" with no regard for other peoples or the broader political context.[88] Because of this mindset, observed Arendt, Zionist leaders seized upon the seductive but patently inaccurate "thought that 'the people without a country needed a country without a people' . . . [so] that they simply overlooked the native population."[89] True to her rejection of nationalism, Arendt also faulted Palestinian Arab leaders for insisting on a unitary Arab state as betraying an illusion that the Jewish settlers could be made to leave.[90] Nor was she impressed with the purported compromise of partition into separate Jewish and Arab nation-states: "It is simply preposterous to believe that further partition of so small a territory . . . could resolve the conflict of two peoples, especially in a period when similar conflicts are not territorially soluble on much larger areas."[91]

A related Zionist affliction Arendt identified was the lack of interest in Palestine's Arabs, including the negative impact of Zionist settlement. She attributed this indifference to Zionism's insular nationalism, which ignored all outside affairs that did not immediately affect statehood prospects. Although Jews interacted with Arabs as neighbors, they regarded the latter "as an interesting example of folk life at best, and as a backward people who did not matter at worst."[92] Consequently, apart from the Brit Shalom and Ihud circles, Zionists gave no priority to Jewish-Arab cooperation.[93] With just a few exceptions, she observed, Jewish economic development in Palestine was hermetically sealed from Arab sectors.[94] But while separate, the impact of land settlement combined with an exclusive Hebrew labor policy brought about a displacement that left many Palestinian fellahin a "potential proletariat with no prospect of employment as free laborers."[95] A more far-reaching blindness of Zionists was the failure to come to terms with what the goal of a Jewish nation-state meant for Palestine's Arabs. Indeed, the Revisionists' advocacy of forced transfer was being "earnestly discussed." The Arabs, presciently warned Arendt, were faced with the choice of either "minority status in Palestine or voluntary emigration."⁹⁶ Zionists should have expected fierce resistance. Tragically, she concluded, Zionists "overlooked . . . that Arabs were human beings like themselves and that it might be dangerous not to expect them to act and react in much the same way as Jews."⁹⁷

The final Zionist affliction Arendt highlighted was the preference for seeking favor from great powers over solidarity with oppressed actors. Zionists foreclosed the pursuit of a "working agreement with Arabs and other Mediterranean peoples" in order "to establish themselves from the very beginning as a 'sphere of interest.'"⁹⁸ Such a policy, she granted, might enjoy temporary success, but in "the long run, there is hardly any course imaginable that would be more dangerous." One crippling fallout was having others regard Jews as the tools of imperialist powers. "Jews who know their own history," warned Arendt, "should be aware that such a state of affairs will inevitably lead to a new wave of Jew-hatred; the antisemitism of tomorrow."⁹⁹ Equally worrisome, such a state forged in conflict would demand a Sparta-like military regime. Arendt provided a grim forecast:

> The land that would come into being would be something quite other than the dream of world Jewry, Zionist and non-Zionist. The "victorious" Jews would live surrounded by an entirely hostile Arab population, secluded inside ever-threatened borders, absorbed with physical self-defense to a degree that would submerge all other interests and activities. The growth of a Jewish culture would cease to be a concern of the whole people; social experiments would have to be discarded as impractical luxuries.¹⁰⁰

In sum, a Jewish state could "only be erected at the price of the Jewish homeland."¹⁰¹

Arendt's Support for a Humanist Zionist Alternative

Up through 1948, Arendt hoped the humanist, non-statist Zionist vision could prevail and produce a Jewish homeland devoted to spiritual renewal, internal liberation, and a transformed global order. Most important was to advance solidarity with Palestine's Arabs. She implored the two peoples to collaborate on a new model of inclusive political organization that broke with the nation-state model. Rather than face off in a zero-sum game, Jews and Arabs could "show the world that there are no differences between two peoples that cannot be bridged." By "the working out of such a modus vivendi," the two peoples could show others "how to counteract the dangerous tendencies of formerly oppressed peoples to shut themselves off from the rest of the world and develop nationalist superiority complexes of their own."[102]

Arendt had no illusions that Zionist or Palestinian Arab politics could readily make such a shift given decades of separate development and mutual recrimination. She hoped for an awakening of two potentially sympathetic Jewish actors, the many non-Zionist Jews outside of Palestine and the left-wing socialist Zionist pioneers. Non-Zionists were the sizable "loyal opposition" within the Jewish Agency, who had reluctantly accepted a Jewish state as a fait accompli following the UN partition resolution. Arendt urged them to continue "to insist that the only permanent reality . . . was the presence of Arabs in Palestine" and to sound the alarm of the "consequences of partition and the declaration of a Jewish state."[103] Closer to Arendt's heart were the kibbutz pioneers and allied actors. She faulted them not for being chauvinist nationalists but for being oblivious to the nationalist conflict: "They did not even stop to think of the very existence of Arabs."[104] So content were the kibbutz pioneers with the just communities they had created within their contained collectives that they withdrew interest in the outside world, with the best among them "afraid of soiling their hands" with politics.[105] Arendt granted that the Hashomer Hatzair Party formally supported an appealing non-nationalist, binational platform. But it offered no practical alternative program of collaboration with Palestine's Arabs under the alibi that the latter were immersed in a "feudal" society. Accordingly, the party abstained on the "vital questions of Palestine foreign policy."[106] She implored this potentially large sector of committed Zionists to become protagonists on behalf of emancipation for the Jews and the broader global community.

Arendt mostly avoided involvement in direct Zionist politics, opting instead to focus on essay writing for a variety of Jewish publications. Yet, despite some reservations, she came to align herself with the political vision of Ihud, singling out Magnes for praise.[107] Her sketching of a federalist alternative to the nation-state model attracted Magnes's attention.[108] The general idea was a federation where sovereignty would be dispersed across national communities while governance for the territory at large required mutual action. Agreeing with Magnes that the situation was too volatile to implement such a plan, Arendt supported his call for a UN trusteeship whereby the two communities would gain experience in shared governance and deepen their trust and interaction. Such a system would follow up on Arendt's proposal for "local self-government and mixed Jewish-Arab municipal and rural councils, on a small scale and as numerous as possible."[109]

She, of course, experienced the same failure as Magnes, Buber, and the anti-statist Zionists. Naturally, Arendt focused on the new statelessness tragedy. Whether as a "consequence of Arab atrocity propaganda or real atrocities or a mixture of both," the war caused the displacement of hundreds of thousands of Palestinians "followed by the Israeli refusal to readmit the refugees to their old home."[110] As a result, lamented Arendt, the Zionists made true the long-standing Arab claim that Zionism by definition sought the expulsion of Arabs, not coexistence. In a characteristically ironic tone, she later remarked that the Jewish question of statelessness had been "solved—namely by means of a colonized and then conquered territory—but this solved neither the problem of minorities nor the stateless."[111] In fact, "the solution of the Jewish question merely produced a new category of refugees, the Arabs, thereby increasing the number of the stateless and rightless by another 700,000 to 800,000 people."

Arendt's Post-1948 Zionist Reflections: Despair Mixed with a Distant Identification

Arendt's active involvement in Zionist politics ended with the failure to attain anything other than an armistice after the 1948 war. Sealing her disillusionment were the murder of UN envoy Folke Bernadotte by the militant Zionist group Lehi and the death of Magnes.[112] Arendt saw the deaths of these two valiant proponents of reconciliation as marking the triumph of chauvinistic forces. Magnes, she remarked, "*was the conscience of the Jewish people* and much of that conscience has died with him."[113] "A people that for two thousand years had made justice the cornerstone of its spiritual and communal existence," she added, "has become emphatically hostile to all arguments of such a nature." Further disheartening was Israel's 1953 raid on the West Bank village of Qibya, which demolished forty-five homes and killed sixty-nine civilians.[114] Arendt found this "absolutely nauseating" and declared, "I do not want to have anything to do with Jewish politics any longer."[115]

Her revulsion transitioned into resignation. Arendt accepted that life in Israel would not contribute to the political awakening of the Jewish people in a broader emancipatory direction. Her disappointment was most acute with regard to the European Jewish experience. After all, the Holocaust, followed by mass migration of the survivors, had pretty much ended the Jewish experience in most of Europe, outside of the Soviet Union. "At the present moment," she wrote an old Zionist mentor, "the Zionist movement is dead. . . . There is no European Jewry anymore. . . . There is no chance for a renaissance of Zionism."[116] Arendt concluded that the once-exciting new modes of social organization in Jewish Palestine had run their course because of the victory of statist Zionism. The kibbutzim now "play no role whatsoever," she wrote her husband in 1955.[117] Accordingly, Arendt directed her hopes for new models of social organization elsewhere, such as the participatory councils that formed briefly in Hungary during the 1956 uprising.[118] Nevertheless, she retained an interest in and attachment to Israel, which led to occasional assessments of Israel's character and ideas for reformation.

Arendt most fully articulated her revised approach in what became her most famous and controversial publication, *Eichmann in Jerusalem*, her report on Israel's 1961 trial of the most notorious Nazi bureaucrat Adolf Eichmann. The book primarily examined the broader European setting in which Eichmann operated and the limits of conventional jurisprudence for comprehending the state-sanctioned crimes against humanity he facilitated. But Israel's resolve to politicize the trial to justify mainstream Zionism prodded Arendt to revisit and update her critique of Zionism's pathologies and rework her appeal for an internationalist orientation.

She focused on Prime Minister Ben-Gurion—the "stage master"—to highlight Israel's politicization. He helpfully listed in various newspaper articles a series of "lessons" the trial would impart.[119] Arendt's lead onstage actor was the chief prosecutor and attorney general, Gideon Hausner, assigned to deliver the script at the trial and press conferences.[120] Ben-Gurion's featured lesson was the unrelenting antisemitism in the diaspora, whereby for "four thousand years," Jews had encountered a "hostile world," rendering them a weak, degenerated people.[121] Following the stage master, Hausner proclaimed at his opening statement, "It is not an individual that is in the dock at this historic trial, and not the Nazi regime alone, but antisemitism throughout history."[122] A concomitant lesson from Ben-Gurion was that "only in Israel could a Jew be safe and live an honorable life."[123] On cue, Hausner praised Israel's presence as enabling "Jews to sit in judgment on their enemies" in a trial that would feature "the tragedy of Jewry."[124] At last, so the lessons concluded, Jews were no longer at the mercy of others but would confront the Nazis on their own.

Arendt offered a devastating rebuttal to each of these justifications and the underlying mentality. The Zionist rendering, she objected, used the horrors of the Holocaust to justify a dangerously simplified comprehension of political dynamics and social trends in the outside world and within Jewish communities. Consistent with their belief in a permanent antisemitism where Jew-killing is the norm simply awaiting adequate opportunity, Zionists saw the Holocaust "as not much more than the most horrible pogrom in Jewish history."[125] Hence, the Jews in exile "went to their death like sheep," because the eternal hatred had reduced them to passivity.[126] Such a tendentious narrative, she lamented, left Jews unable to form a sophisticated or reflective understanding of their encounters with the outside world.

Arendt's desire to gain a rich and self-critical comprehension of the Jewish experience in the Holocaust explains why she included harsh scrutiny of the Jewish Councils. As she wrote to former friend Gershom Scholem in response to his attacks, her point was not to shame the leaders as individuals or to equate them with Nazis: "What needs to be discussed are not the people so much as the arguments with which they justified themselves in their own eyes and those of others."[127] Beyond the specific setting faced by the council leaders, Arendt was reasserting her argument that European Jewish communities were poorly equipped to combat the new genocidal antisemitism, given their insularity and internal hierarchies. Reflecting a recurring penchant for rhetorical excess, she overshot her mark in the bluntness and sweeping nature of her attack. "In the matter of cooperation," she asserted, "there was no distinction between the highly assimilated Jewish communities in Central and Western Europe and the Yiddish-speaking masses of the East."[128] But rather than discrediting the Jewish people, Arendt was following Lazare's spirit of challenging both external and internal oppression. Notably, when the Nazis looked for pliable leaders on the councils, they usually chose the established local leaders, who embraced their new power of selection. The councils, she caustically remarked, spared Jews "'who had worked all their lives for the *zibur* [community]'—i.e., the functionaries—and the 'most prominent Jews.'"[129] The elevating of "prominent Jews" over others, lamented Arendt, had still not been confronted by the time of the trial, nor was there reason to think such hierarchies had been laid to rest with the establishment of a Jewish state.[130]

Arendt also attributed Israel's fixation on self-help to the eternal antisemitism mindset. Israel, she observed, focused on crimes against the Jewish people, as opposed to crimes against humanity, and attacked those who wanted to transfer the trial to a specially created international court. Under this defiant insularity, Israel forfeited a great opportunity to contribute to a much-needed transformation in the international community with regard to understanding and addressing crimes against humanity. After all, as Arendt had extensively demonstrated in *Origins of Totalitarianism*, the Nazi genocide was not so much an especially gruesome outbreak of a timeless antisemitism as a product of a series of interacting forces, including the nation-state form of political organization, the rise of tribal nationalism, and the surge in overseas and continental imperialism.

Arendt favored using the category of crimes against humanity to denote the underlying crimes Eichmann had furthered because it would educate the global community on the broader dynamics at stake. While the victims in the matter before the Jerusalem court were the Jewish people, for which the history of antisemitism would have some relevance, the nature of the crime was a product of frightening new global trends.[131] The world had reached the point, she decried, where it became conceivable to implement a plan across a continent to eliminate an entire national group. Such actions were "more than a crime against the Jewish or the Polish or the Gypsy people" but a crime in which "the international order, and mankind in its entirety, might have been grievously hurt and endangered."[132] Crucially, warned Arendt, there was no reason to believe that this new crime was a one-time event: "The unprecedented, once it has appeared, may become a precedent for the future."[133] Hence, she underscored the urgency to go beyond the familiar nation-state approach, whereby each Nazi victim state held trials on behalf of its victim nationals, and develop a collective and robust global approach. Arendt left unresolved what form such an approach should take. In the book's epilogue, she supported the establishment of a system of international criminal jurisprudence backed by an international tribunal. Employing the latter—albeit an ad hoc one—for the Eichmann trial, she argued, would have done more to convey the scale and "monstrousness" of the crime than "a tribunal that represents one nation only."[134] But in the postscript added a year later, Arendt expressed doubts toward the criminal law path. Prevailing juridical concepts, she concluded, were manifestly inadequate "to deal with the facts of administrative massacres organized by the state apparatus."[135]

Although unsure as to the modalities of an international approach, Arendt had no doubt that Israel should embrace international collaboration. For this to happen, the Jewish people needed to undergo a profound transformation by purging itself of the eternal antisemitism syndrome fueled by Herzlian Zionism.[136] By the time of *Eichmann in Jerusalem*'s publication in 1963, Arendt had accepted the reality of Israel as a self-defined Jewish nation-state. She defended Israel's right under the current global system to judge Nazi crimes against Jewish people on the logic that Israel represented Jews in a manner analogous to Poland representing Poles.[137] She therefore concluded that a transformation in Jewish consciousness had to be anchored in Israel's behavior as a global actor. Rather than behaving as a tribal nationalist, which confronted an undifferentiated hostile world of gentiles, Israel needed to not only make distinctions between friends and foes—that were not reduced to realpolitik calculations—but take part in a common endeavor for a more just global order. Given the book's topic, Arendt focused on a concerted global policy toward crimes against humanity. "If genocide is an actual possibility of the future," she proclaimed, "then no people on earth—least of all, of course, the Jewish people, in Israel or elsewhere—can feel reasonably sure of its continued existence without the help and the protection of international law."[138] In other words, to fulfill the promise of "Never Again," Israel has to depend not on its might but on the forging of a more solidarist and humane global order.

Ironically, although *Eichmann in Jerusalem*'s no-holds-barred approach had made Arendt an outcast in Israel and among establishment American Jewish groups and respectable Jewish intellectual circles, her stance on Zionism had softened.[139] She now accepted Israel as a representative of Jewish identity and developed an overall concern for Israel's welfare. Notably, Arendt distanced herself from the anti-Zionist American Council for Judaism when declining a lecture invitation:

> You know that I was a Zionist and that my reason for breaking with the Zionist organization was very different from the anti-Zionist stand of the Council. . . . I know . . . that should catastrophe overtake the Jewish state, for whatever reasons (even reasons of their own foolishness) this would be the final catastrophe for the whole Jewish people.[140]

Similarly, her fears for Israel's future prompted her to express support for the state during the 1967 and 1973 wars.[141] Nevertheless, Arendt retained a critical distance from both Israel and the Jewish people in general. As she explained in a heated exchange with Scholem regarding *Eichmann in Jerusalem*, "I do not 'love' the Jews, nor do I 'believe' in them; I merely belong to them as a matter of course."[142] This belonging meant a commitment to criticism and a heightened sadness for the wrongs done by Jews.

Conclusion

Arendt, who lived until 1975, did not apply her critical lens to Israel's early post-1967 developments as an occupier. This is a pity because Israel embarked on a path that heightened the negative tendencies she had foreseen two decades earlier: chauvinist triumphalism, a celebration of militarism, attachment to the global imperial power, and the scorning of both regional comity and internationalism. Uncharacteristically, Arendt was swept up in the initial euphoria following Israel's military victory in 1967. In a visit to Israel, she wrote to Karl Jaspers that it was "really quite wonderful that an entire nation react[ed] to a victory like that not by bellowing hurrah but with a real orgy of tourism . . . I was in all the formerly Arab territories and never noticed any conqueror behavior in the stream of Israeli tourists."[143] To summon Arendt's powerful spirit, one had to look then to a younger generation of Jewish pariah, such as Noam Chomsky, Uri Avnery, and Yeshayahu Leibowitz.

But while Arendt provided no new insights, her powerful interjections in the years leading up to Israel's establishment provided the normative scaffolding for the new wave of dissenting Jewish approaches that gradually emerged after 1967. In considering Arendt's distinct value for an updated critical Jewish vision, I return to the three most valuable lessons identified in this chapter's introduction: renouncing the equation of Jewish self-determination with hegemonic Jewish nationalism, overcoming Zionism's foundational pathologies of an eternal antisemitism syndrome and tribal nationalism, and linking the welfare of the Jewish community to that of the global community.

Arendt did overreach in predicting the imminent demise of the nation-state model, to be replaced in either the "form of empires or the form of federations."[144] Nevertheless, her diagnosis of the deadly and unstable potential of the nation-state system retains its force, especially in the multiple states across the world having two or more national identities with contentious histories. One need only review the breakup of the Balkan states in the 1990s and the turmoil across the Middle East unleashed by the U.S. invasion of Iraq and the accompanying surge in supposed counterterrorist operations. Moreover, the homogeneous nation-state model remains a poor fit for Israel-Palestine given the overlapping attachments of Jews and Palestinians to the same land. As reviewed in Chapter 1, Israel has maintained a Jewish nation-state only through the establishment of a massive security, administrative, and legal apparatus, which has come at the expense of the state's commitment to equality and human rights. In sum, Arendt's plea to find innovative modes of political organization remains imperative for the prospects of both a just peace and a desirable Jewish homeland.

Arendt's second valuable lesson is to confront the twinned Zionist pathologies of an eternal antisemitism syndrome and tribal nationalism, which result in a constant perception of the outside world as implacably hostile. Israel has carried out a decades-long stance of transforming political adversaries, such as Egypt under President Nasser, the Palestinian Liberation Organization (PLO), Iran, and even BDS advocates, into Nazi-like existential threats. As I show in the next chapter, this mindset has consistently impeded the state from dealing justly and sensibly with Palestinians or overcoming deep tensions with its neighboring states. To be sure, Israel has managed to develop a prosperous economy, a qualified liberal democracy within its 1967 borders, and a lively intellectual and cultural scene. Yet, as Chapter 1 addressed, Israel's pathologies have in the past two decades reached a new level that has even many respected Israeli observers worried about the state's long-term prospects as a liberal democracy. To break from this path, the original sin of an eternal antisemitism syndrome will have to be recognized and purged.

Arendt's third enduring lesson concerns replacing a Jewish politics of insularity with one committed to global reformation. Writing in the 1940s, she hoped that Jews would at last appreciate that their redemption was inseparable from a global redemption of all oppressed peoples. She implored Jews to collaborate with Palestinians on a new model of multinational coexistence that broke from the nation-state and imperialism. To her great disappointment, mainstream Zionists chose instead to attach their fortunes to the worst elements of the status quo, nationalism and imperialism. In her review of Israel's response to Eichmann, Arendt retained her conviction that the long-term fortunes of the Jewish community were intertwined with a more just and cohesive global order. Yet, as discussed in the next chapter, Israel has continued to see the international community and international law as a threat rather than an opportunity for a more secure and stable existence. Any success at advancing a very different vision of Jewish self-determination will need to return to a joint local-global struggle for a very different political and socioeconomic order.

Granted, Arendt had her blind spots. Even as she movingly castigated the Zionist leadership for dismissing the needs and aspirations of Palestinians and other Arabs, she sometimes demonstrated her own insensitivity. One noteworthy instance was a comment in personal correspondence to her longtime mentor and friend Karl Jaspers while covering the Eichmann trial:

> My first impression. On top, the judges, the best of German Jewry. Below them, the persecuting attorneys, Galicians, but still Europeans. Everything is organized by a police force that gives me the creeps, speaks only Hebrew and looks Arabic. . . . And outside the doors, the oriental mob, as if one were in Istanbul or some other half-Asiatic country.[145]

Even if one wishes to minimize this bigotry as a more visceral reaction not meant for public consumption, her undeniable Eurocentrism resulted in a lack of interest in the experiences of Arabs or Mizrahim. Yet Arendt's Euro-Jewish bias does not undermine the power of her critique and alternative vision. Rather, its primary harm was preventing her from seeing a fuller range of possibilities for productive collaboration among Jews and Arabs in Palestine and the region. Chapter 6 takes up this task by engaging the insights of Arendt and Buber with those of the respective pioneers of Palestinian and Mizrahi scholarship, Edward Said and Ella Shohat. Importantly, both Palestinians and Mizrahi Jews have a "pariah" tradition—consisting of actors seeking liberation from both external and internal oppression—which can readily be enlisted in the type of comrade-in-arms solidarity Arendt favored.

In sum, contemporary Jewish dissenters have rightly settled on Arendt as the most inspirational of the foundational Jewish critics of Zionism. What marks her is an outsider-insider iconoclasm, as she combines penetrating scrutiny of the Jewish community's failings with a deep attachment to its long-term health. Her embrace of an outsider role, avoiding what she regarded as cheap sentimental expressions of love for the Jewish community, has no doubt contributed to her attaining a reputation in certain Jewish circles as either a self-hating Jew or at least lacking emotional attachment, as Scholem charged. Unlike Buber, she received no accolades from top Israeli officials or Zionist leaders elsewhere after her death. But for dissenting Jews confronting the grave crisis of actually existing Zionism in the Jewish community, Arendt's manner of belonging offers the most productive model for moving forward. She is the outstanding Jewish pariah.

4

Missing Every Opportunity for Peace and Reconciliation

There are no refugees—there are fighters who sought to destroy us root and branch. The Arab states . . . still refuse to make peace or to recognize us. . . . Shall we bring back the refugees so they can exterminate us for the second time.

—David Ben-Gurion, diary entry[1]

Buber and Arendt feared for what Zionism would become if it took the form of a nation-state in the European tradition, especially the tribal nationalist variant. They correctly anticipated the negative long-term impact both on Palestinians and on Israel's moral character of forging a nation-state through military conquest. Arendt in particular foresaw a state marred by an enduring belligerency and insularity. This chapter highlights the extent to which the Humanist Zionist diagnosis played out in practice for Israel's first half-century. I identify the following recurring features. First, Israel has regularly subjugated Palestinians within Israel and, all the more so, in the post-1967 occupied territories. Second, it has accorded enhanced rights, benefits, and symbolic status to its Jewish residents and diminished the Palestinian attachment to the land. Third, Israel has been belligerent toward its neighbors, frequently initiating cross-border attacks. Finally, it has treated the UN and the international community in general with contempt. All of these traits follow from the core pathologies Arendt identified, the eternal antisemitism syndrome and tribal nationalism.

This chapter examines three pivotal eras. One is Israel's first decade, in which it institutionalized a hegemonic Jewish nationalism and a hard-line stance toward Palestinians and its neighboring states. The second is the period from the 1967 war through 1980, when Israel formed a special relationship with the United States; instituted a still-enduring occupation of the West Bank, East Jerusalem, and the Gaza Strip; and rejected global appeals for a Palestinian state. The third is the decade from 1991 through 2001. It began with tantalizing prospects for Israeli-Palestinian peace and ended in the second intifada and the harsh Israeli crackdown. Collectively, this chapter demonstrates the enduring cogency of Humanist Zionism in diagnosing what to expect of a state wedded to insular nationalism and an eternal antisemitism mindset. In each era, Israeli leaders failed to take advantage of promising opportunities both to mitigate conflict with Palestinians and neighboring Arab states and to minimize injustices inflicted on Palestinians.

Prioritizing a Strong and Jewish State over Peace: Israel's Early Years

After the 1948 war, Israel possessed all the territory allotted it in the partition resolution (55 percent), and another 20-plus percent. While it had armistice agreements with the Arab states it had fought in the war, Israel was seen as a hostile and illegitimate entity in the region. Due to the Nakba, the land was now overwhelmingly Jewish. The bulk of Palestinians were refugees, concentrated in neighboring Arab states, especially Jordan and the Jordanian-controlled West Bank. Most resided in refugee camps administered through the UN Relief and Works Agency.[2] Israel faced a number of important choices in its early years about how it would interact with the global community, the region, Palestinian refugees, and the minority of Palestinians remaining in Israel. It chose a pathway of opposition to the global consensus, belligerency with its neighbors, and subjugation of all Palestinians.

Two widely approved UN General Assembly resolutions set the terms for the postwar global consensus. One was Resolution 181 from 1947, the partition resolution.[3] Its main features included delineating borders for the new states of Israel and Palestine and making Jerusalem a *corpus separatum* administered by the UN. The second was Resolution 194, which reaffirmed the partition borders and internationalization of Jerusalem and instructed Israel to permit "at the earliest practicable date" the return of all refugees "wishing to return to their homes and live at peace with their neighbors."[4] Guided by these resolutions, UN-appointed mediators focused on a land-and-refugees-for-peace settlement, whereby the Arab states would enter into a peace treaty with Israel while the latter would withdraw from the additional land it had conquered and allow the return of all refugees. Although there was no formal repudiation of Resolution 181's call for a Palestinian state, it did not become a feature of international negotiations. The Palestinians were too weak politically to advance their cause, while Jordan's King Abdullah sought to absorb the West Bank for his own ends.[5]

Israel rejected the first postwar global peace initiative at the UN-sponsored conference in Lausanne, Switzerland, in 1949. There, the three-member Palestine Conciliation Commission (PCC) of the United States, Turkey, and France aimed for a comprehensive regional settlement.[6] The PCC managed to get the parties to agree on a protocol that acknowledged UN Resolutions 181 and 194 as a basis for working out a comprehensive peace. Yet Israel and other states added reservations that diminished the protocol's practical significance.[7] To be sure, the Arab states were reluctant to recognize Israel or meet with its delegates and called for unconditional Israeli withdrawal to the partition resolution borders and admission of all refugees. Nevertheless, they showed flexibility on borders and were willing to absorb a sizable portion of refugees if provided financial support.[8] Overall, as the head of the U.S. delegation complained, Israel was far more recalcitrant.[9] It rejected any proposal that involved ceding any territory, accepting a significant number of refugees, or internationalizing Jerusalem.[10] It even declared as "garbage" a proposal from the U.S. delegate for Israel to withdraw from the southern part of the Negev.[11]

Israel was no more availing in negotiations with individual states. At one point, Egypt floated the idea of a peace treaty in exchange for Israel keeping the Galilee (which the partition resolution allotted to Palestine) but ceding the Negev (which the resolution allotted to Israel). The Negev would then be combined with the West Bank to form a buffer area where many refugees could relocate.[12] Israel summarily dismissed the proposal, noting that it would not give up any of the Galilee or Negev. Most forthcoming was Husnei Zaim, who briefly seized power in Syria in 1949. He proposed direct talks with Ben-Gurion to work out permanent borders, which included an offer to admit three hundred thousand refugees. Despite U.S. urging, Ben-Gurion resisted doing so and was spared of further pressure when Zaim was deposed.[13] Israel's head of the Foreign Ministry's Middle Eastern Department candidly summed up his state's attitude: "The Jews think they can achieve peace without any price—either maximal or minimal. They want the Arabs to cede the territory occupied by Israel; to absorb all the refugees in the Arab states; to accept frontier modifications favorable to Israel to control Palestine."[14]

Rather than cooperate with the international community, Israel carried out a foreign policy oriented toward acquiring greater resources and regional military predominance. As Arendt anticipated, it continued to court outside powers at the expense of peaceful relations in the region. Israel most coveted an alliance with the United States, the dominant global power and home to the largest Jewish population. It openly aligned with the U.S. sphere of influence when the Korean War broke out in 1950.[15] When the United States declined to provide significant military aid, Israel turned to France in the mid-1950s.[16] The two shared a common opposition to the anti-imperialist Pan-Arabism and especially to Egypt's president, Gamal Abdel Nasser, who was providing logistic and political support for the Algerian liberation struggle against France. This alliance led to a collusion between France, Britain, and Israel to invade Egypt with the hope of reversing Nasser's nationalization of the Suez Canal and precipitating his overthrow. The operation failed because of great political backlash, despite Israel's successful invasion.[17] Although Nasser's international prestige soared while Israel was perceived as an imperialist tool, the latter had no regrets. It forged closer military ties with France and persuaded leading U.S. figures of Israel's potential as a regional ally.[18]

Israel's uncompromising commitment to Jewish predominance was most pronounced with regard to the Palestinians. Helped by the waning of international pressure to establish a Palestinian state, Israel abandoned its pragmatic acceptance of the partition resolution.[19] The signing of the armistice between Jordan and Israel effectively buried the idea for two decades by legitimizing Jordan's control over the West Bank and East Jerusalem.[20] Israel did once propose to absorb one hundred thousand refugees in response to a sharp rebuke in 1949 from President Harry Truman.[21] This number, however, appeared to include thousands who had already managed to sneak back in, while Israel would choose where to resettle the new refugees.[22] Archival evidence suggests that it made the proposal to placate the United States but never intended to follow through.[23] Israel soon withdrew the offer and rejected all other appeals to admit refugees. It then imposed martial law to prevent refugee infiltrations and passed an absentee property law to appropriate their property.[24]

Israel followed a more nuanced policy for the Palestinians who remained. It did not openly defy UN Resolution 181's call for full equality, but its compliance was mostly symbolic. In a nod to international opinion, Israel endorsed full equality in the Declaration of Independence and guaranteed individual political rights to Palestinian citizens.[25] Yet Israeli officials created a set of institutions and practices that prioritized the needs and status of Jews. As a foundational step, they declared martial rule over the areas where Palestinians were concentrated. This enabled Israel to relocate Palestinians to closed zones—making room for Jewish immigrants—and strictly regulate their movement and economic activity.[26] Because any travel outside a closed zone required applying for a military permit (a time-consuming process), Palestinians found themselves cut off from each other, isolated from Israelis, and dependent on occupation authorities.[27] Of equal importance, Israel formed a land-use system, administered in part through the Jewish National Fund, that reserved over 90 percent of all land for Jewish ownership and use.[28] This dislocation of internal Palestinians was complemented by the extension of Israel's absentee property law to "present absentees," meaning those still in Israel who had temporarily left their residence on or after November 29, 1947.[29] The state also diminished the Palestinian heritage and attachment to the territory. To begin with, it destroyed many of the mostly emptied Palestinian villages and gave them Hebrew names. Next, the state avoided the term *Palestinians*, preferring *Israeli-Arabs*.[30] It further passed a Law of Return, which granted citizenship to all Jews seeking immigration but denied the opportunity for Palestinians.[31] Finally, Israel passed a nationality law, which created separate categories of "Jewish" and "Arab."[32]

Why Israel Did Not Pursue Opportunities for Easing Tensions

Israel had ample opportunities in its first decade to lessen tensions with its neighbors, mitigate the Palestinian refugee crisis, and foster positive Jewish-Palestinian relations at home. To begin with, Israel enjoyed a favorable political setting for reaching a settlement with the Arab states. In the wake of the Holocaust, the state enjoyed great sympathy, including from the major powers. The new global consensus recognized Israel and carved it a path for long-term acceptance in the region. None of the frontline neighbors, individually or collectively, posed a military threat. During the war, each fought not for the Palestinians but for their own interests.[33] After the war, Arab state leaders supported a settlement based on the global consensus and showed receptivity to modified proposals.[34] Israel thus could have attained modest adjustments to the global consensus with regard to its specific borders and the amount of refugees admitted. The potential payoff was a full peace backed by international security guarantees and financial assistance.

Although a full resolution of the Palestinian situation was doubtful, given Jordan's opposition and the disarray of Palestinians, Israel could have followed Buber's advice to "prepare the ground" for long-term reconciliation.[35] To start, the state could have proposed a creative compromise on the Palestinian refugees that did not pretend to undo all injustices from the war but sought to fulfill the genuine needs of Palestinians and Jews. Namely, Israel would commit to a significant absorption of refugees and solicit the input of the region and of the UN for a comprehensive solution that also addressed the thousands of displaced Jewish persons from postwar Europe.[36] Because the UN mediators at Lausanne were open to such a compromise, as were specific Arab state leaders, the prospects for resolution were promising.

Israel could have attempted similarly creative measures to integrate the Palestinian minority within its borders. Even if, as Buber acknowledged, exigent circumstances precluded full equality in the short term (particularly on security matters), Israel had means to make Palestinians more welcome. For starters, the Declaration of Independence could have announced equal regard for the state's Jewish and Arab heritage. Next, the state could have enacted laws and policies designed to improve the living situation of Palestinians, further individual and collective equality, and foster Jewish-Arab interactions and collaboration. In addition, Israel's endorsement of an internationalized, united Jerusalem would have opened up opportunities for shared governance there. Although Jordan's King Abdullah opposed such unification, he would have been hard-pressed to resist an Israeli-supported plan.

Israel's refusal to pursue any of these opportunities is rooted in the insular nationalism and endemic distrust of outsiders diagnosed by Arendt. This national identity revealed itself in the way Ben-Gurion ranked Israel's "vital interests" at a government meeting in 1952:

> First and foremost, we have to see to Israel's needs, whether or not this brings improvement in our relations with the Arabs. The second factor in our existence is American Jewry and its relationship with us (and the state of America since these Jews live in it). The third thing—peace with the Arabs.[37]

As Zeev Maoz establishes, "Israel's needs" meant forming a strong and unified Jewish nation-state in which militarism and the IDF would serve as the focal point, especially for socializing the mass influx of Jewish immigrants.[38] The combination of a nation-building-militarism nexus and the existential distrust of outsiders led Israel to adopt a security approach based on what Maoz calls a "siege mentality." It viewed itself as a small state confronted by potentially powerful neighbors who ultimately sought its destruction.[39] Accordingly, Israel implicitly adopted the Iron Wall policy of the Revisionist Zionists, which assumed that peace would be possible only once the collective Arab will had been broken.[40] It maintained a large active and reserve military force, treated peace overtures as traps, and responded to perceived threats with conflict escalation, which featured free-fire shootings of infiltrations from Palestinian refugees and collective reprisals on their home villages.[41]

Guided by this siege mentality, Israel assumed an adversarial approach toward the UN, international mediation, and international law. During the Lausanne talks, U.S. State Department officials rebuked Israel's rejectionist stance on refugees and territorial adjustment as being contrary to the partition resolution and to what motivated the UN's support of a Jewish state.[42] Ben-Gurion was unmoved by this appeal: "The State of Israel was not established as a consequence of the UN Resolution. Neither America nor any other country saw the Resolution through, nor did they stop the Arab countries . . . from declaring total war on us in violation of UN Resolutions."[43] Israeli officials maintained that their state's well-being depended on military prowess and an aggressive stance. Hence, they deemed it folly to rely on the UN or on international resolutions. "International law," declared Ben-Gurion, "does not require that Israel commit suicide."[44] When the UN reaffirmed in December 1949 that Jerusalem should be a separate internationalized city, Israel's Knesset voted to relocate from Tel Aviv to Jerusalem.[45] Similarly, it provoked strong UN rebukes for its harsh cross-border reprisals against Palestinian infiltrations. Rejecting UN mediation, Ben-Gurion mocked the UN, *Oom* in Hebrew, as "*Oom-shmoom*."[46]

Because of a combined siege mentality and tribal nationalist insistence on an exclusive Jewish nation-state, Israel chose to exacerbate its subjection and marginalization of Palestinians. Much to Buber's disappointment, Israeli officials did not sympathize with Palestinians as fellow exiles or accept responsibility for precipitating the crisis.[47] To the contrary, Israel's leaders rejoiced at the elimination of the perceived demographic threat to a Jewish state. Foreign Minister Moshe Sharett credited the "wholesale evacuation of its Arab population" as enabling "a lasting and radical solution of the most vexing problem of the Jewish state."[48] He and other leaders deemed it unthinkable to allow the refugees back. For one thing, the mass return and absorption would require significant state resources and thereby impede the primary goal of absorbing Jewish immigrants.[49] For another thing, Israelis regarded Palestinians as irredeemable Jew-haters who should not get another chance to destroy the Jews. In a diary entry, Ben-Gurion stated the following: "There are no refugees—there are fighters who sought to destroy us root and branch. The Arab states . . . still refuse to make peace or to recognize us. . . . Shall we bring back the refugees so they can exterminate us for the second time."[50] Israel was no more obliging to the relatively small remnant of Palestinians—roughly 14 percent as of 1949—who still resided in Israel.[51] Rather than take the steps outlined above to make the minority welcome, Israel cordoned off the Palestinians, subjected them to military rule, and tried to erase the territory's Palestinian heritage altogether.

To be sure, a far more receptive approach by Israel would have faced great challenges. Peace treaties with neighboring Arab states would not have eliminated all conflict, though they would have diminished the frequency of cross-border infiltrations from Palestinians and Israeli reprisals. Yet a serious commitment to resolving tensions and minimizing injustices would not have endangered Israel's survival or impeded the fostering of a distinct Jewish community. The potential payoff, by contrast, was significant. Israel's security would have been grounded in an international normative framework designed to foster better relations in the region. Accordingly, there would have been enhanced prospects for a durable peace and thereby an easing of Israel's military footprint. Because it was unable to shed its core pathologies, Israel set itself on a course of perpetual hostility with its neighbors and the entrenchment of a highly militarized society attached to great-power pursuits.

No to Land-for-Peace and Palestine, Yes to Occupation and Expansion: 1967–1980

The June 1967 war, whereby Israel took control of all the Palestine Mandate along with Syria's Golan Heights and Egypt's Sinai, is rightly viewed as a seminal moment. Israel became a major military power, a close ally of the United States, and a society with a formidable religious nationalist camp. Most dramatically, it launched an enduring and extensive occupation. Israel assumed nearly complete sovereignty over East Jerusalem while maintaining a separate status for its Palestinian residents. For the West Bank and Gaza Strip, Israel combined a conventional belligerent occupation with an extensive settlement project. Under this still-existing bifurcated apartheid system, Palestinians became subjects of military rule while Jewish settlers remained Israeli citizens, living in separate communities and governed by Israel's legal order.[52] Nevertheless, as important as the post-1967 developments have been, they followed long-standing traits. As in its first decade, Israel rejected a global consensus that offered a path for long-term peace with its neighboring states and, eventually, with Palestinians.

Phase One: Opposing the Land-for-Peace Global Consensus

The post-1967 global consensus went through two phases. The first, which lasted through the early-mid-1970s, focused on peace between Israel and the Arab states. Its foundational document was the unanimously approved Security Council Resolution 242. Beginning with an emphasis on the "inadmissibility of the acquisition of territory by war," 242 called for Israel's withdrawal from the territories conquered in the war, respect for all states' "sovereignty, territorial integrity, and political independence," and a "just settlement of the refugee problem."[53] The resolution relegated Palestinians to unnamed refugees. The other new aspect of the global consensus, codified by Council Resolution 237, was a declaration that the laws of belligerent occupation applied to all newly conquered territories.[54]

Following an initial period of ambiguity, Israel settled on rejecting any concessions. In 1969, Prime Minister Golda Meir rebuffed a variant of the peace-for-withdrawal plan formulated by U.S. Secretary of State William Rogers and declared that Israel would not withdraw to the 1967 lines.[55] Israel turned down similar offers over the next several years. One was Jordan's proposal for a peace treaty between Israel and a new federated Jordan, to be called the United Arab Kingdom, which would include the West Bank and East Jerusalem.[56] In 1971, UN Special Representative Gunnar Jarring proposed a simultaneous implementation of mutual recognition between Egypt and Israel and Israel's withdrawal to the 1967 lines. While Egypt accepted the proposal, Israel proclaimed that it would not "withdraw to the pre-5 June 1967 lines."[57] To preclude any deal on East Jerusalem, Israel defied multiple UN resolutions by asserting direct sovereignty over the area, expanding its borders, and launching projects for its Jewish residents that displaced Palestinians.[58]

To Israel's delight, its foreign policy of courting great powers had succeeded by 1970 in establishing a close strategic relationship with the United States. Granted, the United States supported some of the critical UN resolutions, and Israel considered the Rogers Plan an irritant. Yet what mattered for Israel was the close alliance in practice. U.S. military and economic aid ensured it a substantial quantitative and qualitative military superiority over the frontline Arab states. Impressed by Israel's convincing military victory in 1967 and in need of "regional cops" while bogged down in Vietnam, the United States solicited Israel's assistance in containing Pan-Arab nationalism and checking Soviet influence.[59] Unlike Secretary of State Rogers, President Richard Nixon and National Security Adviser Henry Kissinger generally welcomed Israel's belligerent stance. They believed a regional stalemate would help convince Arab states, especially Egypt, of the futility of relying on Soviet aid.[60] By fully embracing the alliance with the United States, who most valued Israel's military capabilities and had little regard for UN-led multilateralism, Israel became more entrenched in a siege mentality and in the type of "imperial sphere of interest" Arendt foresaw, one "which trusts a distant imperial power for protection, while alienating the goodwill of neighbors."[61]

Israel's hostility to the international community and reliance on the United States to shield it from sanctions intensified as the global consensus shifted in the mid-1970s. For roughly twenty-five years, Israel had faced no real international pressure to yield on Palestinian political rights. This happy situation soon came to an end thanks to the efforts of a newly energized PLO.

Phase Two: The Rise of the Two-State Global Consensus and Israel's Defiance

Because of their weak political status, Palestinians were marginalized in Resolution 242 and initial post-1967 global discussions.[62] Ironically, Israel's crushing defeat of the frontline Arab states, especially Egypt, sparked the growth of an assertive, independent Palestinian movement. The PLO's amended charter in 1968 proclaimed, "The Palestinian Arab people assert the genuineness and independence of their national revolution and reject all forms of intervention, trusteeship and subordination."[63] It first gained the support of the Nonaligned Movement (NAM), a coalition of recently decolonized states advancing a common front at the UN and elsewhere. Attracted by the message of an indigenous movement seeking to liberate itself from colonial-style rule, NAM advocated for full Palestinian political rights and mobilized support at the UN General Assembly.[64] Subsequently, the Arab League, to Jordan's disappointment, declared the PLO to be "the sole legitimate representative of the Palestinian people."[65]

The PLO's initial categorical opposition to Israel's existence, however, limited its broader appeal.[66] Prodded by the Soviet Union and internal factions, the PLO announced its receptivity at the 1974 Palestinian National Council to an intermediate "ministate" that would exist alongside Israel.[67] Global support sharply expanded. In November 1974, the UN General Assembly granted the PLO observer status and enacted Resolution 3236, which endorsed Palestinian national independence.[68] By the next year, support expanded in Latin America for Palestinian self-determination, while France and other European states became receptive to an independent Palestinian "homeland."[69]

In 1976, the PLO further moderated its stance in conjunction with launching a new normative offensive at the UN Security Council. Recently empowered by the General Assembly to participate as a nonvoting actor in all Middle East–related deliberations, the PLO collaborated with NAM member states holding rotating seats in the council on a series of council resolutions.[70] One linked Palestinian statehood and refugee rights to the clauses in Resolution 242 that declared the inadmissibility of the acquisition of territory by war, called for full Israeli withdrawal, and affirmed the territorial integrity of all states in the region.[71] In agreeing to the latter clause, the PLO indirectly accepted Israel's existence along the pre-1967 war borders. It recognized that the United States would veto the resolution. Yet the PLO understood that because of the council's prestige on global security matters, its favorable deliberation on Palestinian statehood would boost the cause.[72] The PLO succeeded in its goal. Of the thirteen states voting, nine voted yes, while the United States cast the only no vote.[73] The accompanying debate established universal support outside of the United States and Israel for adding Palestinian self-determination to the global consensus. While Britain, Sweden, and Italy abstained because the resolution did not explicitly endorse 242, they agreed that Palestinian self-determination was "a basic prerequisite for a just settlement of the conflict in the Middle East."[74] As the French delegate concluded, "We do not believe that this has been a sterile or vain debate . . . the framework for a just and stable solution for the Middle East has become clearer . . . all parties to the settlement should hereafter take this into account."[75]

The PLO also lobbied against Israel's settlement project by drafting with NAM a series of council resolutions in 1979 and 1980. The first affirmed "that the policy and practices of Israel in establishing settlements in the Palestinian and other Arab territories occupied since 1967 have no legal validity and constitute a serious obstruction to achieving a comprehensive, just and lasting peace in the Middle East."[76] Because the language mirrored its prior statements, the United States abstained, allowing the resolution to pass. The PLO-NAM coalition secured the passage of several subsequent critical council resolutions, which proclaimed the "overriding necessity to end the prolonged occupation"[77] and directed states to halt settlement-related aid to Israel[78] and remove their diplomatic missions from Jerusalem.[79]

Cumulatively, the PLO's normative offensive prompted a substantial modification of the global consensus. To begin with, there was now universal agreement, apart from Israel and the United States, that there should be an independent Palestinian state on all of the Gaza Strip and West Bank.[80] Sealing this transformation was the European Economic Community's (EEC's) release of the Venice Declaration on June 13, 1980. In part, it consolidated previous position papers by denouncing the settlements and supporting full Israeli withdrawal from the occupied territories. The declaration broke new ground by demanding freedom for the Palestinian people "to exercise fully its right to self-determination," which meant an independent state.[81] The EEC's turn was particularly significant because of the close relations many of its states had with Israel and the United States.[82] The other modification in the global consensus was near-unanimous agreement that the primary obstacle to peace was Israel's ongoing settlement enterprise.

As the global consensus shifted, Israeli society moved sharply in the reverse direction. In 1977, Israelis elected a new governing coalition, led by the Likud Party, which inaugurated a further hardening in Israel's stance toward peace and reconciliation. The Likud Party and allies proclaimed a categorical rejection of all territorial withdrawal and ratcheted up the state's hostile rhetoric toward Palestinians, the UN, and the international community at large. Most concretely, the state dramatically increased the population of Israeli settlers and expanded settlement locations to densely populated areas in hopes of precluding the possibility of territorial partition.[83]

At first glance, the new hard-line government seemingly turned a new leaf by entering into a peace treaty with Egypt in 1978–1979. After all, the prior Labor-led government had rejected a similar plan in 1971.[84] Yet this partial reversal should be understood in the context of Israel's determination to circumvent the new global consensus on settlements and a Palestinian state. What enabled the deal was Egypt's foreign policy shift in the 1970s under President Anwar Sadat. Rather than remain a leading voice in NAM and a Soviet ally, Egypt sought better relations with the United States in order to regain the Sinai. After Israel and the United States rebuffed its initial overtures, Egypt joined with Syria in a surprise attack in 1973 that enjoyed early military success. The United States took notice and initiated a shuttle diplomacy, which prodded a moderation in Israel's stance and brought Egypt into its strategic orbit.[85] In November 1977, Sadat broke from the Arab common front by announcing his willingness to visit Israel's Knesset.[86]

Israel then revised its foreign policy toward Egypt. It had long sought a separate peace, but not at the cost of substantial territorial withdrawal. Yet with Egypt moving away from Pan-Arabism, Israel became receptive to a land-for-peace deal as part of a broader strategy to consolidate control over the West Bank, weaken the PLO, and bypass UN-led diplomacy. Sadat did initially demand that a peace be linked to full withdrawal from the Palestinian-occupied territories and an eventual Palestinian state, while the United States sought a settlement freeze.[87] But because Sadat prioritized regaining the Sinai and President Jimmy Carter did not want the talks to collapse, Israel extracted maximum leverage. At the 1978 Camp David summit, the parties agreed to two frameworks. One was a treaty between Egypt and Israel of mutual recognition and Israeli withdrawal from the Sinai. The second was an Israeli promise to grant an undefined political autonomy for Palestinians in Gaza and the West Bank—but not East Jerusalem—to be worked out through a new, non-UN institutional channel that excluded the PLO and granted Israel veto power.[88] Israel thus secured its goals. Helped by U.S. security guarantees, it no longer had to worry about an Egyptian attack and retained full freedom to expand its settlements. Invoking the autonomy accord, it insisted that all negotiations over Palestinian rights be conducted in the friendly Camp David–created channel rather than through the UN.[89] President Carter later acknowledged that the Camp David accords "gave the Israelis renewed freedom to pursue their goals of fortifying and settling the occupied territories."[90] Not coincidentally, Israel launched an ambitious invasion of Lebanon in 1982, which aimed, unsuccessfully, to destroy the PLO.

Why Israel Rejected the Post-1967 Consensus for Peaceful Resolution

Notwithstanding its track record, Israel could still have shifted from a foreign policy of courting power and aggressive interventionism to one of substantive international cooperation throughout the 1967–1980 era. The immediate post-1967 setting was especially opportune for a peaceful reset with the Arab states. Israel's international standing was respectable. It was not yet a U.S. strategic outpost and had cordial relations in most of the world outside the Middle East and other Muslim-majority states.[91] Most importantly, the global consensus had shifted markedly in Israel's favor. Its UN ambassador in that era, Abba Eban, acknowledged that Resolution 242 "corresponded more closely to our basic interests than we could have dared to expect from the United Nations a short time before."[92] He was impressed that the USSR and most of the international community had for the first time accepted Israel's post-1948 territorial expansion by calling for withdrawal from only the newly conquered territories. Moreover, unlike Israel's 1956 invasion of Egypt, the UN did not demand unconditional Israeli withdrawal but one linked to the region's recognition of Israel. One might add that Resolution 242's "just settlement" formulation implied greater flexibility than General Assembly Resolution 194 on how to resolve the Palestinian refugee crisis.

Along with a receptive global consensus, Israel faced no real security threat. The 1967 war made clear that the frontline Arab states, notwithstanding an increase in belligerent rhetoric in the years preceding the war, had no viable military option. Thus, Egypt and Jordan quickly expressed their support for the new global consensus. Even at the Khartoum Conference in November 1967, where the Arab heads of state proclaimed their opposition to recognition of or negotiations with Israel, Egypt and Jordan declared their intent to rely on diplomacy rather than military force to regain land.[93] Both also proved more obliging in practice by cooperating with international efforts to reach a peace treaty based on the terms of 242. If Israel had embraced 242 and UN mediation, its prospects of reaching a full treaty with Egypt and Jordan would have dramatically improved. Under such a deal, Israel would have withdrawn from the newly conquered territories and admitted a sizable amount of Palestinian refugees, while Egypt and Jordan would have formally recognized

Israel's standing in the region.[94] In addition, Israel could have secured international security guarantees and financial support.

Up through the early 1970s, there was little opportunity to resolve the larger Palestinian situation because the PLO adamantly opposed Israel's existence.[95] Yet Israel was positioned to prepare the ground for long-term reconciliation by absorbing refugees in the manner outlined above and undoing its long subordination of its Palestinian residents.[96] Doing so required the removal of discriminatory laws, reparations for nearly two decades of martial rule and land appropriation, formal honoring of the land's Palestinian heritage, and affirmative steps to improve the economic and political status of Palestinians. Finally, with Jerusalem reunited (albeit under military occupation), Israel could have used the opportunity to revive the international plan to make Jerusalem a united and internationalized city open to all Israelis and Palestinians.

With the shift in the global consensus by the mid-late 1970s, backed by the PLO, Israel could have proposed a peace treaty with the PLO that included joint recognition of two states, Israel's dismantling of settlements, a phased withdrawal from the West Bank and Gaza Strip, and joint management of a united Jerusalem under international guarantees. Even if success was not guaranteed, the risks of making the effort were minimal, and international cooperation would have been robust. The PLO had little military capability, while Israel could take focused measures to protect its civilians from acts of violence. The potential gains were considerable. Israel would have achieved an enduring peace that would usher in a new policy of international cooperation and regional comity. It would have hence moved closer to Arendt's appeal to a "modus vivendi" with the Palestinians that "counteract[ed] the dangerous tendencies of formerly oppressed peoples to . . . develop . . . nationalist superiority complexes of their own."[97]

As in its first decade, Israel's refusal to pursue promising peace opportunities in the dozen years following the 1967 war is best explained by the pathologies Arendt and other Humanist Zionists identified. While governing coalitions shifted, along with the parameters of the global consensus, Israel's political culture retained a tribal nationalism and unyielding hostility toward both its direct adversaries and the international community at large. Similar to its stance toward the 1949 Lausanne summit, Israel regarded the Jarring mission and even the mediation efforts of the U.S. secretary of state as traps, not opportunities. Israel thus ratcheted up its disdain for the UN and international law. In 1971, UN ambassador Yitzhak Rabin denounced the UN for manifesting the "hostility of the world" and being "useless and meaningless."[98] After the council's passage of Resolution 478 in 1980, which directed states to remove their embassies from Jerusalem, Israel's Foreign Ministry remarked,

"We are all disappointed that very important free countries lent their hand to the decision.... This resolution will encourage extremism, blackmail, and incitement to war."[99]

What both Labor-led and Likud-led governments considered the greatest affront was any expression of support for Palestinians. Committed to a tribal nationalism that yielded no collective status to other national groups, Israelis refused to even acknowledge a separate Palestinian people. Prime Minister Meir remarked in 1969, "It is not as though there was a Palestinian people in Palestine ... and we came and threw them out.... They did not exist."[100] Around this time, Israel began its demonization of the PLO as the latest incarnation of an implacable antisemitic enemy. It fixated on PLO violence and ignored the group's moderation by the mid-to-late 1970s. After the passage of UN General Assembly Resolution 3236 in 1974, Prime Minister Rabin promised that Israel would "refuse any attempt to detach the Palestinian problem from Jordan" and would "never negotiate with the so-called PLO."[101] In 1976, its UN ambassador characterized the council's favorable deliberation on Palestinian statehood as "a tragedy of major international proportion."[102] The new hard-line prime minister Menachem Begin continued this rhetorical trope by equating the PLO with Nazi Germany.[103] In reaction to Europe's move in 1980 to support a Palestinian state, Begin defiantly replied, "We shall not recognize the neo-Nazi murderous PLO nor shall we ever agree to the formation of a Palestinian state."[104] Unable to break from its pathologies, Israel entered the 1980s as a leading international pariah, deeply reliant on military might, self-help, and U.S. protection.

The Rise and Fall of the Oslo Peace Process

In August 1993, Israel stunned much of the world by agreeing to sign an accord with the PLO. At the White House lawn the next month, Prime Minister Rabin and PLO chair Yasser Arafat sealed the deal with one of the most famous handshakes. For the first time, Israel and the PLO were engaged in direct talks, while the PLO leadership was cleared to establish a governing authority of sorts in Palestinian territory. Yet this period of optimism was fleeting. In less than a decade, the Oslo-initiated peace process came to a definitive halt amid a violent second Palestinian intifada, a brutal Israeli crackdown, and a surge in popularity of extremist actors on both sides. Although all sides, including the U.S. government, share culpability for Oslo's collapse, it was Israel's aggressive stance from the outset that doomed the prospects for a successful resolution.

Entering the Oslo era, the global consensus was unchanged. The PLO leadership unequivocally supported two states based on the pre-1967 war boundaries, though there had developed a significant Islamist opposition movement led by Hamas. The Rabin government was willing to cede the Gaza Strip and a large part of the West Bank but opposed a Palestinian state and maintained its right to retain and even expand so-called security settlements. One significant change was the weaker political status of Arafat and the PLO leadership by 1993 due to two blows.[105] First, because they had not denounced Iraq's 1990 invasion of Kuwait, the Gulf States had curtailed their financial support. Second, the PLO had become overshadowed by independent movements in the occupied territories waging a successful intifada. To regain relevance, it was willing to grant significant concessions.

The accord consisted of a Declaration of Principles and letters of mutual recognition from Rabin and Arafat. The letters indicated how skewed the accord was in Israel's favor. Arafat recognized Israel's right to exist and renounced both terrorism and the PLO Charter's commitment to "armed struggle."[106] Rabin, by contrast, simply recognized the PLO as the representative of the Palestinian people. He did not commit to a Palestinian state or to full compliance with international humanitarian law. The Declaration of Principles provided for Israel's military withdrawal from the Gaza Strip and Jericho and the creation of a Palestinian Interim Self-Government Authority (Palestinian Authority or PA) in parts of the occupied territories on a restricted set of issues.[107] This arrangement would serve as a transition to "permanent status" negotiations that would resolve the issues of Jerusalem, refugees, settlements, security arrangements, and borders. In the interim, Israel would retain exclusive authority over these issues. Notably, the declaration placed no constraints on Israel's right to maintain or expand its settlements. Nor did it incorporate references to international laws on occupation.[108]

The 1995 follow-up accord, known as Oslo 2, brought specificity to the interim arrangement and retained the asymmetrical relationship. It divided the West Bank into Areas A, B, and C. The PA had nearly full sovereignty over Area A (apart from external security), partial sovereignty over Area B, and almost none over Area C.[109] Oslo 2 called for gradual transference of Area B lands to Area A and of Area C lands to Area B. To satisfy Israel, the accord initially allotted Area C roughly 70 percent of the West Bank and did not specify how much of it would be transferred.[110] With eventual U.S approval, Israel assumed unilateral discretion.

Overall, Oslo 2 substantially furthered Israel's aims. By giving it full control of the bulk of the West Bank, the accord reaffirmed Israel's ongoing settlement population expansion in the areas it intended to maintain permanently.[111] Oslo 2 also enabled the further expansion of bypass roads that linked the settlements to each other and to Israel proper. Most significant, the accord gave Israel structural power by virtue of the state's control of overall security, of the timing of scope of land withdrawals, and of the movement of Palestinian people and goods. Israel freely employed this power to withhold taxes, block commerce, and cancel planned redeployments in response to acts of violence from Palestinians.[112]

For all of Rabin's shortcomings, his government had become Israel's most moderate government, which invited great hopes from the state's peace camp. His assassination in November 1995 inflicted a severe blow to these hopes. Shortly thereafter, the Likud Party regained control of the government. The new prime minister, Benjamin Netanyahu, stopped short of categorically repudiating the accord, but he aggressively moved to halt progress. His government further expanded Israel's settlement population, created more bypass roads and checkpoints, halted or delayed planned Israeli transfers of land to Palestinian authority, and responded disproportionately to Palestinian acts of violence.

The Oslo process seemingly received one last lifeline when a Labor-led government regained power in May 1999 under Prime Minister Ehud Barak. Yet Barak's first year in office, leading up to Camp David, set a bad tone. Like Rabin, he adopted an adversarial stance on implementation. His government facilitated another surge in settlement population growth and bypass roads and checkpoints.[113] Similarly, Barak reneged on prior commitments by delaying transfers of land to PA jurisdiction and the release of prisoners and launching disproportionate reprisals to Palestinian acts of violence.[114] In March 2000, after a failed effort at peace negotiations with Syria, Barak turned his attention to the Palestinians. Backed by President Bill Clinton, he demanded a definitive summit with Arafat. He hoped to prove to the Israeli public his ability to secure a final and favorable agreement that would preclude Palestinians from raising further claims. To forestall a demand for new elections, which he would likely lose, Barak insisted on a quick timeline. Camp David would be a "take it or leave it" summit.[115]

At the Camp David summit in July, Barak refused direct substantive talks with Arafat but conveyed to Clinton a series of tentative proposals. They included a Palestinian state, eventual Israeli withdrawal from over 90 percent of the West Bank, Palestinian sovereignty over the Christian and Muslim areas of East Jerusalem, and a "permanent custodianship" over Haram-al-Sharif. Although a good distance from the global consensus, Barak's tentative offer could have advanced negotiations. Yet he insisted that Arafat unequivocally accept the terms without specifying the meanings of key terms, such as *permanent custodianship*, or how they would be implemented.[116] In fairness, Arafat lacked a coherent negotiating approach. But if he had accepted Barak's offer, Arafat would have perpetuated a pattern of trusting in Israeli-dictated terms and in Israel's willingness to implement the terms in good faith. Even if Arafat had been willing to do so, he would have likely been unable to overcome popular resistance.

What killed the Oslo process was Camp David's aftermath. Multiple parties were at fault, including Hamas, for carrying out suicide bombings and other acts of violence, as well as the PLO leadership for acquiescing in violent actions of its affiliated militias.[117] But Israeli behavior was the most damaging given its structural power. For starters, Barak persuaded Clinton to release joint statements that placed all of the blame for the Camp David impasse on Arafat. He thus heightened Israeli beliefs in the irredeemable nature of Palestinians and Palestinian doubts about the value of the peace process. The next costly action was Likud opposition leader Ariel Sharon's visit to the Temple Mount-Haram-al-Sharif in September 2000, which aimed to rally opposition to any concessions, especially on Jerusalem. Because his visit included a thousand Israeli security officers, it provoked Palestinians to throw rocks and burn tires in protest.[118] True to its siege mentality, Israel responded with a massive show of force, which unleashed the second intifada and the harsh Israeli crackdown. Although negotiations resumed through the Taba meeting in January 2001, they came too late to reverse the situation. Sealing Oslo's death was Israel's overwhelming vote that same month for Sharon as Israel's prime minister.

Why Israel Prioritized Victory in Negotiations over Peace

The scale of Israel's failure during this era to achieve a peaceful resolution is indicated by how ripe the circumstances were for a breakthrough by the early 1990s. The most important precipitating development was the eruption of the Palestinian intifada in December 1987, whereby a grassroots movement in the occupied territories linked mass civil disobedience with support for Palestinian sovereignty, international law, and greater internal democracy. Helped by its largely nonviolent focus, the intifada inspired great international support. In January 1988, its leaders called for an independent state and a UN-sponsored conference to work out a full peace with Israel.[119] Seeking to regain the initiative, the PLO declared the existence of the state of Palestine at the Palestinian National Council meeting in November 1988.[120] Its declaration for the first time expressly accepted Israel's existence along its pre-1967 war boundaries and supported an international conference to implement a full peace treaty. More than ever, Israel had willing Palestinian partners for peace at both the grassroots and elite levels. In addition, Israel still faced no significant security threat. Indeed, its primary vulnerability was its global image as an outlaw occupier that defied global norms. The Palestinian opening offered Israel a chance, then, not only for peace but also for global rehabilitation of its image.

To take advantage of this opportunity, Israel should have seen negotiations not as a high-stakes adversarial process but as an opportunity to foster better relations, improve the living situation of Palestinians, and further the prospects for a modus vivendi between Jews and Palestinians across Israel and a new state of Palestine. Before the closed-door Oslo talks, the official Palestinian delegation at the Madrid and DC talks had held firm to an accord that halted settlements and set international legal norms as the benchmark.[121] By rebuffing these efforts, the Rabin government foreclosed the possibility of grounding a comprehensive settlement in a robust and accountable international process guided by a widely supported body of international norms.

While negotiations proceeded, Israel was positioned to prepare the ground for a stable, long-term resolution by alleviating injustices and fostering greater trust. One way to do so was to reduce the settlement population and Israel's occupation footprint and accept the applicability of the Fourth Geneva Convention to all of the occupied territories. To enable closer relations in which Jews and Palestinians lived not only alongside but, in Buber's formulation, "together with" each other, Israel had a number of promising routes to pursue. One was encouraging more grassroots cross-national interactions in economic, cultural, academic, and religious areas rather than just top-down collaboration between Israeli and Palestinian security forces. Another was to lay the foundation for shared governance on areas of strong cross-border concern, including Jerusalem, migration, tourism, and the management of water and other natural resources. A third was reaching out to the democratic resistance movement in the occupied territories rather than repressing them. The latter, after all, had the potential to be partners for a broader vision of coexistence that featured democracy, social justice, and regard for a normative international order.

Had Israel taken this constructive approach when the new opportunity for peace first emerged, it is far less likely that there would have been such a flawed summit at Camp David, followed by the subsequent explosion of violence and hatred. This is not to argue that Israel on its own could have been assured of attaining a lasting peaceful resolution. There still would have been fierce resistance from both Israel's hard-line nationalist sector and Hamas-led

Islamic resistance. But an Israel committed to internationalism, equal regard for the interests and wishes of Palestinians and Jews, and a long-term goal of substantive coexistence would have been better prepared to overcome the opposition. In addition to strong international support, accompanied by security support and financial assistance, the affirmative bonds fostered by Israel in conjunction with Palestinian actors would have engendered greater trust and goodwill. Hard-line rejectionist actors would have encountered a less receptive population for mobilizing opposition to reconciliation. Hence, selected violent outbursts on either side would have been less likely to provoke the sustained outbreak of violence from late 2000 through 2004 and the general state of despair that prevails to the present.

While there are a number of valuable postmortems of the crucial missteps taken by Israeli, Palestinian, and U.S. officials,[122] the Humanist Zionist diagnosis of mainstream Zionism's core pathologies explains why Israel's political culture more generally was poorly equipped to reach a just and enduring resolution. I focus on Rabin's government, which set the pattern for Israel's adversarial negotiating stance and tough-minded implementation of the various interim measures. To be sure, his government was considerably more forthcoming than the prior and subsequent Likud-led governments. Rabin broke the taboo of not talking openly with the PLO, supported the land-for-peace principle, and opposed the establishment of what he considered "political" settlements.[123] Nevertheless, his government retained a siege mentality, which demanded a highly skewed agreement divorced from international norms and responded disproportionately to perceived Palestinian infractions of Oslo, and a tribal nationalism, which held no empathy for Palestinians and aimed to reduce the Palestinian presence in Israel. In sum, Rabin sought a victor's peace—what Buber would call political surplus—rather than one based on goodwill and mutual regard. Consequently, Netanyahu did not have to stray far from his predecessor's modus operandi.

Notwithstanding Rabin's political courage in entering into direct negotiations with the PLO, his stance still followed a long-standing siege mentality. What primarily spurred his government to talk with the PLO was not its recognition of Israel. After all, the PLO had long been moving in this direction. Rather, it was Arafat's desperate need for political recognition and a base of operations in the occupied territories. Rabin saw the opportunity to extract maximum concessions from the leadership and preserve maximum flexibility throughout the extended negotiation period to control facts on the ground.[124] Hence, Rabin was readily persuaded to bypass the official negotiations with Palestinian delegates unwilling to compromise on matters such as settlements and international law, and authorize direct and secret talks with Arafat's most trusted agents.[125] As discussed above, Rabin's venture paid off in a very favorable accord from his perspective. He could therefore publicly boast the following:

> On four or five major issues, they agreed to [things] I had doubted they would agree to. First, [keeping all of] Jerusalem under Israeli control and outside the jurisdiction of the Palestinians for the entire interim period. Second, [retaining all Israeli] settlements . . . Third, overall Israeli responsibility for the security of Israelis and external security. Fourth, keeping all options open for the negotiations on a permanent solution.[126]

Rabin's aggressive bargaining stance and implementation were joined to a tribal nationalist desire to both shed responsibility for governing the bulk of the Palestinians and reduce daily Jewish-Palestinian interactions in the occupied territories. True to the state's lack of regard for Palestinian concerns, Israel's segregation of Jews from Palestinians took the form of an extensive network of checkpoints and roadblocks, which disrupted daily life, cut off Palestinian contiguity, and impeded the PA from developing a coherent and effective system of governance.[127] Crucially, this pattern persisted through the Netanyahu and Barak administrations, along with the carrying out of disproportionate reprisals and the reneging on interim withdrawal agreements. Such steps cumulatively generated wide despair and discontent among Palestinians by the spring of 2000, leading to fears of an imminent outburst of violence.[128] As usual, Barak dismissed Arafat's accurate observation that the high level of Palestinian distrust did not bode well for such an ambitious summit in the summer of 2000.

Ominously, the aggressive stances of Rabin and Barak, which subordinated Palestinian aspirations to Israeli objectives, did not spare either from vicious accusations of betrayal by Israel's hard-liners, especially its surging religious nationalist camp. The latter first came to notoriety in February 1994 when a resident of a nearby militant settler community killed twenty-nine Palestinians at Hebron's Mosque of Abraham.[129] The religious nationalist sector then convened mass demonstrations, which depicted Rabin as a Nazi and accused him of treason.[130] Believing himself an enforcer of a Jewish religious law that justified the killing of Jews who threatened Jewish lives, Yigal Amir killed Rabin on November 4, 1995.[131] Barak did not pay the ultimate price, but his political career effectively ended in early 2001 when he suffered a landslide election loss to Ariel Sharon. With the collapse of Oslo, Israel's tribal nationalism had reached a frightening new level of intensity that endures to the present.

Conclusion

Mark Twain purportedly once said, "History doesn't repeat itself but it often rhymes." True to this adage, the three historical eras reviewed above have distinct features but all the more striking parallels. In each era, Israel enjoyed ripe opportunities to foster a favorable modus vivendi with Palestinians and the neighboring Arab states but failed to take advantage of them because of Zionism's deep-rooted pathologies. On the one hand, Israel's siege mentality, rooted in tribal nationalism and an eternal antisemitism syndrome, prevented even Israel's most moderate governments from taking the steps necessary for reaching a sustainable peace with the Palestinians. On the other hand, the government's willingness to conduct any substantive negotiations with Palestinians was enough to spark a dangerous and violent Jewish religious nationalist movement. Even if the latter was a new development—at least in the amount of support it attracted and the influence it wielded on Israeli society—its emergence was fueled by its resonance with Israel's underlying pathologies. Consequently, the most salient legacy of the Oslo era has been the potency of extremist, intolerant domestic forces. As reviewed in Chaper 1, such forces have become more potent over the past two decades. Israel has now reached a point of crisis. Although it remains a military power with a prosperous (albeit increasingly unequal) economy, its political culture is incapable of escaping from a permanent state of belligerency. This entrenched belligerency renders precarious Israel's liberal democratic features. Arendt's prophecy of doom quoted at the outset is proving increasingly accurate.

Having established the perspicacity of pre-state Humanist Zionism in making sense of central developments from Israel's founding up through the breakdown of peace talks, I turn to amending and updating the vision into a transformed program of Jewish dissent attentive to both the grave problems confronting contemporary Zionism and the new avenues for revitalizing Jewish self-determination and Palestinian-Jewish coexistence. The next chapter engages Humanist Zionism with the range of approaches taken by leading contemporary Jewish dissenting voices over the past half-century.

5

Toward an Updated Critical Jewish Vision on Zionism

Engaging Humanist Zionism with Contemporary Critical Jewish Voices

As established in the previous chapter, the Humanist Zionist diagnosis of a state founded on tribal nationalism and an eternal antisemitism mentality has proved remarkably effective at explaining Israel's repeated failure to take advantage of multiple opportunities across different eras for reconciliation with its neighboring states and with Palestinians. Moreover, its call for a Jewish self-determination wedded to a broader vision of justice and cooperation with Palestinians retains its moral urgency. Regrettably, the Humanist Zionist movement quickly dwindled after Israel's establishment despite Buber's efforts. It fell victim to the general waning of Jewish dissent on Zionism during Israel's first two decades.[1] By the time substantial Jewish-based criticisms of Israel and of Zionism reemerged in the 1970s, the pre-state Zionist dissenters had been relegated to a footnote. Although Jewish activists and scholars in recent decades have taken greater interest in Arendt and other Humanist Zionists, they have not enlisted their insights on behalf of a transformed critical Jewish perspective. This chapter does so by employing Humanist Zionism as an anchor and then mining insights from contemporary critical approaches to account for major post-1967 developments and redress gaps and shortcomings in the original Humanist Zionist framework.

I begin with an appreciation of the early interjections of the two most influential figures from the first wave of post-1967 Jewish dissent, Noam Chomsky and Uri Avnery. They confronted a pivotal stage of history. On the one hand, Israel was just deepening its militarist-imperialist direction by colonizing new territory and embedding itself in the U.S. sphere of influence. Concurrently, support for Israel and the emerging U.S.-Israeli special relationship was becoming the basis of a new litmus test for much of the American Jewish community. On the other hand, the immediate aftermath of the war seemingly presented new opportunities for pursuing Jewish-Arab reconciliation and rethinking the mission of Zionism. Although not directly influenced by the Humanist Zionists, Chomsky and Avnery carried on their spirit of combining harsh evaluations with bold new visions for self-determination and Jewish-Palestinian reconciliation. Chomsky laid out the ominous moral and political implications of Israel's enhanced militarism and close security relationship with the United States and decried the chilling of dissent within American Jewish circles. He also articulated a counterhegemonic, internationalist two-state program that remains of great value. Avnery excelled at advancing a comprehensive two-state program, which would link the fates of Israel and Palestine in a new federation and identified the urgent need to delink Israeli and Jewish identity.

The chapter then turns to exemplars from the two dominant critical Jewish perspectives of the past two-plus decades, liberal Zionism and anti-Zionism. Although liberal Zionists typically support a hegemonic Jewish nation-state and regard Israel's establishment in 1948 as a net-positive development, they have carried out an increasingly trenchant critique of Israel's recent trajectory. They particularly excel in denouncing Israel's occupation and its negative impact on both Israeli society and mainstream U.S. Jewish groups. I break this section into two parts. The first part reviews the most common liberal Zionist arguments and draws heavily from the work of Peter Beinart during his more conventional liberal Zionist phase. The second part addresses the more qualified and nuanced ideas of Chaim Gans to tease out the liberal Zionist program for reckoning and reconciliation. For guidance on how to carry out the most penetrating criticism of Zionism, which connects Israel's post-1967 depravities to its pre-state foundations, the chapter looks closely at the recent wave of Jewish anti-Zionist perspectives. I feature the writings of Mark Ellis, Judith Butler, and Ilan Pappé.

Throughout this engagement, I take particular interest in the following components of an updated critical Jewish perspective of Zionism. First, is the diagnosis of ongoing and foundational injustices and the underlying traits enabling them. Second, and related, is an account of the long-standing militarism, belligerency, and imperialist-courting features of Israel. Third is the articulation of an alternative Jewish vision of self-determination and program for Jewish-Palestinian coexistence. Finally, the chapter looks at how to reckon with Zionism's foundational and ongoing sins and bring about a lasting reconciliation with Palestinians.

Assessing Zionism at Its Post-1967 Crossroads: Noam Chomsky's Early Zionist Writings

By the late 1960s, Noam Chomsky was a pathbreaking scholar of linguistics who had recently emerged as the leading intellectual voice of the American left. His political commentary linked a detailed opposition to the war on Vietnam with a searing indictment of U.S.-anchored imperialism and the accompanying apologetics of the "New Mandarins," meaning the establishment liberal intelligentsia.[2] Chomsky also articulated an alternative political vision guided by a libertarian, decentralized socialism. In 1969, he extended his critical inquiry to Zionism, Israeli-Palestinian relations, and the evolving stance of the American Jewish community on these matters. Five years later, he released a collection of essays, entitled *Peace in the Middle East?*

Chomsky's Zionist writings continued many of the same themes introduced in his broader political writings. He offered a detailed denunciation of Israeli injustices, situated them in a broader, U.S.-anchored imperialist pattern, and exposed the enabling role of American Jewish organizations and leading Jewish intellectuals. Yet these essays contained much more personal reflections befitting his long attachment to Zionist politics. As a youth in the 1940s, he affiliated with a Hashomer Hatzair group and was "enormously attracted, emotionally and intellectually, by . . . a dramatic effort to create, out of the wreckage of European civilization, some form of libertarian socialism in the Middle East."[3] Chomsky retained admiration for what he saw as enduring egalitarian features. For him, the kibbutzim represented an "outstanding contribution" to modern history and a model for developing a more just society.[4] Chomsky credited Zionism for creating "the most advanced democratic socialist institutions that exist anywhere."[5] Nevertheless, he became a sharp critic of Israeli policies and actually existing Zionism during a time and place when such interjections were rare. Chomsky did so as one invested in Zionism, who hoped to halt the oppressive and self-destructive tendencies of post-1967 Zionism and recover its progressive aspirations and accomplishments. Overall, his essays in *Peace in the Middle East?* and a follow-up essay in late 1974 mark his most comprehensive assessment of Zionism's perils and promise.[6]

As in his critique of U.S. atrocities in Vietnam, Chomsky situated Israel's post-1967 injustices in a long-standing pattern of behavior. Here he featured the Zionist movement's foundational hegemonic nationalism and racial purity.[7] Chomsky recounted the pre-state Zionist pattern of acquiring land for exclusive Jewish use, displacing Palestinian peasants, and boycotting Arab labor and products.[8] Such nationalism paved the way in 1948 for the Nakba, the denial of a Palestinian national identity, and the expropriation of land. Chomsky particularly upset Michael Walzer and other American Jewish defenders of Israel by exposing the inherent tension in Israel's claims to be both Jewish and democratic. Israel, he observed, "will have to come to terms somehow with the fact that it is a Jewish state governing a society that is in part non-Jewish. . . . If a state is Jewish in certain respects, then in these respects it is not democratic."[9] Chomsky recounted a number of de jure and de facto discriminatory practices long employed in Israel for the benefit of its Jewish heritage and population. True supporters of Israel, he insisted, must confront this "Achilles' heel of political Zionism." "The problems of achieving democratic goals in a multinational or multiethnic society," he concluded, "are not trivial ones. It is pointless to pretend that they do not exist."[10]

Chomsky was one of the first to appreciate the disturbing ramifications of Israel's 1967 military triumph. The conquest, he found, aggravated Zionism's militarism and belligerency and gave new momentum to a racial "mythology," which asserted both a transcendent Jewish claim to all of the land and the inferiority of Arabs.[11] Chomsky highlighted two new dimensions that had not yet received much attention. First, Israel had entered into a dangerous new phase of imperialist politics.[12] Prior to the war, he viewed Israel's imperialist-courting politics as more ad hoc and diffuse. But with its new military prestige, Israel embraced a special relationship with the United States, where it became a valued regional cop for the latter's hegemonic pursuits. Consequently, added Chomsky, Israel was becoming more estranged from the Middle East and the global community, less open to diplomatic overtures, and all the more dependent on military predominance.[13] He foresaw a long-term spiral marked by constant military tension, "occupation, resistance, repression, more resistance, erosion of democracy, internal quandaries and demoralization, further polarization and extremism on both sides."[14]

The second ominous development Chomsky identified was the emergence of an increasingly chauvinistic mood among both mainstream American Jewish organizations and Jewish intellectual circles.[15] This new "pro-Israel" stance meant stridently defending Israeli policies and the new special relationship and attacking all perceived opponents, including Jewish critics, such as Chomsky and I. F. Stone. This enhanced chauvinism, lamented Chomsky, was chilling discussion in American Jewish circles and in the United States more broadly. Chomsky movingly recounted his difficulties in coordinating a speaking tour of Israeli doves at U.S. universities because most faculty declined to sponsor the talks for fear of backlash.[16] Under this enhanced post-1967, "pro-Israel" orthodoxy, American Jews were denied the opportunity to hear from knowledgeable Israeli critics. With pro-Israel being reduced to unconditional support for Israeli policies and the close U.S.-Israeli strategic relationship, supposed defenders of Israel were in fact encouraging Israel's "most dangerous and, ultimately, self-destructive tendencies."[17]

To find a way out of this grim spiral, Chomsky sketched a program that broke from hegemonic nationalism and featured a new model of coexistence for multinational societies. For all the problems presented by the 1967 conquest, he regarded the setting as opportune for reconsidering how to govern all of the original Palestine Mandate now that it was no longer divided between several sovereign states. Impressed by the growth of nonchauvinistic, progressive activism among young Israeli Jews and Palestinian Arabs, Chomsky hoped the two groups could work out a shared vision of socialism and binationalism, which would oppose the conventional nationalism that marred the political programs of all Zionist parties and the PLO and would provide equal regard for each community's national aspirations.[18] He hoped the new generation of Jewish activists could persuade other Israeli Jews that the hegemonic nationalist path adopted in 1948 was a mistake both morally and in terms of advancing the long-term security of Israeli Jews. The progressive Palestinians, in turn, could promote a break from the PLO's proposal of a "democratic secular" state, which Chomsky deemed disingenuous and an "exercise in futility" because of its lack of accommodation for a collective Jewish identity.[19]

While Chomsky left it to the direct protagonists to work out a specific program, he sketched broad parameters for this binational socialism. The binationalism entailed autonomy for each community in certain cultural spheres and at the local level, a unified central government, and joint institutions for encouraging cross-national bonds and collaboration.[20] The socialist part provided the common vision. It encompassed cross-national workers' solidarity, coordinated workers' councils, and an economic integration guided by democratic, egalitarian values.[21]

Like Arendt, Chomsky saw the quest for a just, binational society in Israel-Palestine as part and parcel of a global struggle against the prevailing hierarchical order and hegemonic nationalist model of states. He urged Israeli and Palestinian binational socialist activists to also mobilize for a revitalized socialist international movement committed to fundamental alternatives to the nation-state model and capitalism.[22] Such internationalism would "challenge the destructive concept of 'national interest,'" but not the value of national self-determination.[23] It would "combine a commitment to an end to domination and exploitation with a recognition of national and ethnic bonds within complex multinational societies."[24]

By 1974, Chomsky turned his focus to how to radicalize the then-inchoate two-state program. Initially, he held little regard for it, believing that a two-state program would be the output of great-power imposition and thus bound to a hegemonic U.S. strategic focus.[25] Under such an outcome, he feared, Israel would remain a discriminatory state, loyal to the United States, while the Palestinian counterpart, "founded on bitterness, frustration, and despair," would be equally discriminatory and subordinate to the interests of U.S.-allied Arab states.[26] Having concluded, however, that the Palestinians were invested in gaining their own state, Chomsky proposed a creative strategy for modifying the two-state program into a long-term binational direction. Leftist movements in both communities would still emphasize the federated binational socialist program as the long-term goal. In the short term, however, they would work within the two-state framework and demand full democratization and the elimination of national-based discriminatory practices within each state. Moreover, leftist voices would advocate for cross-national bonds, open borders, and joint governance. Advancing this long-range vision, stressed Chomsky, would make more feasible the "simpler and more immediate steps that w[ould] reduce tensions" and "lay the groundwork for an eventual just and peaceful settlement."[27]

Notwithstanding that Chomsky linked his alternative program to the pre-state one of Hashomer Hatzair, its sensitivity to a collaborative binationalism fit more closely to the Humanist Zionist vision. Hashomer Hatzair, after all, as Arendt astutely observed, lacked a program to advance its binational ideal.[28] As discussed in Chapter 2, it rebuffed an entreaty from Brit Shalom to form a joint position on Jewish-Arab relations and pointed to the reactionary character of the Arab national movement. Although the group eventually adopted an outreach program, it continued to demand unlimited Jewish immigration and a Jewish majority, two conditions that eliminated the prospects of cross-national collaboration. Moreover, Hashomer Hatzair acquiesced to the UN partition resolution and later took possession of expropriated land. As a more resolute advocate of an egalitarian binationalism and critic of hegemonic Zionism, Chomsky effectively picked up Arendt's mantle as the preeminent diaspora Jewish dissenter in the post-1967 era. Indeed, he followed up on Arendt's pleas in 1948 for more scrutiny from American Jews of Zionist politics by offering an alternative perspective on how to be pro-Israel. Rather than enable Israel's increasingly belligerent policies, American Jews genuinely concerned for Israel's welfare should expose rather than deny the profound flaws in really existing Zionism. Only then could a new path be found that would advance a just and secure vision of Jewish self-determination.

Reflecting the narrow mood of the time, *Peace in the Middle East?* was not well received in the mainstream Jewish community. Chomsky came under harsh attack from American Jewish groups and leading Jewish intellectuals, such as Walzer.[29] As Edward Said observed, many American Jews concluded that Chomsky "had pushed his Jewishness too far and too wastefully."[30] Those genuinely concerned for Israel's welfare would be well advised to revisit these essays. They remain of great value, in dialogue with Humanist Zionism, for developing an updated vision of Jewish dissent. Like the Humanist Zionists, Chomsky identified the inherent tension between a hegemonic nationalism and an emancipatory version of Jewish self-determination. He was one of the first to emphasize the incompatibility of a Jewish state with a standard liberal democratic one. Also of lasting value is Chomsky's warning about the corrupting nature of Israel's special relationship with the United States. Like Arendt, he warned genuine supporters of Jewish self-determination not to be seduced by the military resources that a pro-imperialist policy offered because the costs to the health of the society and to comity in the region would be far greater. Lastly, Chomsky's ideas on how to radicalize the two-state program in a way that challenges the status quo and hegemonic nationalism remain a promising alternative to either the standard two-state program or the one-state option.

The Original Post-Zionist and Two-State Advocate: Uri Avnery

Had Arendt looked for post-1948 Jewish conscious pariahs in Israel, she would have featured Uri Avnery, who for Israel's first two decades was one of its lone dissenters. Immigrating to Palestine in 1933 at the age of ten, he joined the hard-line Irgun militia as a teenager. He broke from Zionism in 1946 by forming the group Bama'avak (Struggle), which declared the Jewish immigrants in Palestine to be a new national group, not Jewish but "Hebrew." It called for an "integrated, coordinated Semitic front" with the Arab national movements in Palestine and beyond to "[throw] off the British yoke" and attain "national liberation" throughout the region.[31] Although he fought on the Zionist side in the 1948 war, Avnery retained his distance from Zionism and urged the new state to allow the return of Palestinian refugees. In 1950, he purchased the weekly newspaper *Haolam Hazeh* (*This World*) and made it a prominent and provocative forum for exposing scandals, condemning Israel's treatment of Palestinians and Mizrahim, and advocating for reconciliation with Arabs.[32] In later years, he became a forerunner for both post-Zionism and two-state advocacy while remaining a courageous dissenter up to his death in 2018. Over the ensuing decades, he denounced Israel's rightward shift, brutal crackdowns, and expanding colonization of the West Bank and East Jerusalem, urged negotiations with Palestinians, demanded a full withdrawal, and defended the two-state resolution from critics on the right and anti-Zionists on the left, such as Ilan Pappé.[33]

Avnery's most comprehensive formulation of his approach is found in *Israel without Zionism*, first published a year after the 1967 war.[34] There, he became one of the first proponents of an expansive and progressive two-state plan. Like Chomsky, he regarded the post–1967 war setting as an opportune time for a grand reconciliation. His central plank was creating a Palestinian state on the West Bank and Gaza Strip, linked to Israel in a federation with Jerusalem as the shared capital.[35] Fulfilling this plank would allow Israelis and Palestinians to respect each other's national aspirations. For long-term success, Avnery proposed two complementary initiatives. One was resolving the Palestinian refugee situation. He urged Israel to accept the Palestinian right of return, whereby refugees would choose repatriation or compensation. Israel would then absorb refugees the same way as it did for Jewish immigrants, by granting them citizenship and providing housing and economic assistance.[36] The second initiative was making sure the new state of Palestine became a "living organism, a more or less equal partner with Israel."[37] Avnery called for Israel, with international support, to expend the necessary resources to upgrade Palestine's economic infrastructure and standard of living. Moreover, under a federation, a common market and coordinated economic system would further bolster Palestine's economy.[38] Finally, he believed that a successful two-state plan would enable a confederation of Middle Eastern states working toward regional liberation and progress.[39] With this step, Israel would put "an end to the Zionist chapter in its history" and start a new chapter of regional solidarity.[40]

As the title *Israel without Zionism* suggests, Avnery's other central idea was to replace Israel's overarching Jewish national identity with a unified national identity for all citizens. He was among the few Israeli Jews at the time to challenge the inherently discriminatory impact of Israel's official Jewish identity toward the state's non-Jewish residents. As in Chomsky's essays, Avnery recounted the range of Israeli laws and policies that discriminated against its Arab population. Unlike Chomsky, who strived to unpack Zionism's socialist legacy from its hegemonic nationalist one, Avnery maintained that from the outset, "the socialist and the nationalist were not only interrelated, they were one and the same."[41] Socialist Zionists, he added, had established a nationalist iron wall of "Hebrew Labor, Hebrew Land and Hebrew Defense" to ward off any universal socialist appeals.[42] By institutionalizing separate development, socialist Zionists opened a vast gap between the two peoples and fostered a state "which exist[ed] for the solution of the Jewish people" and regarded its Arabs as a "foreign element."[43] With such a hostile stance toward its neighbors, the Zionist leaders naturally aligned with Western great powers and opposed Arab national liberation movements. Hence, concluded Avnery, Zionism engendered a "vicious circle" of increasing bitterness and hostility with Israel regarded as an imperialist tool.[44]

To escape the vicious circle, he urged Israeli Jews to shed their Zionist mindset and embrace their "Hebrew" identity. As Avnery later recalled, he was advancing what scholars later classified as "post-Zionism."[45] Although opposed to Jewish nationalism, Avnery credited Zionists for producing the "first successful war of liberation in the Middle East" against British colonialism.[46] Yet he held that Zionism had become obsolete.[47] Zionists may have established Israel on behalf of Jews in general, but Israeli Jews had formed a qualitatively distinct identity, while most of the world's Jews did not move to Israel. Israeli nationalism was hence rooted in the collective and ongoing experiences and culture of the state's inhabitants.[48] Avnery acknowledged a place for Jewishness in Israel, but simply one of common heritage, allowing for an ongoing symbolic bond to Jews elsewhere. If Israel gave full recognition to this new nationalism, it could finally become the state for all its residents, Jewish and Arab. The state would also "recognize that it belong[ed] to the Region and . . . take a positive attitude toward the national aspirations of the Arab peoples."[49]

Avnery called for this common Hebrew nationalism to subsume the distinct Jewish and Arab national identities rather than coexist alongside them. Unlike the Humanist Zionists, he had no interest in Jewish renewal and rejected a binational program: "Two different nations," he later recalled, "each of which clings to its own national vision, cannot live together in one state."[50] Avnery hoped that the adoption of an exclusive territorial-based national identity applicable to all residents would discredit all laws and practices that accorded a higher status to Israel's Jews. Yet whatever the abstract merits of replacing Jewish and Palestinian nationalism with Hebrew nationalism, he offered no persuasive case that the deeply felt Jewish and Palestinian Arab national identities could readily erode. Ironically, Avnery fell victim to the same mentality for which he derided left internationalists, which was denying the power of nationalist aspirations in Israel-Palestine.[51] Hence, Avnery's Hebrew nationalism offered little promise as a substitute for a hegemonic Jewish nationalism. As the Humanist Zionists and Chomsky recognized, Israel-Palestine has long been binational in practice but has been organized in a hierarchical fashion in which one nation—the Jewish one—subjugates and displaces the other. Accordingly, Humanist Zionism remains a far better baseline for coming to terms with this reality in a way that enables a just coexistence.

Notwithstanding gaps in his promotion of a Hebrew identity, Avnery stands out as a trenchant early critic of Israel's hegemonic Jewish national identity.

Moreover, his conceptualization of an open-border, progressive two-state program remains a welcome alternative to the narrow two-state plans set forth later by liberal Zionists, diplomats, and U.S. officials. He did not seek separation, which would leave Palestine weak and subordinate, but instead sought cross-national comity. Like Chomsky, he offered a potentially appealing counter to both the standard one-state and two-state proposals.

Jewish Dissent during the Rise and Fall of the Oslo Peace Process

Since the first wave of post-1967 Jewish dissent, all the ominous features Chomsky had identified accelerated. Israel's settlements proliferated, along with its matrix of control over the occupied territories. Its national religious camp surged, and its extensive military-security entanglement with the United States solidified. Outside of Israel, Jewish communities, especially in the United States, doubled down on hard-line support for Israeli policies and intolerance of internal dissent. Yet there were some promising developments. Globally, as reviewed in Chapter 4, an overwhelming consensus emerged in opposition to Israel's occupation and belligerent actions and in support of a Palestinian state. In Israel, a significant peace movement took shape, which condemned Israel's settlement expansion, war crimes in the occupied territories, and 1982 invasion of Lebanon. Some came out in favor of a Palestinian state. This momentum opened space for increased dissent in the U.S. Jewish community.

By the early 1990s, the political setting seemed primed for a two-state resolution. In addition to the overwhelming global consensus, the PLO leadership and the bulk of movements within the occupied territories supported such a resolution. Even Israeli society showed signs of receptivity by electing a more moderate government, led by Prime Minister Rabin. The 1993 Oslo accord dangled prospects of a peace settlement, if one downplayed the fine print that enabled Israel to retain its settlements and deepen its colonization. But with the failed Camp David talks of 2000, the second intifada, and Israel's rightward descent, the mood has dramatically darkened. In this new setting, liberal Zionists and anti-Zionists have emerged as the two most prominent strands of Jewish dissent.

It's the Occupation, Stupid: Liberal Zionist Dissent

With the post-1948 constriction in the definition of what constitutes Zionism, liberal Zionists have come to assume the old role of Humanist Zionists, that of dissenters from within Zionism. They mirror the Humanist Zionists in terms of combining a deep attachment to Jewish self-determination with an insistence that such self-determination conform to a set of moral values and with sharp criticisms of prevailing Zionist politics. Yet liberal Zionists also diverge sharply from Humanist Zionists by supporting a hegemonic Jewish nation-state and justifying the events leading to Israel's establishment in 1948. Through a review of conventional and more nuanced versions of liberal Zionism, this section identifies both its most valuable components and its points of departure with Humanist Zionism, in which the latter holds up as a more compelling basis for an updated critical Jewish perspective.

The first prominent liberal Zionist dissenter was Yeshayahu Leibowitz, a distinguished scholar and public intellectual in multiple subjects, including the sciences, philosophy, and theology. Although an orthodox Jew, he came to support the separation of the state and religion, while his Zionist conviction was rooted in a desire for a secular Jewish nation-state. Unlike most liberal Zionists, who did not become sharp critics of Israel until the Likud Party gained power in the late 1970s. Leibowitz raised a powerful challenge as early as 1968 in response to the mood of triumphalism and growing calls to assume permanent control of some or all of the occupied territories. Sounding a lot like Arendt in 1948, he made the following dire prophesy:

> A state ruling a hostile population of 1.5 to 2 million foreigners would necessarily become a secret-police state, with all that this implies for education, free speech and democratic institutions. The corruption characteristic of every colonial regime would also prevail in the State of Israel. . . . There is also good reason to fear that the Israel Defense Force, which has been until now a people's army, would, as a result of being transformed into an army of occupation, degenerate.[52]

This type of criticism, qualified by admiration for Zionism's past and appreciation for Israel's existence as a Jewish nation-state, is now far more common. I turn now to leading contemporary liberal Zionist critics.

While still a conventional liberal Zionist, Peter Beinart opened his influential book *The Crisis of Zionism* by recalling his grandmother's warning that Jews could never be secure, long-term, anywhere but in their own place. Hence, he "[slept] better knowing that the world contain[ed] a Jewish state."[53] "But not any Jewish state," added Beinart.[54] A desired Jewish state follows liberal democratic principles of individual rights, an impartial rule of law, equality of opportunity, and full political participation. Such values, he maintained, reflect the finest moral lessons absorbed by the Jewish people from their history of exile and suffering. As a Zionist, however, Beinart conceded the need for certain deviations to further Israel's Jewish identity and secure a refuge for all Jews. The challenge for Beinart and other standard liberal Zionists is to restrict those inequities to matters "inherent to Zionism," which are immigration, security, and national symbols.[55] Up to the 1967 war, liberal Zionists believe, Israel had flaws but was moving in the right direction.[56] The character of Israel, however, sharply declined once it became an occupier. To realize its promise of becoming both a Jewish state and a democratic one, liberal Zionists demand ending the occupation and reaching a two-state settlement. Although a small core of inequities would persist, they would be balanced by a Palestinian state that privileged its national needs.[57]

The most valuable contribution of liberal Zionists has been their diagnosis of the ways Israel's post-1967 occupation has intensified Israel's subjugation of Palestinians, eroded the state's liberal and democratic foundations, and undermined the liberal ideals of mainstream American Jewish organizations. Blunt rule over millions of people would be bad enough, they argue, but the problem is compounded by civilian settlements. As Beinart summarized, Jewish settlers enjoy full political representation, generous subsidies, the backing of the IDF, and all the rights and privileges of Israeli citizens. Palestinians, in contrast, have no political rights, endure considerable restrictions on travel and work, are governed by military courts and suffer violence and displacement from both settlers and Israeli soldiers. Given this abusive structure, concluded Beinart, "Jewish power runs wild."[58] Equally disturbing, continue liberal Zionists, is the grave impact of the occupation on Israeli society. Gershon Gorenberg blames Israel's post-1967 trajectory of settlement building and military control over millions of hostile noncitizens for unleashing a militarist and chauvinist Zionism and a zealously illiberal religious-Zionist camp. He and other liberal Zionists cite the collapse of the Oslo peace process as a trigger for a further exacerbation of anti-Arab racism and intolerance across Israeli society.[59]

American liberal Zionists have also denounced the deferential stance of mainstream American Jewish organizations with regard to Israel. Echoing Chomsky, they insist that genuine supporters of Israel are obligated to speak out against the state's belligerent and repressive policies. In 2011, Beinart was the leading voice for this alternative pro-Israeli vision. He believed that prior to 1967, American Jewish leaders based their support for Israel in part on a belief that the state was committed to democracy, equality, and individual rights.[60] Regrettably, lamented Beinart, as Israel moved away from its liberal heritage, so, too, did the established American Jewish organizations. Being pro-Israel morphed into support for illiberal Israeli policies, such as uncompromising militarism and demonizing of both Palestinians and critics of Israeli policies. Beinart hence deemed it imperative to reground American Jewish Zionism in a liberalism that speaks out against the occupation and chauvinistic forces and that allies with Israel's liberal democratic opposition.

Despite their increasingly embattled status, liberal Zionists have inspired and staffed a number of effective protest and human rights groups. The longest lasting and most prominent is Peace Now, which formed in the late 1970s. For the past several decades, it has advocated for a two-state resolution and monitored Israel's settlement growth with the aim of mobilizing greater public awareness and resistance.[61] Another prominent group whose agenda, at least until recently, comports with liberal Zionist values is B'Tselem, which documents war crimes and human rights abuses in the occupied territories.[62] Among protest groups formed since 2000, Breaking the Silence has exerted the greatest impact. To the great discomfort of Israeli officials, the group provides firsthand reporting from ex-combatants on the degrading impact of Israel's occupation on the lives of Palestinians and the moral character of Israel's military.[63] Finally, there are liberal Zionist groups focused on Israeli society at large, such as the Association for Civil Rights in Israel, who challenge inequalities and threats to democracy and civil liberties. American liberal Zionists have similarly sparked critical discussion in American Jewish circles. Leading U.S. outlets since the 1980s include, from left to right, the now-defunct New Jewish Agenda, *Tikkun Magazine*, Americans for Peace Now, and J Street. All such groups, to varying degrees, have spoken out against Israel's occupation and various military incursions and urged a wider airing of voices within mainstream U.S. Jewish organizations.

Where most liberal Zionists fall short is the probing of the circumstances leading to Israel's establishment. Some simply hold as a given that Israel's creation justified the displacement of Palestinians. Most blunt is Israeli journalist Ari Shavit in his best seller *My Promised Land*.[64] He starts with the premise that a hegemonic Jewish state was the only means to guarantee a thriving future for the Jewish people. In the immediate postwar setting, continues Shavit, the situation for the Jews had become too urgent to rely on a gradual path forward. War and mass expulsion, at least from Lydda and other central locations, became a necessary evil. Hence, he stands with "the damned" who "did the dirty, filthy work that enables my people, myself, my daughter and my sons to live."[65] What further eases the conscience of liberal Zionists is that Israel provided citizenship to the bulk of the remaining Palestinians. "Arabs were not only subjects of the military government," argues Gorenberg; they "were also citizens."[66] Although the Palestinian citizens were far from equal, he allows, Israel set the foundation for a system that would eventually reconcile its Jewish status with its egalitarian democracy aspirations.

Consistent with their lack of scrutiny of Israel's foundation, liberal Zionists generally gloss over the continuities of Israel's post-1967 occupation with its first two decades. By featuring the occupation as a moral turning point, liberal Zionists obscure Israel's preexisting aggressive siege mentality, courting of outside great powers, imposition of martial law, expropriation of Palestinian property, refusal to readmit refugees, and symbolic erasure of Palestinian identity. Israel's post-1967 behavior has shown many similarities. It has pursued a hard line on negotiations, rejected the global consensus, aligned itself to a U.S. regional policy hostile to independent Arab nationalism, taken sovereignty over Palestinian territory, and suppressed Palestinian activism and organization. Indeed, in one respect, Israel's post-1967 behavior has been less extreme. Knowing that resistance would be too great, it has not emptied the conquered territories of most of the Palestinian population.[67] Of course, liberal Zionists correctly identify ways in which Israeli behavior and attitudes have deteriorated, fueled in part by the rise of religious nationalism. Nevertheless, it is more accurate to characterize Israel's post-1967 evolution as an intensification of long-existing trends. Revealingly, Shavit acknowledges in a conversation with a cofounder of the settlers' group Gush Emunim striking parallels in the ideology and practices of the post-1967 religious-nationalist settlers and the pre-state secular settlers: "With horror I realize that the DNA of his Zionism and the DNA of my Zionism share a few genes."[68]

By brushing past Israel's pre-1967 history, including the Nakba, most liberal Zionists lack a plan for advancing a far-reaching reckoning and reconciliation of Jews and Palestinians. Most regard it sufficient to end Israel's occupation and establish a Palestinian state on the occupied territories. Consequently, liberal Zionists offer little guidance on a number of crucial challenges that would persist. First, how would Israel acknowledge its culpability in causing the Nakba? Second, what would be done to ensure the long-term economic and political viability of the new Palestinian state? Third, what would be done to facilitate the myriad of interconnected dynamics, including Jerusalem, family ties, cultural-religious sites, the environment, tourism, economic transactions, migration, and the management of water and other natural resources? Finally, how would the presumed maintenance of a Jewish nation-state in Israel be made consistent with a commitment to full equality and friendly relations between Jews and Palestinians in Israel? Notwithstanding its support of Palestinian minority rights, the liberal Zionist commitment to a hegemonic Jewish state, underpinned by a substantial Jewish majority, sharply constrains the prospects for Jewish-Palestinian comity. When condemning the occupation, liberal Zionists do not simply condemn the subjugation of Palestinians.

They also emphasize the demographic threat of the large Palestinian population in the occupied territories, which explains Peace Now's common appeal to maintain a state that is "Jewish and democratic." In effect, liberal Zionists demand a peculiar form of democracy in which the Palestinian presence is sufficiently restricted to prevent any measurable changes in Israel's Jewish character. This stance sends a signal of collective suspicion, whereby, as Bernard Avishai wryly observed, "every Israeli Arab, like every Palestinian, has a little mufti inside struggling to get out."[69]

In fairness, a few liberal Zionist thinkers provide more probing and nuanced reflections on the issues reviewed above. The most comprehensive among them is the moral philosopher Chaim Gans, as expressed in his book *A Just Zionism*.[70] By combining a careful defense of hegemonic Zionism with a demand for extensive reforms, he shows a liberal Zionist pathway for redressing certain common gaps and advancing a reckoning and reconciliation.

A Conditional Case for Hegemonic Zionism: Gans on a Just Zionism

Although Gans defends the establishment and maintenance of a hegemonic Jewish nation-state, he departs from conventional liberal Zionists in both offering a considerably more qualified justification and acknowledging the moral validity of Palestinian opposition to such Zionism. He starts with the premise that Jews shared sufficient attributes of a common national identity to lay claim to the right of self-determination in order to preserve their distinct culture.[71] Because Jews were not concentrated in one territory, Gans identifies the land of ancient Israel as the most appropriate unifying site for realizing self-determination due to its symbolic importance.[72] Yet he acknowledges that neither of these claims justifies a hegemonic Jewish state in Palestine. To begin with, a right to self-determination can be realized by less intrusive means, as the Humanist Zionists well appreciated. Moreover, Jews would not normally have been entitled to a hegemonic Jewish state, because its realization would have caused an intolerable level of injustice and bloodshed on the people already living there.[73] It was only the dire situation faced by Europe's Jews in the 1930s and 1940s, maintains Gans, that justified a Jewish state.[74] In an ideal world, he adds, the global community would have found an equitable solution that did not place the burden on the region's Arabs. Hence, "Jews have a special moral obligation to understand Arab opposition to the Land of Israel and to try to contain it by way of conciliation."[75]

If the Jewish right to hegemonic self-determination was simply circumstantial, what justifies the maintenance of a hegemonic Jewish state, given the considerable diminishment of global antisemitism in the ensuing years? Gans skillfully dismisses an argument invoked by Walzer in the latter's attack on Chomsky's *Peace in the Middle East?*, which holds that many states, including democratic ones, implement policies that favor a dominant ethno-cultural group. Besides amounting to a fallacious "everybody does it" excuse, Gans agrees with Chomsky that Israel's level of explicit discrimination goes well beyond that of other liberal democratic states.[76] He is also not persuaded by the argument of an open-ended threat of new outbreaks of virulent antisemitism.[77] The one compelling argument for Gans is the enduring Jewish-Palestinian conflict. Because of the lack of trust between Jews and Arabs, "Jews have good reasons to believe that the Arabs in general and Palestinians specifically would ultimately not respect the Jewish people's interests in their survival as a distinct society."[78] Hence, until the conflict is resolved and there develops an enduring trust, Jews are entitled to their own state.

Like other liberal Zionists, Gans urges a two-state resolution partitioned along the pre-1967 war boundaries. Yet he departs from the standard view in two ways consistent with his downplaying of absolutes. To begin with, Gans does not regard the pre-1967 war boundaries as inherently superior to more narrow ones, such as those drawn by the UN partition resolution.[79] He settles on the 1967 lines because they reflect the overwhelming global consensus and do not require significant demographic adjustments. More significantly, Gans does not posit the two-state plan as the necessary endpoint. If the plan eventually eased tensions between Jews and Arabs in the region, Jews could exercise self-determination without a hegemonic state.[80]

Gans further departs from standard liberal Zionists in imposing a much higher moral obligation on Israeli Jews to reckon with the Nakba. Notwithstanding that a Jewish hegemonic state was justified in 1948, the Palestinians should not have borne the sole burden of rectifying the Jewish situation, and Israel went too far in perpetrating mass expulsions and "confiscation of land and houses that had been left by those who fled in fear of the war."[81] Although opposed to the mass return of Palestinian refugees, Gans calls for acknowledgment of culpability, financial compensation, and the welcoming of a modest amount of refugees to the areas of their family homes.[82] He is similarly more forthcoming than most liberal Zionists on other fundamental matters. Gans approves of modest immigration preferences to Jews, but not the unrestricted acceptance of all Jewish applicants and categorical denial of Palestinian applicants.[83] He also faults Israelis for their insensitivity to the historical and ongoing costs of Jewish immigration on the lives of Palestinians.[84] Lastly, Gans gives an unusually stark account of the moral costs if Israel fails to make amends: "Israel must bring all of this to an end not only because the occupation of the West Bank and the inequality between Jews and Arabs in Israel is bad in and of themselves and corrupts Israel's present and future moral standing, but also because these practices render Israel's good faith in relying on the justice of Zionism's past questionable."[85]

Overall, Gans goes a long way toward reshaping liberal Zionism along Humanist Zionist lines. Yet he still lacks the probing Humanist Zionist scrutiny. To begin with, he does not address Zionist developments prior to the onset of the Nazi terror. As reviewed in Chapter 2, the Yishuv leadership had from the outset embarked on a path demanding Jewish predominance and the subjugation of Palestinians. Moreover, even if just focused on the immediate post–World War II setting, Gans's existential argument for a hegemonic Jewish state is questionable given that the Nazi reign was over. True, there were hundreds of thousands of displaced European Jews, but creating a Jewish state was not the only way to deal with this need. As Humanist Zionists and the Anglo-American Committee understood, converting a territory with no clear national divisions—particularly in the land allotted to Israel—into two distinct hegemonic nation-states would unleash violent conflict and forced displacement. The Anglo-American Committee sketched a trusteeship plan that would have admitted one hundred thousand displaced Jews and fostered institutions for an eventual binational federation. To be sure, it was vague on details and rejected by the Palestinian and Zionist leaders. But what if the Zionist leaders, who easily had the upper hand, had embraced the plan and encouraged American Jewish groups to lobby the Truman administration to commit adequate resources for implementation? Crucially, the Zionist leadership rejected the plan not out of feasibility concerns but because it was prepared to win a Jewish state by force.[86] Driving this hard-line stance was an enduring tribal nationalism and insensitivity to its neighbors that have prompted Israel to maintain a siege mentality and great-power alliance aimed at countering independent nationalist dynamics.

Nevertheless, Gans has carved out a distinct liberal Zionism that, without explicitly addressing Buber, Magnes, or Arendt, upholds most of the central Humanist Zionist premises. Similar to Buber, he acknowledges that while the Jewish attachment to Palestine could not avoid the inflicting of injustices, the Zionists have failed to take steps to make amends. In particular, he echoes Buber's idea of political surplus, which obliges Israel to atone for the actions during the war and after that went beyond what was necessary for secure Jewish self-determination. Gans has thus opened the door for an extensive moral reckoning that would boost the prospects for a more appealing and egalitarian coexistence. Finally, Buber would also appreciate Gans's concession that Zionism's prevailing hegemonic form would no longer be warranted if Jewish-Palestinian relations were to substantially improve. In sum, Gans has provided a constructive liberal Zionist program for aiding in the development of an updated critical Jewish perspective.

The Problem Is Settler Colonialism: Contemporary Jewish Anti-Zionism

The contemporary Jewish anti-Zionists are the radical successors to the Humanist Zionists. They are principled outsiders who challenge the foundational premises of Zionism, condemn ongoing Israeli atrocities, and offer an alternative ethical vision informed by a mix of Jewish and outside beliefs and practices. Jewish anti-Zionists share the following tenets. The first is a renouncing of the entire pre-state Zionist experience as a settler-colonial project. The second is regarding the Nakba as a foundational sin for which Israel must answer through the full recognition of the Palestinian right of return. The third is making no moral distinction between the post-1967 occupation and prior Zionist actions. All are part of a settler-colonial trajectory. The fourth is a conviction that Zionism has stained the moral character of Judaism. I focus on the works of Ilan Pappé, Mark Ellis, and Judith Butler. Among Israel's original "New Historians" of the state's early years, Pappé has become the most prominent anti-Zionist. Butler and Ellis are two leading American Jewish anti-Zionist thinkers and among the few contemporary dissenters to engage Arendt and Buber extensively. Each draw from the latter in diagnosing the pathologies of Zionism and developing a Jewish-inspired ethical vision of resistance. Both go further, however, by highlighting the settler-colonial dimension of Zionism.

Most fundamentally, Jewish anti-Zionists identify settler colonialism as Zionism's paramount feature. As Pappé declares, once Zionists settled in Palestine as a distinct national movement, the humane impulses of escaping antisemitism and fostering Jewish renewal no longer mattered.[87] Zionism became a settler-colonial project where Jews steadily subjugated and displaced Palestinians with the help of the British imperial overseer. This categorical repudiation of the Zionist project explains the importance Jewish anti-Zionists accord to the Nakba. Although Buber and Arendt also condemned the Nakba, neither saw it as intrinsic to the Zionist project. Pappé, by contrast, characterizes the Nakba as the most damning and defining feature because it fulfilled the Zionist "desire to turn the mixed ethnic Palestine into a pure ethnic space."[88] This ethnic cleansing became the "DNA of Israeli Jewish society" that has "motivated Israeli policy throughout the years."[89] He chides liberal Zionists for divorcing the occupation from Israel's creation because all are "part of the same ideological infrastructure on which the ethnic cleansing of 1948 was built, for which the Arabs of Kufr Qassem were massacred [in 1956] for which lands are confiscated in both the Galilee and the West Bank."[90]

Another way Ellis and Butler have extended Arendt's warnings on statist Zionism is highlighting the corrosive impact of Zionism on the health of the Jewish people at large. As an advocate of a new Jewish liberation theology, Ellis has been the most resolute. He follows up on two themes Arendt raised.[91] One is the Zionist belief in an eternal antisemitism impeding Israel or Jewish supporters elsewhere from pursuing a constructive relationship with others, least of all Palestinians. Two is Arendt's fear that the insistence on a hegemonic Jewish state would elevate militarism and state power over all other Jewish values. Ellis adds an important new dimension, which follows up on a concern raised early by Chomsky and later by Beinart, that a narrow-minded pro-Zionist mentality has taken over much of organized American Jewish communal life. He characterizes the post-1967 mindset as a "Constantinian Judaism," "reminiscent of the ties that Christianity has had in nation-states after it was elevated from a persecuted sect to a state religion."[92] In the Jewish variant, worship of a powerful Israeli state has replaced both the Rabbinic tradition and secular liberal values as the overarching American Jewish identity. Caustically, Ellis suggests that synagogues replace the "Torah in the Ark of the Covenant with helicopter gunships."[93] Fueling this identity, he adds, is a new "Holocaust theology," where the Holocaust embodies eternal Jewish suffering, while Israel's rise as a powerful state reflects the redemption.[94] Under Constantinian Judaism, the prevailing American Jewish spirit has become subservient to power, hostile to Palestinians, intolerant of dissent, and uninterested in the Jewish prophetic tradition.

Seeking to reverse this trajectory, Ellis and Butler have sketched new counterhegemonic Jewish ethical visions grounded, like that of Buber, in a mix of Jewish and outside beliefs and secular traditions. Both are influenced by Arendt's retrieval of the Jewish pariah and exile legacies, while Ellis also expands on Buber's efforts to revive spiritual and ethical teachings from Jewish religious texts. Ellis appeals to what he calls "Jews of Conscience," who closely resemble Arendt's "conscious pariahs" and Buber's ancient Jewish prophets.[95] These principled dissenters challenge power and its courtiers in the outside world and within the Jewish community, be it in Israel or in American and other diaspora Jewish institutions.[96] By denouncing the prevailing Constantinian Judaism, Jews of Conscience have been exiled from the Jewish mainstream and joined exiles across the world "in the difficult attempt to birth a new political and economic order."[97] Butler's vision of contemporary Jewish resistance shares an appreciation for the ethical qualities inherent in the Jewish diaspora experience. She agrees with Arendt that the Jewish experience of statelessness and recurring dispossession demands forging cross-national ethical relations "in a socially plural world under conditions of equality."[98]

Butler and Ellis deem it urgent to develop a new Jewish ethics that confronts the sins of Zionism and finds a just path for coexistence. The first step is exposing what they see as the bankrupt two-state program. Generally, Jewish anti-Zionists target the type of post-Oslo two-state plan, what Pappé calls the "real Two States formula."[99] Under the skewed Oslo framework, Israel has consolidated control over the bulk of the West Bank and East Jerusalem, making Israel-Palestine in effect a single but highly stratified political entity.[100] U.S.-mediated proposals have, in turn, incorporated these new facts on the ground to allot Israel the settlement blocs, most of Jerusalem, and an open-ended security buffer deep in the West Bank. Ellis persuasively concludes that the two-state program has become a "fraud" for Palestine.[101] Rather than serving as an acceptable compromise, adds Pappé, the two-state program has enabled Israel to invoke its nominal support for the peace process as leverage to deepen its colonization and put off outside pressure, especially from the United States.[102]

While the more resolute wing of liberal Zionism would share the displeasure with the diluted two-state program introduced in the diplomatic path unleashed by Oslo, Jewish anti-Zionists extend their opposition to the much different version favored by the global community—commonly known as the global consensus—which calls for a Palestinian state over the entire West Bank and Gaza Strip with special status reserved for Jerusalem. Their root objection, as Butler observes, is retaining the "framework of colonial power" and ethnic homogeneity as a "precondition of coexistence."[103] Not only will Palestine be a poor, subordinate state; Israel will fully efface the Palestinian attachment to the territory constituting Israel.[104] Moreover, the two-state framework will reinforce Zionism's demand for an overwhelming Jewish majority and relieve Israel of any obligation to settle Palestinian refugees, beyond a symbolic token amount. Israel, continues Butler, will maintain an "active [process] of minoritization and dispossession."[105] To keep the appearance of "Jewish and Democratic," adds Pappé, Israel will ensure that its Palestinian population remains small with only a light footprint on Israeli politics or society. In a debate with Avnery, he taunts two-state advocates by asking, "Shall we send inspectors to make sure that they will never pass the 20 percent level?"[106] The only acceptable path forward, conclude Jewish anti-Zionists, is to embrace a one-state framework "where all enjoy full rights, equality, and partnership."[107] Only then will Jews break from the Zionist legacy of colonization and ethnic purity, redress the refugee situation, and reconcile with Palestinians.

To foster the enabling conditions for a just one-state resolution, Ellis follows up on Buber's call for a Jewish reckoning, a candid cross-national dialogue, and a joint collaboration. Under Ellis's reckoning, "Israelis and their Jewish enablers in America . . . [would] confess their sins against the Palestinian people" and commit to a "new path characterized by equality and shared responsibility."[108] His hope is that Palestinians would then embark on a "revolutionary forgiveness," a term he encountered from a Christian liberation theologian in response to a meeting of visiting American seminary students with Nicaraguans in the 1980s.[109] Here, Palestinians would join with their former victimizers "*on a new social and political project of inclusion and justice.*"[110] Such forgiveness appreciates that history "is complicated and filled with suffering" and that no return to the pre-Zionist era is possible.[111]

Following a reckoning and revolutionary forgiveness, the final task is collaborating on a shared vision and program for the single state. On one level, Ellis and Butler follow up on the Humanist Zionist call for shared governance based on equal regard for both peoples. Yet Ellis and Butler appreciate the need to break from the Euro-Jewish centrism embedded in the ideas of Arendt and Buber. As Ellis observes, the two "shared certain prejudices inherent in their formative years as Jews and Europeans in the twentieth century" that made them see "Arabs as backward and in need of uplift."[112] Ellis and Butler show how to adapt the underlying call for a new and jointly formulated polity in a genuinely collaborative manner. They still appreciate the lessons of the Jewish exile and prophetic tradition but no longer make them the benchmark. For Butler, a joint project would draw from the distinct exile experiences of Jews and Palestinians "to produce a postnational polity based on the common rights of the refugee and the right to be protected against illegitimate forms of legal and military violence."[113] To recover the once-salient Jewish identification with the most vulnerable, Ellis urges Jews to learn from the Palestinians because they "have become our interlocutors and prophets."[114]

Most anti-Zionists appreciate that the path to a one-state and egalitarian vision faces daunting obstacles. Some respond by emphasizing the moral virtues of an egalitarian single-state program. As Butler states, "A world in which no one held out for a one-state solution . . . would be a radically impoverished world."[115] But she and others also show how a one-state vision can inspire prefigurative forms of Palestinian-Jewish collaboration in opposition to the status quo. The best BDS campaigns, she argues, focus not just on the occupation but on issues that implicate the broader Zionist colonial rule and oppress all Palestinians, including those living in Israel and those residing in the diaspora. It is through such comprehensive campaigns of resistance, in which both dissenting Jews and all Palestinians are invested, concludes Butler, that "we might catch a glimpse of what substantial coexistence could mean."[116]

Ellis's and Butler's interjections underscore the richness of contemporary Jewish anti-Zionism in combining a thorough denunciation of the Zionist experience with an attractive vision for both redeeming Jewishness and advancing reconciliation between Jews and Palestinians. In so doing, they have taken on the mantle of radical dissent pioneered by Arendt and Buber and have developed valuable new insights on setter colonialism, Constantinian Judaism, and reckoning and reconciliation. Jewish anti-Zionists also stand out for their thorough dissection of the moral shortcomings of standard two-state programs, including their implicit legitimization of hegemonic nationalism. Any effort to carve out a progressive two-state version will need to account for these concerns.

There are, however, two notable areas where the Jewish anti-Zionist perspective offers little guidance. First, it typically lacks a fully developed alternative vision of Jewish self-determination because Jewish anti-Zionists fear that doing so will implicitly legitimize the Zionist experience.[117] Second, it has little interest in retrieving any of the ostensibly egalitarian and participatory Zionist institutions and ideals from the pre-state era. In the final chapter, I more fully contest the stance of Jewish anti-Zionists on these issues and reiterate the value of both developing an alternative, non-statist vision of Jewish self-determination and appreciating the appealing, nonhegemonic features of the pre-state Yishuv. Suffice it for now to note that any updated critical Jewish vision is well advised to both recover pre-state Humanist Zionist ideas and temper them with the sharp Jewish anti-Zionist critical lens.

Toward an Updated Critical Jewish Vision of Zionism

Humanist Zionism still holds up as the best anchor for an updated critical Jewish perspective on Zionism because none of the post-1967 critical Jewish voices match its breadth. Flaws notwithstanding, Buber and Arendt integrated a probing diagnosis of the Zionist movement's foundational failings, an appreciation of the egalitarian and spiritual dynamics that inspired many Zionists, the development of an alternative Jewish self-determination, and the articulation of a program for reconciliation and coexistence with Palestinians. The relative shortcomings of contemporary dissenting approaches correspond to the post-1948 constriction in the discourse on Zionism. Before Israel's establishment, Zionism included camps who opposed a Jewish nation-state. Subsequently, it has narrowed to those who support a hegemonic Jewish nation-state.[118] As a result, contemporary Jewish dissenters have tended to situate themselves into pro- and anti-Zionist camps or deflected the issue altogether. Reinserting Humanist Zionism into the critical discussion disrupts this binary divide in favor of a more expansive framework.

My updated critical Jewish vision uses Humanist Zionism as the frame of reference while incorporating insights from later dissenting Jewish perspectives to refine and update the perspective. In particular, I seek to account for new and evolving major trends that have shaped Israel and the Jewish communities globally over the past half-century, such as the following:

- Seven-plus decades of Palestinian exile and subjugation coupled with the continued failure of Israeli Jewish society to reckon with its actions
- Israel's post-1967 shift to an occupier and a major military power embedded in a U.S.-centered imperial order
- The diminishment of Zionism's social democratic and humanist features and growth in its illiberal characteristics
- The prevalence of a "Constantinian Judaism" in the United States and elsewhere
- The rise and fall of the prospects for a two-state resolution accompanied by the diminishment of Israel's peace camp

The first component of my vision is to expand on the foundational failings of the Zionist project and its long-term legacy. The Humanist Zionists captured the disruptive and insensitive nature of Zionism and the root pathologies of tribal nationalism and a fixation on an eternal antisemitism. Their diagnosis effectively anticipated the state's ongoing siege mentality, disregard of Palestinians, militarism, and embeddedness in an imperialist politics. All of these factors have rendered Israel incapable of taking the needed steps toward a just and peaceful reconciliation with Palestinians. Jewish anti-Zionism builds on this diagnosis by emphasizing Zionism's settler colonialism and the enduring legacy of the Nakba in entrenching a program grounded in the subjugation and displacement of Palestinians. Moreover, Jewish anti-Zionist insights draw out the continuities of Israel's post-1967 injustices and belligerent practices with its foundational ideologies and practices.

Just as the continuities need to be appreciated, so do the post-1967 deteriorations in Israeli society and the underlying Zionist ideology. Arendt powerfully warned that a Jewish state founded on tribal nationalism and a fixation on outside hostility, and beholden to distant imperialist powers, would be obsessed with survival and militarism and thereby clash with the goals of a broader Jewish cultural renaissance.[119] Her dire forecast is looking increasingly accurate with regard to Israel's subsequent decision to colonize the post-1967 occupied territories. As Yeshayahu Leibowitz prophesied in 1968, the decision to dominate hundreds of thousands of additional Palestinians without even nominal citizenship status markedly aggravated Israel's militarist, nationalist, and oppressive features.[120] Contemporaneously, Chomsky recognized that Israel's decision to became fully embedded in a U.S.-dominated global order would push it irretrievably to an imperialist outpost at perpetual odds with its neighbors. It is important, then, for an updated Jewish vision of dissent to take stock of the depravities of an escalating colonization and domination of the occupied territories, dependent on a powerful and aggressive military, which casts a heavy shadow over Israeli society at large. The human rights group B'Tselem provided an especially helpful assessment in its comprehensive report at the beginning of 2021. Long focused on the occupation, it concludes that the perpetuation and extent of colonization has collapsed the neat distinction between Israel proper and the occupation, to render the entire state an "apartheid" regime.[121]

The costs of the Zionist project are, as discussed above, not confined to Israel-Palestine but extend to Jewish communities globally, especially in the United States. As cultural Zionists, the Humanist Zionists hoped Zionism would revive and enrich Jewish life globally. Yet they appreciated, especially Arendt, that a tribal nationalist variant would exert a corrosive impact. American contemporary Jewish dissenters have added important dimensions to this dynamic. Chomsky spoke to the post-1967 surge in a narrow "pro-Israel" mentality, which has stifled dissent and critical discussion. Beinart targets the correlation between a chauvinistic Zionism in Israel and an undermining of American Jewish liberal values. The sharpest diagnosis is Ellis's Constantinian Judaism. It deftly captures the underlying state-worship dimension that has devastated the moral and spiritual character of Jewish life in the United States and elsewhere.

The other essential elements for a new Jewish vision of dissent concern how to move forward. As Buber understood, a redemptive vision of Jewish self-determination would be impossible if Jews failed to forge a path of just coexistence with Palestinians. His demand for a thorough reckoning of the Zionist program's injustices remains a vital element of an updated program of Jewish dissent. Such a reckoning would enable a reconciliation in which Jews and Palestinians learn about each other and find a new path forward. Ellis best follows up on how to carry out such a searing self-scrutiny in the wake of seven more decades of Israeli subjugation. Particularly valuable is his idea of revolutionary forgiveness, which overlaps with Edward Said's call for a shared history, to be discussed in the next chapter.

Contrary, however, to the view of most Jewish anti-Zionists, moving forward also requires an updated emancipatory vision of Jewish self-determination free of the hegemonic nationalism that has, in practice, exclusively defined Zionism since 1948. To do this, it is of both moral and tactical value to make connections to the pre-state Zionist features that excited Buber, Arendt, and Chomsky—namely, the spirit of direct democracy, socialism, and the flourishing of new cultural and educational Jewish institutions and practices. With regard to a formal vision, Humanist Zionism presents the best point of departure. Informed by a blend of Jewish and outside teachings and experiences, it integrated social justice and cultural renewal for the Jewish people with just coexistence, solidarity with oppressed peoples, and a transformed global order. Yet, as Butler and Ellis correctly observe, the emancipatory vision of Jewish self-determination needs to free itself from a Euro-Jewish centrism and extend its sources of inspiration to the experiences of Mizrahim and other non-European communities, especially those with long and dynamic histories of resistance to imperialist structures. I follow up on this extension next chapter.

Also important is asserting a Jewish ethical and political framework to oppose the Constantinian Judaism in the United States and elsewhere. Arendt's appeal to a tradition of conscious pariahs remains a valuable frame of reference. As Ellis observes, there is a long history of Jewish dissent, inspired by religious and secular values, in the United States, which has confronted broader societal injustices and the shortcomings within the establishment Jewish community. Guided by Butler and Ellis, Jewish voices of conscience can readily draw from the Jewish exile experience to empathize and practice solidarity with the marginalized and oppressed communities. With respect to Israeli policies and Zionism, an updated ethical Jewish vision stresses the added moral responsibility of Jews to speak out against injustices done ostensibly in their name and on behalf of the victims. In so doing, Jewish dissenters would offer a radically transformed interpretation of what it means to be pro-Israel. As Chomsky argued, a genuine pro-Israel stance acts in solidarity with Palestinians and Israeli Jewish resistance groups committed to a socially just coexistence and a secure future for all. To honor this vision, American Jews would stand in solidarity with social justice advocates in Israel-Palestine and advocate for a foreign policy that holds Israel accountable for its occupation, human rights abuses, and subjugation of Palestinians.

The final dimension of an updated critical Jewish vision is forming a shared framework with Palestinians for living, in the words of Buber, "together with" rather than simply alongside each other. To accommodate a land where two communities have deeply held distinct identities, it makes the most sense to pursue the Humanist Zionist blend of autonomous cultural and political institutions for Jews and Palestinians and shared ones, which foster cross-national bonds and values attentive to the long-standing disparities in power and resources. Critically, as the Humanist Zionists and Chomsky urged, this joint living should be anchored in an appealing set of underlying values. Chomsky's formulation remains compelling, which is to build "free, collective forms of social organization" in the political, socioeconomic, and cultural spheres opposed to imperialism, concentrated power, and oppression. For guidance, Jews and Palestinians would draw from their peoples' most promising values, movements, and practices and from the outside. As discussed by Ellis and Butler, this new policy would be shaped by the past and ongoing experiences of exile and marginalization among Jews and Palestinians to remain vigilant against arbitrary state violence. Following Chomsky's suggestion, the common struggle to make this new society would be attached to a broader global campaign to break down imperialism, nationalism, and oppressive transnational forces generally.

The next chapter follows up on the themes of reckoning, reconciliation, and a shared vision forward by engaging the respective pioneers of critical Palestinian and critical Mizrahi scholar-activism, Edward Said and Ella Shohat.

6

Lessons from Edward Said and Ella Shohat on Reconciliation and Coexistence

As Ellis and Butler correctly observe, Buber and Arendt had Eurocentric blind spots, which led them to neglect Palestinian and other Arab experiences and values. As reviewed in Chapter 3, Arendt even slipped into racism in a private correspondence with Karl Jaspers. Nevertheless, Arendt and Buber presented the lone Zionist perspective that both decried the parochialism of mainstream Zionism and of conventional nationalism in general, and insisted on a just coexistence. Regrettably, neither Buber nor Arendt put much effort into learning about the rich history and diverse set of beliefs and practices in Palestine and the region. As a result, neither probed for complementary experiences and nationalist visions that would strengthen the prospects for an inclusive and cooperative coexistence.

To his credit, Buber did implore the Zionist community to reach out to Palestinians, learn of their culture and religion, and interact much more extensively with them. By contrast, other than an occasional passing reference, he and other Humanist Zionists ignored the experiences of the Jews who had lived for centuries in majority-Arab communities across the greater Middle East. Indeed, it was not clear if Arendt felt any shared identity with Mizrahim. This lack of interest is particularly disappointing given that various Jewish communities participated in the culture and politics of their broader societies while maintaining distinct religious and cultural practices. The Mizrahim presented a rich set of lessons for developing the type of Jewish-Arab coexistence sought by the Humanist Zionists.

To redress the Eurocentrism of Buber and Arendt, this chapter summons the respective pioneers of critical Palestinian and critical Mizrahi scholarship, Edward Said and Ella Shohat. Said's work from the mid-1970s to his death in 2003 sets forth the most comprehensive complementary perspective to Humanist Zionism. In addition to recounting the devastating toll of Zionism on Palestinians and the underlying Orientalist ideology, he situated Palestinian-Israeli relations in a broader imperialist context, articulated an emancipatory vision of Palestinian self-determination, scrutinized the failings of the Palestinian community (especially its leadership), and offered a nuanced framework for attaining reconciliation and a just coexistence. Although Said initially described his project as narrating Zionism from the perspective of its victims, this chapter demonstrates how he also articulated a vision for modifying the emancipatory and coexistence spirit of Humanist Zionism from the perspective of Zionism's victims. Inspired by Said, Shohat has reframed the history of Zionism and of Israeli-Arab relations from the perspective of the Mizrahi victims, whose mixed identities clashed with the homogeneous conceptions of both Zionism and Arab nationalism. By focusing on the heterogeneous Mizrahi heritage, she identifies both new dimensions to Zionism's core pathologies and new insights into advancing a just coexistence.

Said and Shohat carry on a critical orientation very much aligned with the Humanist Zionist vision of Buber and Arendt. They too oppose conventional nationalism and imperialism, articulate an alternative outward-oriented nationalism, demand full equality and democracy, challenge outside subjugation and internal failings, and seek a shared future that accommodates the fluid national identities of Jews and Palestinians. Hence, Said and Shohat demonstrate the continued vitality of Humanist Zionism and identify new challenges and pathways for attaining reconciliation and sustained coexistence. Reading Said and Shohat together with Buber and Arendt allows me to further refine a transformed vision of Jewish dissent and develop a program for reckoning and reconciliation sensitive to the intersecting experiences of European-origin Jews (Ashkenazim), Palestinians, and Mizrahim.

Reckoning, Liberation, Reconciliation, and a Shared Future: Edward Said's Path Forward

There is no better Palestinian counterpart to the exiled European Jewish Humanist Zionist of the 1930s and 1940s than Edward Said. At the conclusion of an interview with the Israeli journalist Ari Shavit, he remarked, "I'm the last Jewish intellectual. You don't know anyone else. All your other Jewish intellectuals are now suburban squires."[1] Like Arendt, Said was a cosmopolitan thinker with a secure perch in the United States but also part of a long-marginalized group. "To be a Palestinian" in the United States, he remarked, "is to be an outlaw . . . an outsider."[2] To be sure, Said enjoyed greater respectability in the Palestinian community than did Arendt in Israel or in the U.S. Jewish establishment. Yet he eventually became a formidable iconoclast unwelcome among the official Palestinian leadership. He first attained prominence with the publication of *Orientalism* in 1978, which helped launch postcolonial studies. Blending literary and historical analysis to uncover the cultural dimensions of imperialism, he dissected the simplistic and patronizing patterns by which Western scholars, essayists, and novelists depicted life in the Greater Middle East and Asia.[3] One year later, Said published *The Question of Palestine*, which quickly became a seminal text in Palestine studies. The book exposed the underlying racist premises and practices of Zionism and the persistent Western demonization and marginalization of Palestinians. It also presented a vision for an emancipatory Palestinian nationalism and a framework for Jewish-Palestinian reconciliation and coexistence. While Said pursued these same themes in subsequent writings, he substantially modified his analysis in two ways following the 1993 Oslo accord. First, he sounded the alarm at the emergence of a disturbing version of Palestinian nationalism that catered to prevailing global forces and abandoned the cause of substantive liberation. Second, Said reconceived how to pursue Palestinian liberation and a just coexistence with Israel's Jews. To fully appreciate his evolution in thinking, I devote separate sections to his insights in *Question of Palestine* and to those in his post-Oslo essays.

Assessing Zionism, National Liberation, and Reconciliation from the Perspective of the Victims

Said wrote *Question of Palestine* at a time of robust U.S. popular and elite support for Israel and little sympathy for the Palestinian cause, even in most liberal-leftist outlets. The book appeared while the just-completed Camp David peace accord between Egypt and Israel was widely acclaimed despite its sidelining of the Palestinian issue. "For too long," remarked Said, "we have been outside history, and certainly outside discussion." He aimed "to make the question of Palestine a subject for discussion and political understanding."[4] To do so, Said confronted the prevailing Western Zionist narrative, which viewed Israel-Palestine as a clash between a heroic affirmation of the Jewish people and the resistance of an "essentially repellant population of uncivilized Arab natives."[5] Most Americans were therefore unaware of a Palestinian people with a long and deep attachment to the land. To disrupt this view, Said set out to relate the Palestinian experience and reinterpret the Zionist story "from the standpoint of its victims."[6] In doing so, he exposed the grave toll of Zionism and a toxic Orientalism that enabled this subjugation. At the same time, *Question of Palestine* presented a hopeful vision of emancipation and reconciliation. "Only if [the Palestinians'] values and history are taken account of," he noted, "can we begin to see the bases for compromise, settlement, and finally, peace."[7]

The book was among the first in the West to identify Zionism as a settler-colonial ideology rather than one of national liberation. He summed up the ideology as follows:

> Palestine's colonization was to be accomplished simultaneously for and by Jews and by the displacement of the Palestinians; moreover, that in its conscious and declared ideas about Palestine, Zionism attempted first to minimize, then to eliminate, and then, all else failing, finally to subjugate the natives.[8]

Most fundamental was the permanent displacement of over seven hundred thousand Palestinians, facilitated by forced evacuations, psychological terror through well-publicized massacres, the instituting of machinery to prevent the return, and the obliteration of all remnants of emptied Palestinian villages.[9] The Nakba, argued Said, was not simply an ad hoc reaction to war but integral to the Zionist settler-colonial mission. The logic that drove the Nakba continued to shape Israel's approach in the ensuing decades, as manifested in Israel's expropriation of Palestinian lands for resettling Jewish immigrants, implementation of martial rule over the bulk of remaining Palestinians, and enactment of laws and policies that drew sharp lines between Jew and Arab and furthered Jewish supremacy. Israel's then-decade-long occupation of the West Bank, East Jerusalem, and Gaza Strip, continued Said, followed the established framework.

To legitimize the displacement and subjugation of Palestinians, Said probed Zionism's dehumanizing of Palestinians. The Zionists "considered the Arab problem as something either to be avoided completely, or denied (and hence attacked) completely."[10] One recurring avoidance practice was to write out Palestinians from Zionist history. Taking on the mythical stature of the kibbutzim in Zionist lore, Said pointed out what was omitted: that "Arabs were never admitted as members, that cheap (Arab or Oriental Jewish) hired labor is essential to kibbutz functioning, that 'socialist' kibbutzim were and are established on land confiscated from Arabs."[11] Where avoidance was not possible, Said showed how Zionists followed the European imperialist pattern of contrasting the civilized "Occidental" to the backward "Oriental." The Jews were portrayed as the Westernized Easterners in Palestine who would redeem the land from the stagnant and treacherous Arabs.[12] Convinced of the righteousness of their cause and that the Arabs could not be trusted, even moderate Zionist leaders, such as Chaim Weizmann, accepted that severe measures were justified to fulfill the Zionist mission.[13] Through this combination of denial and denigration, Israelis and their supporters minimized the significance of the Nakba and exempted themselves from any blame.[14] The persistence of this Orientalist approach has, in turn, justified and sanitized Israel's subsequent aggressions. To be sure, allowed Said, the post-1967 occupation of another million Arabs has made it impossible for Israel to "dodge the problem of the new Palestinian actuality."[15] But, aided by a still-popular Orientalist narrative, shared by the *New York Times* editorial page, Israel's supporters still managed to frame the occupation as an earnest effort to develop good relations between Jews and Arabs rather than as a conquest.

Said demonstrated how readily the Zionist binary narrative of enlightened-versus-savage resonated in the West. Notably, the Balfour Declaration's support of Zionist settlement in Palestine established the Zionists as the worthy transmitters of European values. As lord Balfour approvingly remarked, the great powers deemed Zionism "*of far profounder import than the desire and prejudices of 700,000 Arabs who now inhabit the ancient land.*"[16] For both British political elites and Western intellectuals, Zionism comported with a common Western liberal rationale for colonialism. Said cited the interjections in the late 1940s of the preeminent American theologian and public intellectual Reinhold Niebuhr as an outstanding case in point. In a coauthored public letter to the *New York Times* in 1947, Niebuhr and others described "Jewish Palestine" as the "one vanguard of progress and modernization in the Middle East" and the "Arab-Moslem Middle East" as a "hopeless picture."[17] Said traced the deepening of this Orientalist perspective, especially in U.S. political discourse, leading to a "complete hegemonic coalescence between the liberal Western view of things and the Zionist-Israeli view."[18] Consequently, most Israeli and U.S. intellectuals and journalists would "celebrate Israel and Zionism unblinkingly," while those few who spoke out against Israeli injustices and on behalf of Palestinians were branded as "anti-Semitic, or an apologist for Islam and the Arabs."[19]

To help rescue the image of Palestinians and make them full protagonists, *Question of Palestine* celebrated a post-1967 rebirth of a cohesive and emancipatory national identity. Despite being "geographically dispersed and fragmented," he observed, "we have begun . . . to construct a political identity and will of our own; we have developed a remarkable resilience and an even more remarkable national resurgence."[20] The aftermath of the 1967 war provided the spark. For one thing, noted Said, Israel's acquisition of additional Palestinian territory in which a million Palestinians resided gave the Palestinian cause new global prominence. Unlike the pre-1967 setting, Israel could not obscure the Palestinian presence or the forceful Israeli subjugation in the West Bank and Gaza Strip. The occupation became a new rallying point.[21] Moreover, he added, the Arab states' decisive military defeat put an end to subsuming the Palestinian cause to a broader Pan-Arabism. Marking the birth of a new assertive Palestinian-led resistance was the defense waged by Palestinian militias to an Israeli raid in 1968 on the Jordanian town of Karameh. Suddenly, a resurgent and independent PLO had wrested leadership of the resistance from Nasser's Egypt.[22]

Part of the PLO's success, explained Said, was forming an umbrella organization that accommodated all of the distinct Palestinian constituencies—those in the occupied territories, those in Israel, and the majority who were scattered across the region and beyond—and most of the ideological strands.[23] He singled out the Palestinian National Council for instituting robust deliberation and critical scrutiny of the PLO leadership. It marked the first "broadly representative national body in the Arab world actually debating important matters in a totally democratic way."[24] In addition, the PLO gave birth to a "startlingly active array of Palestinian organizations" including "students' organizations, women's groups, trade unions, schools . . . [and] a vast health and supply network."[25] Through this largely consensus-based network of institutions, observed Said, the PLO established a distinct and rich Palestinian identity. Moreover, by attaining international legitimacy, the Palestinian people became a leading global protagonist, especially in the Middle East and the broader nonaligned world.[26]

Underlying this consensus-based approach and active grass roots was a new vision of national liberation, which Said called the "Palestinian idea." Rather than simply seek return to a pre-Zionist Palestine, the Palestinian idea envisioned an *"entirely new* place" "responsive to the dramatically changed realities of the post-1967 era."[27] This vision broke from the prevailing regional model of modern nationalism by calling for a multiethnic secular democracy sensitive to the pluralistic nature and history of Palestine. Said welcomed the PLO's guarantee of full equality for Jews and all other residents based on "secular human rights, not on religious or minority exclusivity."[28] The Palestinian idea also encompassed a "refusal to sell out, to give up the struggle, to accept tutelage of occupation without protest."[29] Palestine, he proudly noted, became the focal point of global anti-imperialist struggles and inspired resistance movements in Iran, Egypt, and elsewhere.[30] In sum, concluded Said,

> No Arab community has in so short a period of time . . . reflected so deeply and so seriously as a community on the meaning of its history, the meaning of a pluralistic society given the dismal fate of multiethnic communities in the world, the meaning of national independence and self-determination against a background of exile, imperialist oppression, colonialist dispossession.[31]

While much of *Question of Palestine* was aimed at giving voice to the Palestinian experience, it also marked one of the first internal exhortations to Palestinians to understand the Jewish historical experience and its impact on Zionism. Here, too, Said mirrored Buber and other Humanist Zionists who had reproached Palestine's Jews for showing no interest in Palestinian Arabs. Said, however, faced the challenge of a highly asymmetrical relationship in which the other was not primarily a largely unknown community but an oppressor. Helped by his deep familiarity with the European Jewish experience and the meaning of Zionism for Jews, he articulated a sensitive and compelling case for outreach. To be sure, Said found the Zionists' ignorance of Palestinians far more severe and destructive to the cause of a just peace because of the power they wielded. Palestinians had at least come to realize that "the Israeli-Jewish people is a concrete political reality with which they must live in the future."[32] Nevertheless, he faulted Palestinians for not trying to understand the depth of the Israeli Jewish experience. He urged Palestinians to appreciate that Israeli Jews were the most morally complex of colonial oppressors because they belonged to a group constituting "the greatest victims of racism in history."[33] Such a trauma had led Israeli Jews and their supporters to regard Israel's establishment as a major accomplishment for Jews, including as a "protection against further genocidal attempts."[34] By understanding how the Jewish people could be both victimizers and scarred survivors, argued Said, Palestinians would gain a sophisticated understanding of their enemy, which could inspire not just better resistance but a more productive path toward reconciliation and coexistence.

Said demanded much more of the Israelis given their long record of dehumanizing Palestinians but urged both to "reckon with the existential power and presence" of the other, including their collective traumas and "emotional and political investment" in the land of Israel-Palestine.[35] While their relationship was one of victimizers and victims, Said insisted that both sides accept that their histories had made them "fully implicated in each other's lives and political destinies."[36] If the two peoples would commit to seeing "each other within a common historical perspective" that both reckoned with the grave costs Zionism inflicted on Palestinians and appreciated the struggles and national aspirations of both, they could find a path of reconciliation.[37]

Notwithstanding his praise for the PLO's proposal of a united, nonsectarian state, Said supported the establishment of an independent Palestinian state on the occupied territories to exist alongside Israel. His rationale was twofold. Like the majority of the PLO leadership by the mid-1970s, Said recognized that there was little global support for the one-state option. Yet he also reasoned "that an independent and sovereign Palestinian state is required at this stage to fulfill our history as a people during the past century."[38] Said welcomed a Palestinian state as a means to declare the enduring Palestinian attachment, not to further rigid national divides. Similar to Arendt, he implored not just Israel but all states in the region to move away from a nation-state focus in which the central government privileges the majority and instead to prioritize human rights and common citizenship.[39] Hence, his version of two states was similar to what Chomsky proposed in the mid-1970s, one that downscaled nationalism and emphasized cross-national collaboration. A Palestinian state would mark not a divorce between Jews and Arabs but a foundation for breaking down tensions and facilitating extensive cross-national exchanges to foster a shared future.[40]

Question of Palestine holds up well for its dissection of the profound harms inflicted by Zionism, its articulation of an appealing new Palestinian national vision, and its identification of a path forward for reconciliation and coexistence. But unlike the work of the Humanist Zionists, the book lacked a systematic internal critique. Said interspersed occasional criticisms of Palestinian leaders and society but provided no elaboration. Because the book was one of the first efforts to present the Palestinian story to the United States, where Palestinians were routinely marginalized or demonized, Said may have chosen to soften his critical edge and emphasize what genuinely impressed him. As he later recalled, "There wasn't and has never been a Palestinian lobby in the West, so what one did at the outset was fairly solitary. It became part of my purpose to keep up support for Palestine, to inform, explain, interpret what was otherwise unreported, misrepresented, or falsely portrayed."[41] Consequently, *Question of Palestine* offered little guidance for diagnosing and countering negative nationalist and leadership tendencies.[42] Said vigilantly remedied this deficiency after the Oslo accord.

Carrying on Liberation and Coexistence in a Time of Dual Oppression

Said maintained good relations with the PLO leadership through the 1980s and was active in the Palestinian National Council. He drafted the English version of the 1988 Palestinian Declaration of Independence, which formally supported a two-state resolution.[43] Yet throughout the 1980s, Said became disillusioned with Arafat and his inner circle for their growing distance from the Palestinian people and their prioritizing of self-interest over national liberation.[44] After the PLO rebuffed his effort in 1991 to assemble a group of activists and officials to work out a set of principles to guide the upcoming negotiations with Israel, Said resigned from the council.[45] His spirited and far-reaching criticisms of the Oslo accord launched his second phase as the preeminent Palestinian intellectual opponent of not only U.S.-backed Israeli rule but also Palestinian elites and the new peace orthodoxy. In this phase, Said's assessment of the promises and perils of nationalism matched or even surpassed the breadth of the Humanist Zionist framework. To begin with, he ruthlessly dissected the prevailing trends of Palestinian nationalism, where what was billed as sovereignty and liberation amounted to cooption, parochialism, and internal oppression. In this regard, Said identified a type of dual oppression analogous to what Arendt diagnosed for Europe's Jews in the nineteenth and first part of the twentieth century. In the post-Oslo era, the Palestinians' primary oppressor was Israel, with full U.S. backing, and the secondary oppressor was a complicit and short-sighted elite sector of Palestinians. At the same time, he provided an inspiring program for reviving the Palestinian idea and advancing a plan for coexistence, which broke fundamentally from Oslo's separate-and-unequal two-state paradigm.

Like the Humanist Zionist opposition to the UN partition plan, Said objected not just to the terms of the Oslo accord but to the underlying political dynamics. Just as the partition plan discredited an alternative inclusive Zionism, Said saw Oslo as ratifying the demise of the Palestinian idea.[46] For roughly a decade prior, he observed, the PLO had deteriorated from a once-consensus-based organization open to robust debate to "a quasi-official Arab state organization, not unlike . . . the bureaucracies and dictatorships it was forced to deal with in the region."[47] Corresponding with the oppressive internal structure was the abandonment of anti-imperialism, replaced by an orientation followed by Egypt's President Sadat and most Arab state leaders of courting U.S. elites.[48] Fittingly, he recalled, Arafat made no outreach to sectors in the United States potentially supportive of the Palestine idea, such as African Americans, students, and civil rights groups. Rather, he solicited "patrons" who could secure him a deal.[49] Arafat got his deal, lamented Said, but at the cost of selling out the Palestinian idea and reducing self-determination to a hollow shell.

In critiquing the Oslo accord, Said emphasized the undemocratic and self-serving maneuvers of Arafat and his inner circle. Arafat's main concern in the era immediately preceding Oslo, noted Said, was regaining his status as the preeminent Palestinian representative. Arafat had been eclipsed during the first intifada by a new grassroots movement in the occupied territories and sidelined from the official Madrid talks initiated in 1991. There, a relatively independent group of West Bank and Gazan delegates had both given favorable visibility to Palestinian concerns and held firm on core Palestinian demands.[50] Consistent with its secretive and unaccountable manner, the PLO leadership proceeded to undermine the Madrid delegation. It initiated separate negotiations without incorporating the work done by the Madrid delegates or soliciting the input of other Palestinians. What Arafat and his circle sought, argued Said, was not a better deal for Palestinians but a restoration as the primary interlocutors.[51] Accordingly, Arafat yielded on most Israeli demands, with the result being a "Palestinian Versailles."[52] The PLO got its formal recognition, but in exchange, it committed to a "whole series of renunciations," including of the right to resist and of all the hard-fought UN and regional resolutions that affirmed Palestinian statehood and the right of return and censured Israeli settlements, annexation, and war crimes.[53] Israel, by contrast, did not declare support for a Palestinian state and retained effective control of the process. The end result of Oslo and the 1995 follow-up accord was a PA subordinate to Israel coupled with Israel's further colonization of the occupied territories through settlement growth, bypass roads, and security checkpoints. Meanwhile, added Said, Oslo precluded any reckoning of what had happened in 1948, including the Nakba.[54]

In establishing the PA, he observed, Arafat and his advisers had completed the process of replacing a once-sincere national liberation movement with an authoritarian regime that resembled that of Egypt and other developing states in the U.S. sphere of influence. In the areas under its control, the PLO bypassed local organizations and governed according to a "one-man rule" with a repressive security apparatus that permitted "no real freedoms and democratic rights."[55] It also suppressed countervailing dynamics, such as a strong civil society, independent political channels, and a robust rule of law.[56] Befitting its lack of substantive sovereignty, the PA was tightly constrained by Israeli rule and subordinate to a U.S.-dominated neoliberal global order. It followed the Washington Consensus of limited public spending, a weak public infrastructure (apart from security), liberalization of investment and trade, and courting of wealthy capitalists and business firms.[57] The result, complained

Said, was a highly stratified society. On one end was a select sector of interconnected political and economic elites, who benefited from a skewed privatization, new international business ventures (often linked to Israeli firms), and preferential political treatment. On the other end was most of the population, whose standard of living deteriorated from local oppression, economic neglect, and expanding Israeli colonization.

Said found further depressing the complicity of most Palestinian intellectuals and other shapers of opinion. He charged those who remained silent with abetting the deteriorating state of affairs: "The condition of Arab and Palestinian politics today is desperate not because of an excess, but because of a poverty, of reason and responsibility."[58] In an argument similar to that made by Chomsky in "Responsibility of Intellectuals" regarding mainstream U.S. intellectuals during the Vietnam War era, Said attacked the mindset of the so-called responsible Palestinian intellectuals.[59] By favoring access to elites over principled opposition, they "internaliz[ed] the norm of power, not those of genuine reflection and analysis." Such intellectuals advanced the agenda of not just Palestinian elites but also the more powerful Israeli and U.S. elites.[60]

Unlike in the time frame of *Question of Palestine*, Said had to think about how to revive a Palestinian idea under attack not just from Israel but from Palestinian elites and intellectuals. His definition of the idea remained the same, which encompassed a multiethnic, multireligious pluralism, robust democracy, emphasis on human rights and citizenship, and resistance to the prevailing global order and to all types of subjugation. Like the Humanist Zionists, Said urged a broad self-scrutiny whereby Palestinians would "look at our history, the history of our leaderships and of our institutions, with a new critical eye. Is there something about those that can perhaps explain the difficulties as a people that we now find ourselves in?"[61] Another challenge was to recover a global consciousness. It was high time "to break out of our self-constructed mind-forged manacles and look at the rest of the world and deal with it as equals."[62] Particularly important was to take part in global struggles for justice and study other resistance movements, past and present.[63] He identified the last challenge as resuscitating the democratic spirit by forging a "mass movement . . . imbued with a vision of participating directly in a future of its own making."[64]

Said looked to what Arendt would have defined as the conscious pariahs to lead the revival. He took pride in a broader Palestinian society that remained "rambunctious and healthily unruly."[65] Operating outside of formal Palestinian political channels, these unruly Palestinians kept alive the Palestinian idea of substantive democracy, popular resistance, and international solidarity despite the suppression and discouragement from Israel and the PA. He singled out for praise a nonsectarian grassroots movement known as the Palestinian

National Initiative (PNI) that emerged early in the second intifada. It consisted primarily of independent intellectuals, political activists, and artists and featured a platform of unconditional resistance to the occupation, internal democracy and freedom, and an independent rule of law.[66] The PNI, continued Said, had carried out political mobilization, training programs and social services, and solidarity outreach with "Israelis, Europeans, Americans, Africans, Asians, and Arabs" to build a movement "that practice[d] the pluralism and coexistence it preache[d]."[67] Through the work of the PNI and like-minded activists, the cause of Palestine remained a global rallying point for resistance movements, including the recently formed anti-imperialist, counterglobalization ones.[68]

Said commended the PNI's openness to collaboration with Israelis. He maintained his conviction that Palestinian liberation could not be complete unless it found a path for a just coexistence. For this to happen, Said identified three prevalent but dysfunctional Palestinian approaches toward Israel to overcome. One was that of the PLO leadership, which solicited the goodwill of ostensibly more moderate Israeli politicians from the Labor and Meretz Parties but ignored Israel's broader civil society. Another more widespread approach was thinking of Israeli Jews only as oppressors rather than as part of a complex community with a rich history. Finally, Said pointed to the reflexive anti-"normalization" stance of many activists that rejected any outreach or collaboration with Israelis.[69] All such tendencies, he persuasively argued, failed to recognize the need to develop a transformed relationship that would enable a just coexistence.

The starting point for a more productive stance, stressed Said, was aggressively relating their experiences and sufferings to an ignorant Israeli Jewish community. He called on Palestinians to "confront the Israeli conscience with the serious human and political claims of the Palestinians" and Zionism's atrocities since the state's establishment.[70] Equally important was becoming far more educated on Israelis. How, Said asked, "could one possibly oppose analyzing and learning everything possible about a country whose presence in our midst . . . had so influenced and shaped the life of every man, woman, and child in the Arab world?"[71] Palestinians should study the Holocaust and the broader history of antisemitism in order to "see how it impinges on the Jewish, and indeed Western, conscience."[72] They should also look inside Israeli society and consider its diversity of constituencies and social institutions. Palestinians would thereby gain deeper insights into the challenges facing them and how to respond effectively. They could then distinguish the oppressive state from a more complex civil society and uncover the "potential for real, as opposed to cosmetic, accommodation with Palestinian national rights in all their historical and moral richness."[73] He pressed Palestinians to "cooperate with sectors who stand for civil and human rights, who oppose the settlement policy, who are ready to take a stand on military occupation, who believe in coexistence and equality [and] who are disgusted with official repression of the Palestinians."[74]

By bringing about a deeper mutual understanding at the grass roots, argued Said, the path would be eased toward a substantive reconciliation, propelled by a shared but asymmetric moral reckoning. As the victimizer, Israel must formally take responsibility for "the destruction of Palestinian society, . . . the dispossession of the Palestinian people . . . the confiscation of their land" and subsequent depredations.[75] Said also insisted that Israel "accept the sovereign existence of a Palestinian people" and its claim to the land of Israel-Palestine.[76] Were Israelis at long last to assume this moral burden, he continued, both peoples could understand how their tragic histories came to intersect. Each would learn about and empathize with the collective sufferings of the other, but not as detached and self-contained experiences.[77] Palestinians would appreciate the enormity of the Holocaust and, together with Jews, reflect on how it yielded moral distortions that prodded the latter to forge in blood and conquest a Jewish state in disregard of the devastating consequences for Palestinians. In sum, the "great virtue of reading Palestinian and Jewish history *together* not only gives the tragedy of the Holocaust *and* of what subsequently happened to the Palestinians their full force, but also reveals how . . . one people, the Palestinians, has borne a disproportional share of the pain and loss."[78] Ultimately, Said viewed a shared history as the way for both peoples to cleanse themselves of ongoing moral distortions and appreciate each other's humanity.[79] The process would push both peoples to admit the "universality and integrity of the other's experience" and commit to a coexistence "that is true to the *differences* between Jew and Palestinian, but true also to the common history of different struggle and unequal survival that links them."[80]

By the mid-to-late 1990s, Said no longer believed that a two-state program could lead to an acceptable shared future. Rather than stemming Israel's ongoing colonization of the occupied territories, he understood the Oslo regime to have further unleashed the process, making impossible a progressive two-state resolution based on equality, open borders, and collaboration. Through settlement expansion, bypass roads, checkpoints, and security zones, Israel had precluded the possibility for Palestine to enjoy normal sovereignty. Even if Israel were to agree to a nominal Palestinian state, noted Said, such a "state" would be bifurcated by Israeli settlements and security zones and economically dependent on Israel for conducting cross-border trade.[81] Besides the physical obstacles Israelis had imposed, Said also considered the cumulative interlocking experiences of Israelis and Palestinians. Each had come to exert a profound impact on the identity of the other. The challenge was to find a "peaceful way in which to coexist . . . as equal citizens in the same land."[82]

Most symbolically marking Said's affinity to the spirit of the Humanist Zionists was his call to revive the binational single-state idea. He too sought a program that would honor the enduring national attachments of Jews and Palestinians to the same land. Unlike most Jewish anti-Zionists, he rejected any demands on Jews to renounce Zionism. As he told Ari Shavit, he was not asking Israeli Jews "to commit hara-kiri. They can be Zionists, and they can assert their Jewish identity."[83] Instead, he called on Jews and Palestinians to accept a reformed view of self-determination that did not diminish either people's attachment to the land but would "soften, lessen, and finally give up special status for one people at the expense of the other." On the highly sensitive topic of immigration, continued Said, the "Law of Return for Jews and the right of return for Palestinian refugees [would] be considered and trimmed together."[84] The idea was to foster distinct but not antagonistic national identities along with a shared political and social project.

Like Arendt in the 1940s and Chomsky in the 1970s, Said connected his alternative vision for Palestine-Israel to a broader global shift from the still-prevailing nation-state and imperialist-friendly model. He focused on the Middle East, where a sectarian nationalism had left a modern legacy of "warring fiefdoms,"[85] autocratic leaders, and a state of affairs in which "no Arab state is free to dispose of its resources as it wishes, or to take positions" that upset the long-dominant imperial power, the United States.[86] Said desired a loosening of state borders in which "the Jews of Israel and Arab peoples in the surrounding regions [would] make a new kind of history based on a politics of integration and inclusion."[87] To Shavit's objection that such a development would leave Israel's Jews vulnerable to a concerted regional hostility, Said echoed Arendt's old argument that it was "folly" for Jews to trust a "distant imperial power for protection, while alienating the goodwill of neighbors."[88] To be sure, he conceded that Jews had reason to worry given the mixed historical record of Arab societies in their treatment of Jews and other minorities.[89] But an integration based on pluralism, he countered, offered far better assurance than a region of antagonistic nation-states. Israel's reliance on overwhelming might and U.S. backing may have brought it security for an indefinite period from military conquest, but at the cost of "paranoia, militarization, and a rigid mindset."[90] A successful integration, he noted, would mean a more attractive and mobile life for Jews.

Said understood the daunting political impediments to attaining a binational single state. "It now seems like a totally long shot," he opined in a 1999 interview, "and completely utopian."[91] But because he regarded the binational egalitarian state as the only pathway for a just and peaceful coexistence, he deemed it urgent to build support for this option. Said found one source of hope in historical precedents within the Arab and Jewish communities. Palestine's "millennia-long history" had been one of heterogeneity consisting of multiple national groups, cultures, and religions.[92] Past Arab culture in general, he added, was one of "catholicism," which managed to endure, albeit in weaker form, "despite mutilation by the nation-state."[93] He was also impressed by the dissenting pre-state Zionists as a "small but important group of Jewish thinkers (Judah Magnes, Buber, Arendt and others) [who] argued and agitated for a binational state."[94] These "international luminaries," Said noted, "realized that there was going to be a clash if the aggressive settlement policies and the unreflecting ignorance of the Arabs pressed ahead."[95]

Moving to the contemporary setting, Said identified two subcommunities uniquely positioned to foster a binational, pluralist spirit of coexistence. The first were younger Palestinian citizens of Israel. Having lived among Israeli Jews as fellow citizens, albeit second-class, they were intimately familiar with Israeli society rather than just the coercive state apparatus. Israel's younger Palestinians did not seek separation, noted Said, but were struggling to gain equal individual and collective rights as Israeli citizens.[96] Less numerous but more complex were the Mizrahi Jewish critics of Zionism, who have been outsiders among outsiders. Like Israel's Mizrahi community in general, as elaborated in the following section, the dissenters experienced a de facto second-class citizenship due to their Arab heritage. Yet they also did not fit in with Israel's mainstream Mizrahim because they had come to challenge the foundational hegemonic ideology of Zionism. Regrettably, lamented Said, many Palestinians and other Arabs had extended their anti-normalization stance to these Jews rather than recognize a promising ideological kinship.[97] These dissenting Mizrahim, he countered, should be welcomed both for their courage and informed scrutiny of Zionism and for embodying a type of fluid and heterogeneous cultural and political identity that would inform a new inclusive binational spirit.

Ultimately, Said believed that Israel's Palestinians and the dissenting Mizrahim could find common ground with a new generation of globally oriented Palestinian and Jewish iconoclasts. Uniting them all was profound dissatisfaction with the status quo and a conviction that a bold transformation was imperative. The lynchpin for such a transformation, he concluded, was a revived and amended binational vision whose essence was "coexistence and sharing in ways that require an innovative, daring, and theoretical willingness to get beyond the arid stalemate of assertion, exclusivism, and rejection."[98]

Below, I address how to further an engagement of critical Jewish and Palestinian perspectives. Before doing so, it is essential to incorporate a critical Mizrahi perspective.

Zionism and Coexistence from the Standpoint of the Arab Jew

Ella Shohat is the first scholar to have carefully considered what was lost both intellectually and politically by the long neglect of the Mizrahi experience. While there is now a burgeoning critical Mizrahi scholarship, Shohat contributes the most far-reaching criticism of the Zionist project's prevailing hegemonic nationalism. Born to an Iraqi Jewish family forced to relocate to Israel in the early 1950s, she internalized a feeling of displacement, which has informed her scholarship.[99] She has published a series of essays since the 1980s that have examined the difficult and multilayered Mizrahi encounter over time with Zionism and Arab nationalism. Collectively, Shohat has revealed a deeper assessment of the distortions inflicted by Zionist Orientalism and tribal nationalism. She has also provided a longer and richer shared history of Jewish-Arab encounters and shown its value for inspiring a renewed spirit of coexistence that will enable a break from the grim impasse of the present.

Shohat's depiction of Zionist Orientalism of the Mizrahim is most comprehensively set forth in her pathbreaking essay from 1988, "Sephardim in Israel: Zionism from the Standpoint of Its Jewish Victims."[100] As indicated in the second part of the title, the essay uses Said's framework from *Question of Palestine* as its point of departure.[101] To fully understand the "Zionist denial of the Arab-Muslim and Palestinian East," argues Shohat, it is necessary to confront the corresponding "denial of the Jewish 'Mizrahim' . . . who, like the Palestinians, but by more subtle and less obviously brutal mechanisms, have *also* been stripped of the right of self-representation."[102] She does not equate Mizrahi suffering under Zionism with that of Palestinians. Rather, she features the crucial role of the Mizrahi experience in facilitating the Zionist Orientalist project. Her ultimate goal is to open up a new framework that will enable the various communities to "move beyond the present intolerable impasse."[103]

Shohat depicts the Orientalism toward Mizrahim as grounded in a Zionist-as-savior mythology. As it does the Palestinians, the narrative casts Mizrahim as illiberal, reactionary, and premodern. Here, Orientalism justifies not a displacement or overt subjugation but a hierarchical relation, in which the Ashkenazi Jewish condition serves as the benchmark Jewish identity. Such Orientalism shaped the character of the Mizrahi absorption into Israeli society. Shohat recalls a number of disparaging remarks from leading officials, academics, and journalists to evince the crudity of the Mizrahim. Prominent scholar Karl Frankenstein, for example, commented on the "primitive mentality of many of the immigrants from backward countries," while Ben-Gurion called Moroccan Jews "savages" and proclaimed, "We are in duty bound to fight against the spirit of the Levant, which corrupts individuals and societies, and preserve the authentic Jewish values as they crystallized in the Diaspora."[104] Notably, adds Shohat, the Ashkenazi elite continue to portray Mizrahim as backward and overlook their multilayered cultural heritage, including in the metropolises of Alexandria, Baghdad, and Istanbul.[105]

Informed by her diagnosis of Zionist Orientalism, she provides a withering portrayal of Zionist depictions of the Mizrahi experience in Israel. The most prominent is the "Zionist Master Narrative" whereby "European Zionism 'saved' Sephardi Jews from the harsh rule of their Arab 'captors.'"[106] Shohat recognizes that the situation for Jews in a number of countries, including her parents' home of Iraq, became highly precarious in the years immediately preceding and following Israel's establishment. What she refutes is the depiction of Zionists as noble rescuers. To begin with, the Zionist leaders originally focused exclusively on Europe's Jews and worried that an infusion of Mizrahim would taint the project.[107] What changed their mind was not concern for the welfare of Mizrahim but practical demographic and economic concerns. First, Israel was not able to attract enough post-Holocaust European survivors to secure an overwhelming Jewish demographic majority.[108] Second, the Israeli establishment wanted an exploitable but Jewish population to settle in undesirable border areas and remote villages and to perform low-paid blue-collar and agricultural labor.[109] Israel's Orientalism conveniently legitimized this arrangement.

Shohat further demonstrates how Israel's exploitative absorption of Mizrahi immigrants undermines the Zionist redemption mythology. Assuming Mizrahim as a group were backward and inferior, the Israeli absorption officials consigned the bulk of them to an entrenched second-class status.[110] As Shohat recounts, officials assigned new immigrants to substandard housing in segregated urban neighborhoods, rural areas, or development towns, all of which lacked quality public education or other adequate infrastructure.[111] The jobs were low-paying with few opportunities to advance, while the children were tracked in educational paths geared toward low-status vocations. Further undermining the redemption narrative, she continues, was the systematic disparaging of Mizrahi Jewish religion and culture. The fluid religious practices of Mizrahim were deemed as fanatical and primitive by secular Ashkenazim and as corrupted and insufficiently Jewish by Ashkenazi religious authorities.

More generally, Israeli officials, journalists, and academics depicted Mizrahim as tainted by a "malignant" and "backwards" Arab heritage.[112] The message they conveyed to Mizrahim was to be rid of all vestiges of Arab culture and adopt the default Euro-Jewish culture. Shohat rebukes contemporary "sociological accounts" for attributing the persistent lower socioeconomic status of Mizrahim to their failure to shed their cultural heritage rather than to the "classed and raced structure" that took root in Israel's early years.[113]

As important as Zionist Orientalism has been, Shohat dissects the deleterious impact of Zionism's exclusionary and homogeneous nationalism and the corresponding Arab variant. "The reconceptualization of Jewishness as a national identity," she writes, "had profound implications for Arab Jews. The Orientalist splitting of the Semite was now compounded by a nationalist splitting."[114] Shohat's characterization of the emerging nationalisms matches Arendt's depiction of tribal nationalism. Both Zionism and Arab nationalism "assumed that the 'national' is produced by eliminating the foreign, the contaminated, the impure."[115] Neither could accommodate "crossed and multiple identities." Even had Zionism been free of Orientalism, she suggests that the tribal nationalism would have propelled state officials to take every effort to de-Arabize the Mizrahim. Indeed, the very idea of an Arab Jew was seen as an "ontological impossibility."[116] More importantly—and consistent with Arendt's warnings—because Zionism assumed a perpetually embattled world, it regarded any outside identity, even in a hybrid form, as a profound threat to the nation.[117] Zionism's tribal nationalism hence engendered not only brutal behavior toward the Palestinian outsider but also enduring internal injustices and bitterness.

Shohat extends her scrutiny regarding tribal nationalism to the postcolonial Palestinian and Arab societies. The anticolonial Arab nationalism that assumed power in the 1950s "paid lip service to respecting the diverse ethnic and religious minorities," but, in practice, it imposed a "hegemonic and essentialist... Sunni-Muslim-Arab notion of what a 'real' Iraqi or Egyptian should be."[118] Arab Jews became especially suspect with the "aggressive advance of Zionism." Within pre-1948 Palestine, notes Shohat, the Arab nationalist movement came to drop the Zionist-Jewish distinction and lumped the Mizrahim "as at least potential Zionists" not to be trusted.[119] Had Arab national movements adopted a more nuanced and differentiated stance, they may have maintained relatively peaceful relations and attracted considerable Mizrahi support. She finds all the more disappointing the continued lack of differentiation among Palestinians and other Arabs, even with regard to strong Mizrahi critics of Zionism. At a 1989 meeting of Palestinians—mostly high-ranking PLO members—and Mizrahi peace activists (including Shohat), the former reacted skeptically to the latter's emphasis on a "common culture" as a basis for a new vision. In so doing, the Palestinians "seemed to echo the Euro-Israeli discourse."[120] More disturbing was a 1998 conference in Beirut on the Nakba, in which the inclusion of a panel of Arab Jews, all strong critics of Israel, prompted strong objections on essentialist grounds, which scared off some of the invited participants. This reaction, she lamented, marked an "ironic victory for Zionism," which also held that all Jews "are genetically Jewish and ideologically Zionist, regardless of historical origins, cultural affinities, political affiliations, and even professed ideologies."[121]

By diagnosing the debilitating effects of Zionist and Arab tribal nationalism, Shohat provides a nuanced reassessment of the most salient collective trauma of the Mizrahim, the mass displacement from their home countries in the decade following the 1948 war. She refutes the two prevailing Zionist interpretations: the perpetual antisemitism of Arab and Muslim societies and the linking of the Mizrahi displacement to the Nakba as an acceptable population exchange. Like Arendt, she attacks Zionism's eternal antisemitism syndrome for reducing Jews to passive victims and outsiders to unyielding Jew-haters and for ignoring historical, political, and social trends. The eternal antisemitism syndrome is all the more damaging with regard to the Mizrahi experience because it erases a rich and dynamic history. One is left with a "trace-the-dot history of pogrom-like episodes" whereby the Mizrahi experience is subsumed within the most well-known patterns of European antisemitism.[122] Consequently, one gains no insight into the chain of events leading to the displacement, the varying circumstances within and across the distinct Mizrahi communities, or the complicity of Zionism and homogeneous nationalism in general. The eternal antisemitism syndrome, she adds, also buries a rich history of positive Mizrahi engagement with Arab Muslim societies. Tragically, Jews are deprived of valuable historical lessons for developing productive relations with Palestinians and neighboring Arab states.

Perversely, suggests Shohat, the eternal antisemitism syndrome enables Zionists to both condemn Arab states for the mass displacement of Mizrahim and welcome the development as confirming the tribal nationalist view that Jews can be secure only in a Jewish state. Zionists invoke the Mizrahi mass displacement as a direct moral trade-off with the Nakba.[123] Moreover, so the argument goes, each displaced group is now better placed, living with its co-nationals. Shohat exposes the underlying fallacies in such reasoning. For starters, she dismisses the claim of a moral equivalency. The Nakba was an unequivocal forced mass exodus of a people "that never wished to evacuate Palestine and have maintained a desire to return, or at least a desire to have the 'right' to return."[124] The Mizrahim, by contrast, left their countries at different times and under divergent circumstances. While some were effectively pushed out, others were motivated by a mix of push and pull factors. Overall, she observes, "the question of will, desire, and agency . . . remains highly ambiguous and overdetermined."[125]

A more significant fallacy of the population exchange view, continues Shohat, is its portrayal of Zionism as the salvation for the displaced Mizrahim rather than as a contributing cause of the displacement. Zionism was complicit in the collective Mizrahi trauma. Most concretely, Israel's Mossad engaged in "various 'on-the-ground' activities, some violently provocative, to dislodge Iraqi, Egyptian [and] Moroccan Jews from their homelands."[126] In Iraq, the Mossad coordinated the planting of "bombs in Jewish centers so as to create hysteria among Iraqi Jews and thus catalyze a mass exodus to Israel."[127] Normatively, Shohat points to Zionism's tribal nationalism, in effective collusion with corresponding Arab nationalism, as a crucial enabling ideology. Neither nationalism looked fondly on a continued Jewish presence in an Arab nation. Indeed, Israel at times collaborated with Arab regimes in the exodus of Jews. Ultimately, "Arab Jews were caught up in the contradictory currents of British and French colonialism, Zionism and Arab nationalism."[128] The Nakba and the Mizrahi mass displacement are not moral trade-offs, concludes Shohat, but the tragic consequences of a tribal nationalism that rules out the possibility of peaceful coexistence.

To overcome the interlocking pathologies of tribal nationalism and Orientalism, she sketches a framework that complements Said's shared moral reckoning and history. Shohat's innovation is to triangulate the project to include the Mizrahim. Because "Palestinians are those most egregiously wronged by Zionism," her reckoning begins with Israeli Jews collectively acknowledging and making amends for the displacement and continued subjugation of Palestinians.[129] Presumably, one part of the shared history would address the intersection of the Nazi Holocaust and the Nakba along with the moral distortions. Shohat's triangulation would then demand a reckoning of the Ashkenazi Zionists' systematic demeaning of and discrimination against the Mizrahi immigrants. Here, too, a shared history calls on Israel's Ashkenazi and Mizrahi communities to study together the historical circumstances that brought them together and the moral distortions unleashed by the Holocaust, imperialism, and the surging tide of exclusivist forms of nationalism.

Finally, Shohat calls for a shared history and reckoning of Mizrahim and Palestinians, which uncovers how two groups with shared cultural roots became hostile toward the other. "What is desperately needed," she asserts, "is a de-Zionized decoding of the peculiar history of Mizrahim, one closely articulated with Palestinian history."[130] Refuting a stereotype held by many liberal Ashkenazi Zionists, she establishes that Mizrahi hostility is both overstated and of recent vintage rather than embedded in Mizrahi history and culture. She cautions observers to attribute high rates of Mizrahi voting for Likud and other hard-line parties not to an enhanced anti-Arab orientation but to a distrust of Ashkenazi-dominated parties, such as Labor.[131] The recent Mizrahi animus toward Palestinians, adds Shohat, "is very much 'made in Israel.'"[132] After all, as Arendt also recognized, anti-Arabism has been integral to Zionism's tribal nationalism. Another made-in-Israel dynamic is the Zionist Orientalism: "Fearing an encroachment of the East upon the West, the establishment repressed the Middle Easternness of Sephardim. . . . Arabness and Orientalism were consistently stigmatized as evils to be uprooted."[133] Having been "taught to see the Arabs, and themselves, as other," many Mizrahim have internalized an "Arab-hatred" that is "almost always a disguised form of self-hatred."[134] One final made-in-Israel factor Shohat identifies is the hierarchy that Zionism established in Israel. The Ashkenazim typically occupy the most prestigious white-collar jobs, while Mizrahim are concentrated in blue-collar and security jobs in the occupied territories. Accordingly, Mizrahim and Palestinians either compete over jobs (with the former clinging to what W. E. B. Du Bois described, with regard to poor white workers in the U.S. South, as a "sort of public and psychological wage" for being Jewish) or are pitted against each other in Israel's occupation regime.[135]

Like Said, Shohat makes a compelling case that reflecting together on the forces that have driven them apart will facilitate a joint project toward peaceful and interactive coexistence. Unlike the Ashkenazi Jewish–Palestinian Arab history, a constructive path forward between Mizrahim and Palestinians benefits from a shared history that long predates the emergence of modern Zionism. Interestingly, Shohat does not emphasize a comprehensive recalling of the vast history of Jewish-Arab relations in the greater Middle East, including very unpleasant stretches—though she does not oppose such a project. Instead, she urges Mizrahim, Palestinians, and Arabs throughout the region to focus on the "relatively convivial" past.[136] Doing so most directly counters the now-popular tribal nationalist view of a timeless hostility and gulf between Jews and Arabs. The idea, explains Shohat, is a joint conjuring of what the Jewish philosopher Walter Benjamin called a "revolutionary nostalgia," which is using "the past for the construction of the future."[137] Such nostalgia entails regretting the loss of a more fluid cultural identity and set of interactions and resolving to create a future that recaptures and updates this spirit. To get there, she concludes, it is necessary to erase "the East/West cultural borders between Israel and Palestine" that modern nationalism in the region imposed and to remap "national and ethnic-racial identities against the deep scars of colonizing partitions."[138]

Shohat finds hope in the persistence of Mizrahi dissenters, who reject tribal nationalism and Orientalism and have been "eager to serve as a bridge of peace to the Arabs and to the Palestinians."[139] The most notable Mizrahi dissenters of the past, she recalls, are Israel's Black Panthers, who were inspired in part by the well-known U.S. organization. In the early 1970s, Israel's Black Panthers not only exposed systematic discrimination, including police repression, but also linked their struggle to that of the Palestinians and demanded that the state engage in a "real dialogue" with the Palestinians.[140] Though the Black Panthers disbanded, there has emerged since the 1990s a lively antiestablishment Mizrahi presence committed to solidarity with Palestinians.[141] What distinguishes Mizrahi activists from most Ashkenazi ones, such as Peace Now, declares Shohat, are their calls for an "integration" with the Palestinians and neighboring Arabs rather than a "divorce."[142] Like Said, she concludes that among Israel's Jews, the Mizrahi activists will assume the vanguard role in advancing a program that breaks from prevailing nationalist divides.

What Said and Shohat Contribute to an Updated Critical Jewish Vision for Coexistence

Notwithstanding that the Eurocentrism of the original Humanist Zionists stood in sharp contrast to the anti-Orientalism of Said and Shohat, all are, at heart, kindred spirits. All reject imperialism and conventional nationalism, support an emancipatory, outward-oriented self-determination, and find the most hope in the nonconformists. Indeed, Said's comment to Shavit, "I'm the last Jewish intellectual," could be more accurately framed as "I'm the last Jewish Humanist Zionist." After all, he did not call for Jews to renounce Jewish self-determination in Israel-Palestine but to redefine it to enable a just coexistence. Moreover, he welcomed the vision promoted by "Judah Magnes, Buber, [and] Arendt" and saw its spirit as "alive today" among the most "innovative [and] daring" Jewish and Arab activists.[143] I close this chapter by incorporating the insights from Said and Shohat, along with those of the contemporary Palestinian scholar Leila Farsakh, to flesh out an updated joint program for reckoning, reconciliation, and coexistence.

On the essential first task of Jewish reckoning, Said effectively followed up on Arendt's powerful rejoinder of the Zionist founders for overlooking "that Arabs were human beings like themselves." A foundational lesson of *Question of Palestine* for contemporary critical Jewish voices is to treat Palestinians as protagonists and therefore reexamine the history of the Zionist project from their perspective. In addition to uncovering the devastating toll of displacement, deaths, and oppression, a full reckoning confronts both the settler colonialism and the accompanying Orientalism of Zionism that has guided this pattern. The end goal is, in part, to enable what Ellis terms a revolutionary forgiveness by Palestinians.

Shohat, for her part, alerts contemporary Jewish dissenters to the need to reckon as well with the impact of Zionism on the other victims, the Mizrahim. The Zionist project, first in combination with Arab nationalists, sparked a massive displacement of Mizrahim from their home countries, and then, following the Mizrahi relocation to Israel, demeaned their cultural heritage and relegated the majority to a subordinate status. Informed by Shohat's analysis, a reckoning means both expanding the diagnosis of Zionist tribal nationalism to encompass intolerance of heterogeneous identities and understanding the distinct harm of Zionist Orientalism to Mizrahim. Guided by Said and Shohat, a comprehensive reckoning of Zionism's injustices and enabling pathologies would triangulate the interactions over time between Ashkenazim, Palestinians, and Mizrahim.

Once Israeli Jews have fully owned up to their past, Said's call for a shared history points the way to Jewish-Palestinian reconciliation. This involves a mutual commitment to learn of the other people's diverse experiences, accomplishments, aspirations, and collective traumas, especially the Holocaust, the Nakba, and the uprooting of most Mizrahim in the decade following Israel's establishment. This shared history is not dialogue for its own sake but part of a social and political struggle for a transformed Israel-Palestine grounded in full equality and a spirit of what Buber referred to as living together with rather than just alongside. To get there, both Palestinians and Jews need to see the richness and diversity of the other and engage in self-reflection on their blind spots toward the other. Most fundamental is for each people to understand the intensity of the other's national attachment to the same land. For Jews, this means coming to terms with the pain of the Nakba and the resilience of Palestinian attachment to Israel-Palestine at large, not just the occupied territories. Palestinians, for their part, as Farsakh explains, need "to address, rather than negate, the continuous presence of the Israeli-Jewish culture and how to live with it."[144]

Farsakh adds a valuable component to this shared history project by highlighting the variety of ways in which Jews and Arabs, in Israel-Palestine and throughout the Middle East, have shaped each other's identity. She extends Said's critique of the pre-state Zionist Orientalism, which treated Arabs as simply the dangerous other, to the pre-state Humanist Zionists. The 1946 Ihud platform, she notes, "did not seem to know either the Arabs or the Palestinians, two terms that it used interchangeably," and did not recognize that the Arab was "an interacting or defining element of Jewish nation-formation."[145] Of equal importance for both Jews and Palestinians, adds Farsakh, is taking stock of the deep Arab roots in Israeli Jewish culture. Following up on Shohat's work, she calls for "rehabilitating the concept of the Arab Jew" to "enable the average Arab and Palestinian to see the Jewish people as part of the broader Arab heritage, not as an alien."[146]

Through a rich shared history, which follows a full reckoning of the Zionist movement's injustices, the prospects markedly improve for a substantive reconciliation and coexistence. A consistent theme in the writings of Said, Shohat, and Farsakh is the need to make room for complex, fluid, and heterogeneous national identities committed to a just coexistence. Such coexistence would accommodate the enduring and distinct attachments of two peoples to the same land, while holding pluralism and multiculturalism as equally essential. All three seek to retrieve and update the cosmopolitan qualities that are a part of Arab and Jewish history rather than retreat to an essentialist Jewish or Arab identity.[147] The pivotal actors in each community are, respectively, the Palestinian citizens of Israel and the Mizrahim, each of whom have had to negotiate a hybrid identity in their everyday lives. Particularly important among the latter are the critical Mizrahim who have both retrieved a heterogeneous Arab-Jewish identity and connected the Zionist establishment's disparagement of their community's Arab heritage with the subjugation of Palestinians. As Shohat has demonstrated, such Mizrahim represent a vanguard who summon a past history of positive Jewish-Arab coexistence in the region to inspire a heterogeneous and ecumenical path forward in Israel-Palestine and the surrounding area.

With regard to a common rallying vision for Jews and Palestinians, Said contributes a rich Palestinian counterpart to the Jewish practices and ideals that inspired Humanist Zionists. One aspect is the Palestinian idea of a democratic, multiethnic society committed to pluralism, secular human rights, equality for all residents, and international solidarity. The other is a resilient resistance to external and internal oppression. Shohat provides a further source of inspiration from the legacy of Mizrahi social and political activism in Israel. Starting with the Black Panthers of the 1970s, such protest has incorporated broader social justice themes, outreach to Palestinians, and international solidarity. In the past decade, inspired by the Arab Spring, a new generation of Mizrahi activists have declared solidarity with Arab movements in resisting both internal oppression and a Western-dominated capitalist global order.[148] In 2016, dozens of Mizrahim presented a manifesto to a coalition of Palestinian political parties in Israel, known as the Joint List, which proposed "an alliance between all those who seek to struggle against a neoliberal social order and the anti-democratic forces rising up to destroy us."[149]

Finally, there is the matter of what political structure to pursue for this transformed society. Said, Shohat, and Farsakh all agree on the need to break from the diplomatic orthodoxy of national-based separation and pursue a type of binationalism. Said sets forth a valuable overall framework, whereby Jews and Palestinians enjoy self-determination while "willing to soften, lessen, and finally give up special status for one people at the expense of the other."[150] Overall, the binational ideal has not only revived but gained a notable following among Palestinian activists and intellectuals. Indeed, the leading contemporary advocates are Palestinian scholars and activists, many of whom are Palestinian citizens of Israel.[151] To be sure, Palestinian binationalists are presently outnumbered among the global left-of-center Palestinian diaspora by a liberal one-state camp, whose followers include Omar Barghouti and other leading BDS advocates. They hold that recognizing Jewish national rights contradicts the anticolonial spirit of the right of self-determination and implicitly legitimizes the settler-colonial project.[152] Farsakh effectively counters this view with two arguments. First, she warns that a single liberal democratic state with no formal accommodation for national identity does not address the risks of majoritarian rule in practice by one national group or, more concretely, the dangers of continued Jewish domination given its great economic advantages.[153] Second, she faults the liberal one-state camp for being in denial of a strong Israeli Jewish national identity that is not reduced to colonialism. Hence, she observes that one can insist on the "dismantling of Israel's settler-colonial structure" without "negating the national culture and heritage that Israel has created over the past seventy years."[154] Whether the pursuit of this egalitarian binationalism demands a categorical repudiation of all two-state proposals, as argued by Said and a growing number of Palestinian and Jewish activists, is considered in the concluding chapter.

Conclusion

How to Further an Ambitious New Vision

Today, two states and one equal state are both unrealistic. The right question is not which vision is more fanciful at this moment, but which can generate a movement powerful enough to bring fundamental change.

—Peter Beinart, "Yavne"[1]

In [Said's] view successfully removing Israel from the West Bank and Gaza Strip, not least by systematically dismantling the settlement project, would deal such a body blow to Zionist pretensions, and have such an impact on Israel Jewish public opinion, that it could and in his view likely would open non-military pathways to the realization of a one-state outcome.

—Mouin Rabbani, "Can the Question of Palestine Be Resolved?"[2]

The last two chapters offer the essential components of an updated critical Jewish vision that builds on the pre-state Humanist Zionist legacy. This vision diagnoses the foundational and ongoing injustices of the Zionist project; the underlying pathologies of an eternal antisemitism syndrome, tribal nationalism, and Orientalism; and the corrupting impact on the Jewish community at large, including the highly influential American Jewish one. The vision's prescription is a Jewish self-determination of social justice, cultural flourishing, solidarity with the oppressed, and antihegemonic internationalism. Especially important is reckoning with the grave harms inflicted on Palestinians and reaching a just and collaborative coexistence based on equal regard for each community's self-determination aspirations.

Although this book's critical Jewish vision faces daunting obstacles toward realization, the time is opportune for advancing it. To begin with, there is a heightened urgency for fundamental change rather than a revival of a more restrained hegemonic Zionism and of the U.S.-led diplomatic route toward a two-state resolution. Recalling the quoted passage from Zeev Sternhell in the introduction, Israeli society has reached a new level of reactionary nationalism, with those in power "striving to delegitimize the left and anyone who does not hold the view that conquering the land and settling it through the use of force are the fundamental foundations of Zion."[3] Meanwhile, as discussed in Chapter 1, the U.S. Jewish establishment continues to enable this extremism by its own intolerance of dissent and devotion to defending the Israeli state. Fortunately, the grave crisis has also sparked a new wave of dissent and openness to challenging once-sacred tenets, particularly among young American Jews. If such Jewish dissent were to gain sufficient numbers and cohesion—which is presently a long way off—it could enable a fundamental break with the status quo. Having a Jewish-informed critical framework can help ground this movement.

The final chapter considers how to advance the book's long-term goals. It addresses the two most polarizing issues among the Jewish left as well as Palestinians and the broader left. One is whether it is necessary to categorically renounce Zionism in order to develop a just vision of coexistence. Two is whether, as demanded not only by anti-Zionists but also by a new crop of reconstructed liberal Zionists (such as Peter Beinart and Ian Lustick), to abandon all advocacy of two-state resolutions. Advocates for this position claim both that it is no longer possible to divide the territory into two states and that two-state advocacy undermines the cause of a just coexistence across Israel-Palestine. On the first issue, I call for a middle ground that both appreciates the appeal that some forms of Zionism once held for Jews committed to social justice and recognizes the overall negative direction assumed by actually existing Zionism. Accordingly, I neither renounce Zionism nor retain it as part of a shorthand label for this book's vision. Rather, I simply affirm support for an inclusive and nonhegemonic vision of Jewish self-determination. On the second issue, I propose a creative and pragmatic advocacy that links the global consensus version of a two-state resolution to a more ambitious and comprehensive binational arrangement for all of Israel-Palestine. Such a program would repudiate the Oslo-derived version of two states, update the antiestablishment two-state program introduced by Jewish peace activists in the late 1960s and 1970s, and engage the long-standing global consensus version of two states to resist Israel's occupation and subjugation of Palestinians. The end goal is an innovative and egalitarian binational polity across Israel-Palestine.

Farewell to Zionism?

Jewish anti-Zionists hold that Zionism needs to be renounced given the history and ongoing nature of the prevailing Zionist project. Judith Butler acknowledges that there were alternative, non-statist versions prior to 1948 but reasons that such variants have long ago been rendered extinct.[4] Consequently, she adds, Zionism has become equated with an ideology that demands a hegemonic Jewish state and has consistently underwritten the "subordination, destruction, or expulsion of the indigenous."[5] Butler thus urges the discarding of Zionism so that "broader principles of justice can be realized for the region."[6] To work out these principles, she continues, one must consider "what form of polity could be regarded as legitimate for lands that are currently inhabited by Jewish and Palestinian Israelis, and by Palestinians living under occupation, and are no longer inhabited by hundreds of thousands Palestinians who were dispossessed of their lands?"[7] A further reason that Jewish anti-Zionists renounce Zionism is the belief that doing so will open up more extensive avenues of collaboration with Palestinians. In this spirt, a coalition of Israeli Jewish activists issued an anti-Zionist manifesto in 2004 to open "a dialogue about the specific political arrangements to be put into place."[8] Similarly, Jewish Voice for Peace, which previously had no formal stance on Zionism, declared itself anti-Zionist in 2018 not simply to reflect the evolving views of its members but to facilitate more robust partnerships with Palestinian groups.[9]

Yet however understandable the call to renounce Zionism may be in light of its dominant manifestation, doing so will impede the shared history that Said correctly identified as essential for a long-term reconciliation and coexistence. It is one thing to demand that Jews reckon with the deadly impact of Zionism on Palestinians. It is a quite different matter to disregard the longstanding appeal of Zionism to most Israeli Jews for realizing self-determination. Edward Said's approach is more sensible. Rather than renounce Zionism, he implored Jews to find a reformation that would draw guidance from prior nonhegemonic visions.[10] Therefore, it is important to recognize the egalitarian and renewal aspects of Zionism that attracted European Jews in the pre-state era. As Arendt observed, the collective settlements of the pre-state Yishuv and other socialist-oriented institutions inspired them "to go to Palestine in the decisive years when immigration to America was the natural escape."[11] All the more important is to take heed of Jacqueline Rose's point that Zionism produced an emancipatory and self-critical strand from within.[12] Disappointingly, the typically nuanced Judith Butler dismisses this alternative Zionist project championed by Buber as fatally compromised because it depended on "conditions established by settler colonialism."[13] But, as Rose reflects, had Buber's vision prevailed, "Zionism might have created a form of nationhood that would slash away politics, face its own dark beast, make room for the foreigner in the midst (or, even more radically perhaps, see itself as the stranger for the Arabs in Palestine)."[14] Retrieving this vision is essential as a foundation for widening support among Jews upset with the present direction of Zionism.

A nuanced view of Zionism's legacy, however, does not mean one should continue to embrace the term. After all, Butler and others are correct that Zionism has come to be equated with support of a hegemonic Jewish state. I am indebted to the pre-state dissenting Zionists for inspiring the foundation of this book's critical vision, but I am not retaining Zionism as a partial modifier. At the same time, I stress the importance of featuring an alternative, non-hegemonic vision of Jewish self-determination. I have thus titled this book *Jewish Self-Determination beyond Zionism*, not *The Revival of Humanist Zionism*. If pressed to come up with a shorthand label to characterize an important component of this book's vision, it would be binationalism. While the term can mean different things, Jewish advocates, past and present, have primarily used it to convey a Jewish self-determination that features a just and collaborative coexistence with Palestinians. As reviewed last chapter, binationalism is no longer confined to Jewish dissenters but has a sizable Palestinian following. Both Palestinian and Jewish binationalists take for granted that the concept incorporates a full reckoning of Zionism's depredations, reconciliation, appreciation of the two peoples' shared history, and commitment to an integrated political arrangement that encompasses Jewish and Palestinian self-determination.

Farewell to All Two-State Advocacy?

Given the centrality of binationalism to this book's critical Jewish vision, there might seem to be no place for a two-state program. After all, the pre-state Humanist Zionists vigorously opposed partition, while many contemporary binationalists agree with Said's post-1999 position that no two-state plan could justly accommodate the overlapping attachment of both peoples to the same land. Nevertheless, as Amnon Raz-Krakotzkin remarks, binationalism is best understood as "a set of values," not "a concrete political arrangement."[15] Recall that Buber made a similar point in 1949 when he proposed the articulation of a new program—"a new juncture of the true path"—to advance the Humanist Zionist values following Israel's establishment. The central questions, then, are could a two-state program advance the binational vision as well as a single state, and would it provide a more promising political pathway? To answer these questions, it is necessary to review the historical trajectory of two-state advocacy starting in the 1970s—contrasting the plan grounded in an overwhelming global consensus with the very different version that emerged from post-Oslo, U.S.-mediated talks—and take stock of contemporary challenges and opportunities.

As reviewed in Chapter 4, the original two-state plan of the post-1967 era emerged from a sustained PLO-NAM global normative offensive in the 1970s. Attached to the norm of self-determination, this campaign became one of the central planks of the global reformist anticolonial movement carried out at the UN.[16] It succeeded in creating a new global consensus, which called for Israel's dismantling of settlements and full withdrawal from the occupied territories, an independent state of Palestine, mutual recognition, special status for Jerusalem, and a just resolution for Palestinian refugees. Notably, the series of UN resolutions underpinning this consensus raised a forceful challenge to Israel and to U.S. support of Israel. They deemed Israeli settlements and overall belligerency as the primary obstacles to peace and insisted on a settlement that fully honored Palestinian political rights.[17]

While the global consensus has endured, it has been sidelined in all U.S.-mediated talks since Oslo. As recounted in Chapter 4, Israel, with U.S. support, exploited the PLO's weak political position in the early 1990s to craft a negotiating framework highly skewed toward Israel's perceived political and strategic interests. The Oslo accords pointedly omitted incorporation of international legal understandings on settlements or occupation, or the repeated UN General Assembly and Security Council calls for a full Israeli withdrawal and establishment of a Palestinian state. They left all matters to direct Israeli-Palestinian negotiations where Israel has held a decided structural advantage and the support of the primary mediator. Israel also succeeded in ensuring a highly constricted governing entity for the Palestinians. Mouin Rabbani convincingly characterizes this situation as one where the PA has had to jump "through an unending series of Israeli-American hoops" designed to satisfy Israel's extensive security concerns, with the end reward not to exceed "a statelet existing in permanent subordination to Israel."[18] Only by the 2000 Camp David talks did Israel accept the idea of a Palestinian state. Yet with each substantive round of negotiations following Taba, this new two-state framework has become a far cry from that envisioned in the global consensus. Rather than governing all of the occupied territories, the proposed state is hemmed in by settlement blocs and an indefinite Israeli security presence in the Jordan Valley. Furthermore, Israeli governments have used the various negotiations as cover for extending Israel's colonization of the West Bank and East Jerusalem.[19] With the Oslo-derived model in mind, it is not surprising that more and more Palestinians and dissenting Jews have renounced the two-state idea.

Particularly noteworthy is the recent renunciation by prominent liberal Zionist public intellectuals of the two-state program. Some, such as Antony

Lerman, have rejected Zionism altogether. In a 2014 op-ed for the *New York Times*, he not only declares the two-state solution politically dead but challenges the fundamental premises of liberal Zionism.[20] "The romantic Zionist ideal to which liberal Jews subscribed," Lerman writes, ". . . has been tarnished by the reality of modern Israel. The attacks on freedom of speech and human rights organizations in Israel, the land-grabbing settler movement, a growing strain of anti-Arab and anti-immigrant racism, extremist politics, and a powerful, intolerant religious right—this mixture has pushed liberal Zionism to the brink." "The only Zionism of any consequence today," he continues, "is xenophobic and exclusionary." Lerman takes his conversion a step further by concluding that the foundational liberal Zionist insistence on a Jewish state was morally bankrupt from the outset because it depended on a "Jewish majority in perpetuity," which "inevitably implies policies of exclusion and discrimination." He calls for a new single-state paradigm based on universal democracy and equality for all. By contrast, other liberal Zionist converts, such as Peter Beinart and Ian Lustick, have not regretted their past advocacy for a Jewish nation-state and remain Zionists. They argue that the transformed dynamic of the past two decades necessitates a new one-state and egalitarian Zionist paradigm to recapture the appealing ideals once reflected in the liberal Zionist two-state program. Because their goals—especially Beinart's—of a transformed Jewish self-determination substantially overlap with this book's vision, I turn to a fuller assessment of their arguments for abandoning two-state advocacy.

Both fundamentally base their argument on the cumulative changes in policies and attitudes of Israeli politics over the past two decades. Looking at facts on the ground, Israel has over six hundred thousand settlers in the West Bank and East Jerusalem, an extensive infrastructure in place for integrating the settlers and much of the territory into Israel, a security apparatus that extends to all of the West Bank, and plans to annex up to 30 percent of the West Bank.[21] What follows from these numbers, agree Beinart and Lustick, is not simply a matter of logistic difficulty in reversing this colonization. Rather, Israel's colonization reflects an unshakable political commitment, no matter the specific governing coalition, to maintain permanent control of the occupied territories. Lustick labels this Israeli political consensus a "One-State Reality" ("OSR"), which imposes crippling "cultural, psychological, and political" structural barriers to any effort to secure Israel's withdrawal from the occupied territories.[22]

In light of this new reality, Lustick and Beinart deem it urgent for peace advocates to disabuse themselves of the two-state option. Two-state advocacy simply enables Israel to maintain the charade of peace negotiations while continuing with its colonization. Such advocacy, adds Lustick, impedes the urgent task of developing new and effective strategies for reversing Israel's subjugation of Palestinians.[23] Beinart offers a particularly ominous assessment of what will come from clinging to a now-impotent political program. Israel will simply deepen its destructive colonization and thereby further immiserate Palestinians and embolden Israel's extremist forces. The end result will be formal annexation, which is "a waystation on the road to hell," meaning ethnic cleansing.[24]

To break from this grim trajectory, Beinart exhorts his fellow liberal Zionists to abandon "the goal of Jewish-Palestinian separation and embrace the goal of Jewish-Palestinian equality" within a unified state. He acknowledges that this goal, in the abstract, is presently less realistic than a two-state resolution because it arouses much greater alarm for Israeli Jews.[25] Beinart's counter is that the question of relative feasibility has become moot because Israel's actions have made even the less-threatening two-state path unrealistic under the status quo. Hence, the "right question" is which vision "can generate a movement powerful enough to bring fundamental change." The right answer is that equality and human rights for all have far greater resonance than separate nation-states.[26] For Lustick, the one-state reality is simply a political fact to confront. Hence, he implores activists to work within this reality and seek "opportunities to argue for the broad and comprehensive application of the same laws to all people under the control of the same state."[27]

Both Lustick and Beinart have made valuable contributions to developing an updated critical Jewish vision. Each starkly details the gravity of the crisis brought about by Israel's long-standing colonization of the occupied territories, ugly nationalist ideology, and manipulation of a fraudulent official peace process. They also correctly identify the urgent need for a new vision of Jewish self-determination and reconciliation. Indeed, Beinart asks the right question of which political platform will most likely advance a path toward a just coexistence. Yet he stacks the deck by comparing the unappealing two-state version promoted by Israel and the United States to a single state where all are equal and enjoy the panoply of individual and collective human rights. The latter, by way of a confederated binational model, is this book's desirable end goal as well. What is not so persuasive, however, is the claim that the best short-term path forward for advancing this goal is an abandonment of all two-state advocacy, including support for the global consensus, in favor of an exclusive focus on a single, egalitarian state.

Much of their claim rests on a point-of-no-return logic. This argument is seductive, given both the steps taken by Israeli governments and settler groups to cement control of the occupied territories and recent avowals from the last two prime ministers of categorical opposition to a Palestinian state. Yet as Lustick acknowledges, the obstacle is not logistic but political. Accordingly, Rabbani offers a compelling response: "If . . . the occupation and all it has produced are not more than [political] obstacles to the application of the international consensus, then there is essentially no 'point of no return' and the Israeli occupation can be reversed . . . through an application of sufficient political will or a transformation of political calculations."[28] Moreover, he continues, there are repeated historical instances where even more enduring and entrenched colonial occupations were terminated, including that of Britain over Ireland, France over Algeria, South Africa over Namibia, and Indonesia over East Timor. Although each case has distinct historical trajectories, Rabbani effectively enlists them collectively to dispute there being a point of no return absent extreme scenarios, such as "wholesale extermination."[29]

Understanding, then, that the obstacle to either the global consensus version of two states or the egalitarian single state is political, it is necessary to inquire further into the nature of this political reality. Lustick defines this reality as an adamant insistence across Israel's political culture to retain the entire West Bank as part of greater Israel.[30] Accordingly, he holds that activists may enjoy success persuading a cross-section of Israelis, including settlers and "Jewish maximalists," to extend full citizens' rights to all Palestinians.[31] His idea seems to be that all things are possible so long as Israelis are assured of a greater Israel. Lustick goes so far as to find hope in the proposals floated by some Jewish maximalists, including a founder of Gush Emunim, for a formal annexation of the West Bank that includes legal avenues by which Palestinians can attain citizenship.[32] Although aware that, under the best of conditions, such avenues would include many hoops to circumvent, he holds out the prospects of "unintended and unimagined consequences" and, in a rhetorical flourish, adds that the "arc of history is long, but it does bend toward integration."[33]

What if, however, the nature of Israel's new political reality is not a simple attachment to a greater Israel but a commitment to systematic Jewish predominance? As discussed in the first two chapters, what stands out in contemporary Israeli society is an illiberal, belligerent, and chauvinistic mentality. Indeed, the damning and comprehensive reports recently issued by B'Tselem, Human Rights Watch, and Amnesty International do not target the occupation per se but focus on a broader set of laws and practices designed to maintain Jewish domination and Palestinian subjugation, albeit to varying degrees, across all of Israel-Palestine. Hence, the commitment to a greater Israel is a product of an overarching commitment to Jewish supremacy and a corresponding growth in intolerance for dissent and liberal values. This is not a reality to which to adjust by finding supposed alliances of convenience with Jewish settlers, which may in some "unimagined" way bend the arc of history. Far more advisable is Rabbani's call "to identify and examine the various factors that obstruct and support the struggle for Palestinian self-determination, and . . . propose a strategy that maximizes strengths, minimizes the influence of weaknesses, and is therefore capable of both responding to immediate needs and achieving core strategic objectives."[34] In short, the question is how to change the reality in which U.S.-backed Israeli obstinacy obstructs progress toward a just coexistence.

There are, of course, a number of areas to pursue for changing the existing political dynamics. Among the ones Rabbani identifies are rebuilding cohesion and a unifying vision across the various Palestinian communities, deepening an already strong international solidarity movement on behalf of Palestinians, and expanding grassroots support in the United States. Consistent with this book's focus, I would add the mobilization of dissenting Jewish voices, especially in the United States. Returning to the theme of this section, one can find ways in which well-focused appeals to the two-state global consensus can bolster the broader struggle.

To see why, it helps to recall what Beinart, Lustick, and other recent one-state converts overlook or only glancingly discuss: a past record of progressive-oriented two-state campaigns, starting with the one launched by Avnery and allies in the late 1960s. For the next two decades, Jewish support for an independent Palestinian state on the occupied territories was concentrated on the left, including those, such as Avnery, who were not Zionists in the commonly understood sense. These dissenters linked two-state advocacy to broader condemnations of Israeli depredations and support for Palestinian rights. Following the lead of Avnery, the two-state plans included an end to Israel's occupation, the dismantling of settlements, full Palestinian sovereignty in all of the West Bank and Gaza Strip, substantial economic aid to Palestine, a comprehensive resolution of the refugee situation, and open borders. Like Chomsky, many saw a two-state settlement as creating political space for advancing democracy and equality, reducing nationalist divides, and fostering cross-national bonds within and across the two states. To be sure, the Jewish two-state proponents failed to gain much support in Israel or in mainstream U.S. Jewish groups through much of the 1980s because of widespread resistance to an independent Palestinian state. Indeed, by the late 1980s, this progressive two-state camp started to get eclipsed by a moderate two-state camp, which emphasized separation to keep Israel "Jewish and Democratic." Yet the progressive Jewish two-state program substantially overlapped with the successful global campaign led by the PLO in alliance with NAM during the 1970s and

1980s to assemble a new global consensus that discredited Israel's colonization and belligerency and legitimized Palestinian political rights.

Another important dynamic that Beinart and Lustick overlook is the persistence of the two-state global consensus. It too is a political reality. By overwhelming majorities, the UN General Assembly and, less frequently, the UN Security Council continue to condemn the settlements and treat the June 1967 borders as the frame of reference for establishing a Palestinian state.[35] In 2004, the International Court of Justice declared the settlements to be in violation of international law and upheld the principle that international laws of occupation apply to all of the territories Israel conquered in the 1967 war.[36] In sum, all of Israel's efforts to disrupt the global consensus, be it through facts on the ground or diplomatic lobbying, have roundly failed.

Significantly, both the official Palestinian leadership and, more to the point, Palestinian solidarity groups have enjoyed recent success in invoking the global consensus to boost the Palestinian profile and impose a cost on Israel's colonization. In 2012, the UN General Assembly overwhelmingly approved nonmember observer state status for Palestine, which gave it leverage to join various international organizations, including the International Criminal Court.[37] Legally empowered by Palestine's granting of jurisdiction over the occupied territories, the International Criminal Court prosecutor reviewed the 2014 Israeli offensive into Gaza and began an official investigation in 2021.[38] As of July 2019, 138 states recognize Palestine.[39] In 2013, the European Union enacted guidelines, described by Israel as an "earthquake," that prohibit the issuing of grants or funding to any Israeli entity active in the occupied territories, including East Jerusalem.[40] Similarly, a growing number of local municipalities, churches, and universities across the globe have divested from companies implicated in the occupation, and the UN Human Rights office compiles a list of such companies.[41] These successes support Rabbani's argument that the global consensus offers a foundation "to leverage Palestinian strengths and overcome weaknesses."[42] Notably, the long-standing appeal of U.S. and Israeli governments to focus on U.S.-mediated talks, rather than global actions, has lost virtually all credibility in light of Israel's open opposition to Palestinian statehood or withdrawal from East Jerusalem and the bulk of the West Bank. Hence, the time is ripe for reinvigorating the global campaign against Israeli colonization, including demands for much sharper sanctions.

The problem, then, with circumventing the global consensus by demanding an immediate transition to an egalitarian single state is the likely short-term negative impact on the most promising global normative attacks on Israeli behavior. The UN resolutions and dominant international legal interpretations are predicated on condemning Israel's colonization of the occupied territories and establishing a distinct Palestinian state. Accordingly, virtually all concrete actions taken by state and nonstate actors against Israel have targeted not Israel as a whole but its settlements and occupation. This pattern has held, observes Nathan Thrall, even among boycott and divestment campaigns conducted under the umbrella BDS movement, notwithstanding that the BDS scope extends to denial of equal rights to Palestinian citizens in Israel itself.[43] As Noam Chomsky argues, a wholesale refocus on transition to a single constitutional state would interject confusion and new divisions into these ongoing efforts and thereby weaken overall support for confronting Israeli depredations.[44]

Another difficulty of featuring a quick transition to an egalitarian single state is that the ground has not yet been prepared. Ran Greenstein correctly observes that outside of a few urban pockets in Israel, there is little horizontal interaction between Jews and Palestinians.[45] Rather, they interact as the oppressor to the oppressed. Because the requisite social and political conditions are absent, Greenstein—who firmly opposes Zionism—effectively explains why demanding a single state in the present is the equivalent of inserting a square peg in a round hole: "Making Israel/Palestine as a whole a state of all its residents" requires "a radical re-alignment of the political scene. It is not feasible in the short-term as there are no serious political forces advocating it, and it cannot be a substitute for the ongoing struggle against the 1967 occupation and for restoring refugees' rights."[46]

Finally, as even Beinart acknowledges, the degree of Israeli resistance to making Israel-Palestine a single egalitarian state would be fierce, considerably greater than the state's likely resistance to simply a full withdrawal from the occupied territories. Indeed, to rally fear and opposition from Israeli liberals and centrists to divestment and boycott campaigns, propagandists for a greater Israel play up not the call for withdrawal but the attacks—real or imagined—on Israel's Jewish state in general.[47] "The hard truth," explains Rabbani, is that the "Israeli state will neither capitulate nor disintegrate in response to mass mobilisation as practiced during the US civil rights struggle, in South Africa, or recent Palestinian uprisings, no matter how much international support is generated."[48] It would then take a credible military option, he continues, which is not foreseeable anytime soon.

By contrast, the forces preventing Israel's withdrawal from the occupied territories are of a lesser degree, albeit still formidable. The main obstacles are a minority constituency, led by the religious nationalist camp, committed to retaining large parts of the occupied territories. This group has helped keep more hard-line political coalitions in power and is willing to take extraordinary steps to prevent land withdrawals. Accordingly, as Thrall observes, the domestic and international settings give Israeli governments little incentive to end the occupation.[49] Although Israel's occupation has made it a global pariah symbolically, put a strain on its military, and impeded some economic and cultural interactions, Israel retains a thriving, sophisticated economy, respectable relations with many states, and robust, bipartisan U.S. support at the elite level. If it were to withdraw from the West Bank, however, it would face massive demonstrations (possibly including violent resistance from Jewish settlers), lose access to water and other resources in the West Bank, and suffer a blow to its intelligence-gathering capabilities.[50] The challenge, then, is to change Israel's incentive structure by dramatically increasing the costs of the occupation. As Rabbani argues, this is a daunting task, but it can be achieved "through a combination of sustained mass mobilisation," the ratcheting up of political, economic, and judicial sanctions, and a change in U.S. policy.[51] Crucially, such sanctions would be grounded in existing international law and long-standing UN resolutions that almost all states have long supported. Moreover, Israel would still have a widely acceptable fallback position, given that its overall economy, social structures, political system, and military abilities would remain intact.

To be sure, the global two-state consensus does not encompass the broader ambitions of this book, shared by Beinart and many contemporary Jewish dissenters, for full equality, reconciliation and collaboration, an inclusive nationalism, the breaking down of state borders, and a concrete program for honoring Palestinian refugees' rights. Yet there is no reason to treat the present two-state global consensus as the end goal. Rabbani reminds us that even Edward Said appreciated the "transformative potential of ending Israel's occupation."[52] In a 2001 interview with Rabbani, Said remarked that "successfully removing Israel from the West Bank and Gaza Strip . . . would deal such a body blow to Zionist pretensions, and have such an impact on Israeli Jewish public opinion that it . . . would likely open non-military pathways to the realisation of a one-state outcome." As reviewed above, a similar aim was what inspired the two-state advocates from the late 1960s through the 1980s, by way of linking two states to an integrated federation of full equality within and across the states. In the concluding section, I sketch a plan for updating a progressive two-state campaign.

Forging Ahead in Dark Times

Notwithstanding the above qualifications on how to proceed in the short term, many are likely to find this book's ambitious vision natively romantic, what

Avnery rebuked as "escaping into the world of idealist solutions for the days of the Messiah."[53] Such a critique, however, holds only if all that is needed are modest reforms to bring about a reasonably stable and morally acceptable outcome. In the real world, the crisis is grave, at least for anyone who seeks a resolution not based on a victor's justice secured by Israel's military and economic superiority. This book's vision is not an escape into utopianism but an effort to recover and adapt an inspiring Jewish vision of engagement with the world. The Humanist Zionists advanced such a grounded idealism. They understood that any desirable Jewish homeland had to acknowledge the reality of Palestinian attachment to the land and reach a just accommodation. In modifying the Humanist Zionist vision through a critical engagement with contemporary dissenters, I have attempted to bring out a comprehensive, long-term pathway for a sustainable Jewish-Palestinian reconciliation. Indeed, it would be utopian to imagine that the simple creation of a Palestinian state, which avoids all other issues, will bring about an acceptable resolution for both Palestinians and Jews.

Strategic appeals to the global two-state consensus remain indispensable as a normative benchmark for condemning Israel's colonization of the occupied territories and accompanying war crimes and human rights abuses. Such condemnation highlights Israel's belligerency more generally and raises the costs for Israel though diplomatic isolation, boycotts, divestments, and sanctions. With regard to what the plan proposes, one should welcome the immediate results: an end to occupation and the establishment of an independent Palestinian state. Yet, it is essential to explain why the creation of two separate and unequal nation-states is far from sufficient for a just and sustainable resolution. The end goal is a lasting reconciliation based on a just and collaborative coexistence within and across the two states. Under this vision, supporters would insist on a comprehensive settlement that attends to such matters as full equality for Israel's Palestinian minority, the rights of refugees, Jerusalem's special status, a truth and reconciliation process, support for Palestine's ability to deliver effective governance, open borders, and collaborative governance on a range of economic, security, and cultural-religious matters.

Although it is premature to advance a full blueprint for a two-state-plus arrangement, a number of Israelis, Palestinians, and others have sketched useful confederation outlines.[54] Particularly promising is an ongoing project of a group of Palestinian and Israeli scholars, activists, and journalists entitled "A Land for All." Guided by the overarching premise that the land consisting of Israel-Palestine is a shared homeland for Jewish Israelis and Palestinians, the group's draft visionary statement proposes a resolution based on three tenets:[55]

- Two sovereign states divided along the 1967 boundaries.
- Respect for the "deep affiliation of both Palestinians and Jews to the land in its entirety."
- The creation of joint institutions "operating on the basis of equality" to address a range of issues, including "security, civil and socioeconomic rights, economic issues, environmental protection [and] climate change."

The draft contains a platform of general proposals, which feature open borders that extend to living and working in the other state, a united and shared Jerusalem, full equality and collective rights for Israel's Palestinian citizens as well as for Jewish settlers wishing to reside in a sovereign Palestine, and an integrated economy attentive to the disparities between Israel and Palestine. On the thorny matter of refugees, the platform affirms full rectification embedded in the right as a citizen in the new state of Palestine to travel, work, and reside in Israel.[56]

Having sketched a path forward to a just coexistence, we are left with the daunting challenge of forging ahead, to borrow from Arendt, in today's "dark times." The initiators of "Land for All" do so by building a growing network of Israeli and Palestinian collaborators. They are not simply drafting a blueprint but engaging in a prefigurative politics where Palestinians and Jews develop and refine a vision and an accompanying set of proposals through extensive dialogue, which includes the type of shared history proposed by Said. Ultimately, as the initiators recognize and Rabbani has stressed, no success is possible without sustained and coordinated mobilization among Palestinians, dissenting Jews, and the global solidarity movement.

Sustained mobilization within the Jewish communities, especially in Israel and the United States, is particularly important for countering the oft-stated claim that Israel's actions are done for the benefit of the Jews. Within Israel, a courageous group of Jewish activists have carried out civil disobedience and direct action campaigns, documented and exposed Israeli war crimes and human rights abuses, and established alternative media channels, such as +972 Magazine.[57] American Jewish dissenters, such as Jewish Voice for Peace, If Not Now, *Jewish Currents*, and coalitions of Jewish scholars, regularly denounce Israeli actions and the U.S.-Israeli special relationship, support BDS, and confront AIPAC, the ADL, and other leading U.S. Jewish organizations. Jewish dissent has benefited from the surge in activism among independent Palestinians and Palestinian-solidarity groups, which includes civil disobedience in the occupied territories, mobilization for full equality in Israel, and the global BDS campaign. Jewish dissenters have regularly linked their protests to this Palestine-solidarity work and thereby linked Jewish-based protest to a broader emancipatory struggle.

Although the conscious pariahs among Jews are still relatively few in number and Jewish-Palestinian collaboration is not yet well advanced, the two groups represent the primary foundation for finding a way out of the deadly status quo. Of course, the range of protesters, even among just the Jewish segment, are not united on what future they want. Yet what stands out is a shared commitment to equality, human rights, and a just internationalism that derives from a blend of Jewish and outside ethical principles, cultural values, and historical experiences. Moreover, few renounce or deny a Jewish attachment to the land. The attraction of a distinct, non-statist vision of Jewish self-determination is its ability to reach the many Jews and non-Jews looking for an alternative that enables self-determination to flourish for both Jews and Palestinians while categorially breaking from the imperialist and nationalism-domination order that has shaped the land since the Balfour Declaration. This book's transformed Jewish vision articulates the desired shape of this transformation. Let us hope, as Arendt concluded in one of her most optimistic essays during the 1948 war, that "it is still not too late."[58]

Notes

PREFACE AND ACKNOWLEDGMENTS

1. Mari Cohen and Isaac Scher, "The ADL Doubles Down on Opposing the Anti-Zionist Left," *Jewish Currents*, May 1, 2022, https://jewishcurrents.org/the-adl-doubles-down-on-opposing-the-anti-zionist-left. Of the 2,717 antisemitic incidents the report identified, only 345 were related to Israel or Zionism. Within that category, 68 were attributed to white supremacist groups, while it is unclear who perpetrated the remaining instances. "Audit of Antisemitic Incidents 2021," ADL, March 5, 2022, https://www.adl.org/audit2021.

2. "Remarks by Jonathan Greenblatt to the ADL Virtual National Summit," ADL, May 1, 2022, https://www.adl.org/news/remarks-by-jonathan-greenblatt-to-the-adl-virtual-national-leadership-summit (emphasis in original).

3. Arthur Goren, ed., *Dissenter in Zion: From the Writings of Judah L. Magnes* (Cambridge, MA: Harvard University Press, 1982).

INTRODUCTION

1. Antony Lerman, "The End of Liberal Zionism: Israel's Move to the Right Challenges Diaspora Jews," *New York Times*, August 22, 2014, p. SR4.

2. "Netanyahu Hails Italy's Salvini as 'Great Friend of Israel,'" AP News, December 12, 2018.

3. Zeev Sternhell, "Why Benjamin Netanyahu Loves the European Far-Right," *Foreign Policy*, February 24, 2019.

4. Ishaan Tharoor, "On Israeli Election Day, Netanyahu Warns of Arabs Voting 'in Droves,'" *Washington Post*, March 17, 2015.

5. David M. Halbfinger and Isabel Kershner, "Israeli Law Declares the Country the 'Nation-State of the Jewish People,'" *New York Times*, July 19, 2018; "A Regime of Jewish Supremacy from the Jordan River to the Mediterranean Sea: This Is Apartheid," B'Tselem, January 12, 2021, https://www.btselem.org/publications/fulltext/202101_this_is_apartheid.

6. Akiva Eldar, "Is Israel Inching Closer to Fascism?," *Israel Pulse*, May 10, 2016, http://www.al-monitor.com/pulse/originals/2016/05/zeev-sternhell-holocaust-fascism-nationalistic-education.html.

7. "Our Approach to Zionism," Jewish Voice for Peace, accessed September 16, 2022, https://jewishvoiceforpeace.org/zionism/.

8. Marc Ellis, "Jew vs. Jew: On the Jewish Civil War and the New Prophetic," in *Wrestling with Zion: Progressive Jewish-American Responses to the Israeli-Palestinian Conflict*, ed. Tony Kushner and Alisa Solomon (New York: Grove, 2003), p. 143.

9. Peter Beinart, "Yavne: A Jewish Case for Equality in Israel-Palestine," *Jewish Currents*, July 7, 2020, https://jewishcurrents.org/yavne-a-jewish-case-for-equality-in-israel-palestine/; Omri Boehm, *Haifa Republic: A Democratic Future for Israel* (New York: New York Review of Books, 2021).

10. Beinart, "Yavne," p. 18.

11. Ran Greenstein, *Zionism and Its Discontents* (London: Pluto, 2014); Jacqueline Rose, *The Question of Zion* (Princeton, NJ: Princeton University Press, 2005); Amnon Raz-Krakotzkin, "Jewish Peoplehood, 'Jewish Politics,' and Political Responsibility," *College Literature* 38, no. 1 (2011): pp. 57–74; Rory Miller, "J.L. Magnes and the Promotion of Binationalism in Palestine," *Jewish Journal of Sociology* 48, no. 1–2 (2006): pp. 50–68; Raluca Munteanu Eddon, "Gershom Scholem, Hannah Arendt and the Paradox of 'Non-Nationalist' Nationalism," *Journal of Jewish Thought and Philosophy* 12, no. 1 (2003): pp. 55–68.

12. Rose, *Question of Zion*, p. 107.

13. Martin Buber, "Nationalism," in *A Land of Two Peoples: Martin Buber on Jews and Arabs*, ed. Paul Mendes-Flohr (Chicago: University of Chicago Press, 2005), p. 56.

14. Susan Lee Hattis, *The Bi-national Idea in Palestine during Mandatory Times* (Tel Aviv: Shikmona, 1970).

15. Judah L. Magnes and Martin Buber, *Arab-Jewish Unity: Testimony before the Anglo-American Inquiry Commission for the Ihud (Union) Association* (Westport, CT: Hyperion, 1976).

16. The next most influential binational Zionist group was the Marxist-oriented Hashomer Hatzair. But because it regarded Arabs as a socially regressive peasant society, the movement did not develop a serious program for fostering cross-national bonds until 1936. Hattis, *Bi-national Idea*.

17. Daniel P. Kotzin, *Judah L. Magnes: An American Nonconformist* (Syracuse, NY: Syracuse University Press, 2010).

18. Maurice Friedman, *Encounter on the Narrow Ridge: A Life of Martin Buber* (New York: Paragon House, 1991); Paul Mendes-Flohr, *Martin Buber: A Life of Faith and Dissent* (New Haven, CT: Yale University Press, 2019).

19. Kotzin, *Judah L. Magnes*, pp. 282–305; *Anglo-American Committee of Inquiry* (Lausanne, Switzerland, April 20, 1946), Lillian Goldman Law Library, Yale Law School, http://avalon.law.yale.edu/subject_menus/angtoc.asp. The quotation is from chap. 1.

20. Benny Morris, *One State, Two States: Resolving the Israel/Palestine Conflict* (New Haven, CT: Yale University Press, 2009), pp. 44–56.

21. Hannah Arendt, *The Origins of Totalitarianism* (New York: Meridian Books, 1958), p. 290.

22. Friedman, *Life of Martin Buber*; Mendes-Flohr, *Buber on Jews and Arabs*.

23. Martin Buber, "Hebrew Humanism," in *Israel and the World: Essays in a Time of Crisis* (New York: Schocken Books, 1948), pp. 240–252.

24. Ibid., p. 248.

25. Martin Buber, "The Meaning of Zionism," in Mendes-Flohr, *Buber on Jews and Arabs*, p. 183.

26. Martin Buber, "A Tragic Conflict?," in Mendes-Flohr, *Buber on Jews and Arabs*, p. 187.

27. Examples include the comprehensive compiling of Arendt's Jewish writings in Hannah Arendt, *Jewish Writings*, ed. Jerome Kohn and Ron H. Feldman (New York: Schocken Books, 2007); Richard J. Bernstein, *Hannah Arendt and the Jewish Question* (Cambridge, MA: MIT Press, 1996); Judith Butler, *Parting Ways: Jewishness and the Critique of Zionism* (New York: Columbia University Press, 2013); Amnon Raz-Krakotzkin, "Binationalism and Jewish Identity: Hannah Arendt and the Question of Palestine," in *Hannah Arendt in Jerusalem*, ed. Steven E. Ascheim (Berkeley: University of California Press, 2001), pp. 165–80; Gabriel Piterberg, "Zion's Rebel Daughter: Hannah Arendt on Palestine and Jewish Politics," *New Left Review*, November–December 2007; Eric Jacobson, "Why Did Hannah Arendt Reject the Partition of Palestine?," *Journal for Cultural Research* 17, no. 4 (2013): pp. 358–81; Shmuel Lederman, "Making the Desert Bloom: Hannah Arendt and Zionist Discourse," *European Legacy* 21, no. 4 (2016): pp. 393–407.

28. Hannah Arendt, *Eichmann in Jerusalem: A Report on the Banality of Evil* (New York: Penguin Books, 2006). For a helpful overview of the wide rebuke she received, see Amos Elon, "Introduction: The Excommunication of Hannah Arendt," in ibid.

29. Hannah Arendt, "Zionism Reconsidered," in Arendt, *Jewish Writings*, pp. 358, 361.

30. Dmitry Shumsky, *Beyond the Nation-State: The Zionist Political Imagination from Pinsker to Ben-Gurion* (New Haven, CT: Yale University Press, 2018).

CHAPTER 1

1. Martin Buber, "Should the Ichud Accept the Decree of History?," in Mendes-Flohr, *Buber on Jews and Arabs*, p. 250.

2. B'Tselem, "Regime of Jewish Supremacy"; "A Threshold Crossed: Israeli Authority and the Crimes of Apartheid and Persecution," Human Rights Watch, April 27, 2011, https://www.hrw.org/report/2021/04/27/threshold-crossed/israeli-authorities-and-crimes-apartheid-and-persecution; "Israel's Apartheid against Palestinians: Cruel System of Domination and Crime against Humanity," Amnesty International, 2022, https://www.amnesty.org/en/wp-content/uploads/sites/9/2022/02/MDE1551412022ARABIC.pdf.

3. Human Rights Watch, "Threshold Crossed," p. 10; Amnesty International, "Israel's Apartheid," pp. 12–13.

4. Human Rights Watch, "Threshold Crossed," pp. 108–9.
5. Ibid., p. 111.
6. Ibid., p. 114.
7. Ibid., p. 113.
8. Oren Ziv, "How Israel Is Turning Sheikh Jarrah into Another Hebron," *+972 Magazine*, June 10, 2021.
9. "Settlement Watch," Peace Now, accessed September 16, 2022, http://peacenow.org.il/en/settlements-watch/settlements-data/population.
10. Human Rights Watch, "Threshold Crossed," p. 92.
11. Ibid., pp. 137–38. Israeli authorities have categorized "communications equipment," "steel elements and construction products," and even medical X-ray equipment as "dual use."
12. Ibid., p. 133.
13. Ibid., pp. 131–32.
14. Ibid., pp. 57–59.
15. Ibid., p. 200.
16. Ibid., p. 17.
17. Aaron Boxerman, "After Coalition Battle, Knesset Reauthorizes Ban on Palestinian Family Unification," *Times of Israel*, March 10, 2022, https://www.timesofisrael.com/after-coalition-battle-knesset-reauthorizes-ban-on-palestinian-family-unification/.
18. Asher Schechter, "Punch a Lefty, Save the Homeland: Israel Rediscovers Political Violence," *Haaretz*, July 24, 2014.
19. TOI Staff, "'Death to Arabs': Nationalist Jerusalem Flag March Held under Ramped-Up Security," *Times of Israel*, June 15, 2021, https://www.timesofisrael.com/jerusalem-is-ours-nationalist-flag-march-held-under-ramped-up-security/.
20. Tamar Hermann, Ella Heller, Chanan Cohen, Dana Bublil, and Fadi Omer, *Israeli Democracy Index 2016* (Jerusalem: Israel Democracy Institute), p. 133.
21. Ibid., 126.
22. "Israel's Religiously Divided Society," Pew Research Center of Religious and Public Life, March 8, 2016, http://www.pewforum.org/2016/03/08/israels-religiously-divided-society/.
23. Jeffrey Heller, "Israeli General Warns of Nazi-Like Jewish Extremists in Holocaust Remembrance Speech," *Forward*, May 5, 2016; William Booth, "Israel's Defense Minister Abruptly Resigns in Slap at Growing 'Extremism,'" *Washington Post*, May 20, 2016.
24. "'Nakba Law': Amendment No. 40 to the Budgets Foundations Law," Adalah, 2011, https://www.adalah.org/en/law/view/496; Jonathan Lis, "Despite Global Criticism, Israel Approves Contentious 'NGO Law,'" *Haaretz*, July 11, 2016; Jonathan Lis, "Israel's Travel Ban: Knesset Bars Entry to Foreigners Who Call for Boycott of Israel or Settlements," *Haaretz*, March 7, 2017.
25. Oliver Holmes, "Israel Bars Entry to US Politicians Ilhan Omar and Rashida Tlaib," *Guardian*, August 15, 2019.
26. Halbfinger and Kershner, "Israeli Law Declares."
27. The Joint List (whose voters are primarily Palestinians) received six seats, while the conservative Islamist Party received four seats.

28. TOI Staff, "What's in the Coalition Agreements Yesh Atid Signed with 'Change Bloc' Partners?," *Times of Israel*, June 11, 2021, https://www.timesofisrael.com/whats-inside-coalition-agreements-yesh-atid-signed-with-change-bloc-partners/.

29. Patrick Kingsley, "Israel Accuses 6 Palestinian Rights Groups of Terrorism," *New York Times*, October 22, 2021.

30. "Jewish Americans in 2020," Pew Research Center, May 11, 2021, https://www.pewforum.org/2021/05/11/jewish-americans-in-2020/.

31. Ken Toltz, "AIPAC's Fall: I Worked at the Pro-Israel Lobby. Now I Have to Call It Out," *Haaretz*, February 16, 2020.

32. "ADL Statement Regarding Recent Violence and Rocket Attacks in Jerusalem," ADL, May 10, 2021, https://www.adl.org/news/press-releases/adl-statement-regarding-recent-violence-and-rocket-attacks-in-jerusalem; "Antisemitic Attacks Spread Like 'Wildfire' in the U.S. during Gaza Conflict," PBS, May 24, 2021, https://www.pbs.org/newshour/show/anti-semitic-attacks-spread-like-wildfire-in-the-us-during-gaza-conflict. To maintain its centrist image, the ADL added a brief criticism of private Jewish extremists. For a critical review of the ADL's approach, see Mari Cohen, "A Closer Look at the 'Uptick' in Antisemitism," *Jewish Currents*, May 27, 2021, https://jewishcurrents.org/a-closer-look-at-the-uptick-in-antisemitism/.

33. "What is Antisemitism," International Holocaust Remembrance Alliance, accessed September 16, 2022, https://www.holocaustremembrance.com/resources/working-definitions-charters/working-definition-antisemitism.

34. "ADL Welcomes Executive Order Combating Anti-Semitism," ADL, December 11, 2019, https://www.adl.org/news/press-releases/adl-welcomes-executive-order-combating-anti-semitism; Toby Tabachnik and Jackson Richman, "Jewish Groups React to Trump's Executive Order on Anti-Semitism," *Pittsburgh Jewish Chronicle*, December 18, 2019.

35. "Anti-Zionism or Criticism of Israel Is Never Antisemitic," Anti-Defamation League, accessed September 16, 2022, https://antisemitism.adl.org/anti-zionism/?_ga=2.195381676.1044677086.1625007206-1373792645.1623097829.

36. Jonathan Greenblatt, "BDS Must Be Taken on with Every Measure of Seriousness," Medium, June 1, 2016, https://medium.com/@J0NATHAN_G/bds-must-be-taken-on-with-every-measure-of-seriousness-d701403ede19.

37. Nathan Thrall, "A Day in the Life of Abed Salama," *New York Review of Books*, March 19, 2021, https://www.nybooks.com/daily/2021/03/19/a-day-in-the-life-of-abed-salama/.

38. Beinart, "Yavne"; Peter Beinart, "I No Longer Believe in a Jewish State," *New York Times*, July 8, 2020.

39. Beinart, "Yavne," p. 8.

40. Boehm, *Haifa Republic*, pp. 38–39.

41. Ibid., p. 42.

42. Ibid., p. 15. While South Africa has dropped racial categories, it retains institutionalized tribal distinctions. Mahmood Mamdani, *Neither Settler nor Native: The Making and Unmaking of Permanent Minorities* (Cambridge, MA: Belknap, 2020), pp. 144–95.

43. Boehm, *Haifa Republic*, pp. 150–53.

44. Ibid., pp. 156–57.
45. Peter Beinart, *The Crisis of Zionism* (New York: Picador Books, 2013); Beinart, "Yavne," p. 18.
46. Shumsky, *Beyond the Nation-State*.
47. Beinart, "Yavne," p. 22.
48. Ibid., p. 18.
49. Boehm, *Haifa Republic*, p. 11.
50. Ibid., pp. 15–16. In quoting from Shumsky's text, Boehm neglects to add that this excerpt was part of a longer letter vociferously attacking Brit Shalom's accommodationist stance. Shumsky, *Beyond the Nation-State*, p. 125. Boehm's citation of Shumsky wrongly locates the Jabotinsky passage at pp. 90–91.
51. Boehm, *Haifa Republic*, pp. 99–100.
52. Ibid., p. 60.
53. Shumsky, *Beyond the Nation-State*, p. 7.
54. Ibid., pp. 212–13.
55. Boehm, *Haifa Republic*, p. 70.
56. Rashid Khalidi, *The Hundred Years' War on Palestine: A History of Settler-Colonialism and Resistance, 1917–2017* (New York: Metropolitan Books, 2020), p. 51.
57. Tom Segev, *A State at Any Cost: The Life of David Ben-Gurion* (New York: Farrar, Straus and Giroux, 2019), p. 158.
58. Khalidi, *Hundred Years' War*, p. 51.
59. "The Palestine Mandate," The Avalon Project, July 14, 1922, accessed September 16, 2022, https://avalon.law.yale.edu/20th_century/palmanda.
60. Shumsky, *Beyond the Nation-State*, pp. 212–13.
61. Ibid., p. 4.

CHAPTER 2

1. Friedman, *Life of Martin Buber*; Mendes-Flohr, *Martin Buber*.
2. For a summary of the first twelve Zionist Congresses, see "Zionist Congress: First to Twelfth Zionist Congress," Jewish Virtual Library, accessed September 16, 2022, http://www.jewishvirtuallibrary.org/first-to-twelfth-zionist-congress-1897-1921.
3. For an extensive critique of this arrangement, see Arendt, *Origins of Totalitarianism*, pp. 269–90.
4. Reproduced in Charles D. Smith, *Palestine and the Arab-Israeli Conflict: A History with Documents*, 8th ed. (Boston: Bedford/St. Martins, 2013), p. 94.
5. Ibid., pp. 100–102.
6. This is not to lose sight of intense conflicts over political ideology, diplomatic approaches, openness to compromise, tactics, religion, and other matters. For an overview of pre-state Zionist politics, see Tom Segev, *One Palestine Complete: Jews and Arabs under the British Mandate* (New York: Henry Holt, 1999).
7. Hattis, *Bi-national Idea*, p. 37.
8. The British rejected Zionist lobbying to incorporate language in the Balfour Declaration that referred to a Jewish "state." They used the compromise language of a Jewish "homeland" in Palestine, which left open what specific political arrangement the declaration foresaw. Segev, *One Palestine Complete*.

9. Ibid., p. 183.

10. Mendes-Flohr, *Buber on Jews and Arabs*, p. 10. Most statist Zionists, including the hard-line Revisionists, were willing to grant collective minority rights for the remaining Arab population in Palestine once Jewish predominance was secured. Shumsky, *Beyond the Nation-State*.

11. Friedman, *Life of Martin Buber*, pp. 120–21. Like Buber, the youth group from central Europe was not religious in the conventional sense of strict observance of Jewish laws. Rather, they were attracted to the spiritual message and underlying values of Judaism.

12. Shalom Ratzabi, *Between Zionism and Judaism: The Radical Circle in Brith Shalom, 1925–1933* (Leiden: Brill, 2002), pp. 188–234; Bernard Avishai, *The Tragedy of Zionism: How Its Revolutionary Past Haunts Israeli Democracy* (New York: Helios, 2002), pp. 45–66.

13. Avishai, *Tragedy of Zionism*, p. 48.

14. Zohat Maor, "Moderation from Right to Left: The Hidden Roots of Brit Shalom," *Jewish Social Studies: History, Culture, Society* 19, no. 2 (2013): pp. 79–108.

15. Ratzabi, *Between Zionism and Judaism*, pp. 337–77.

16. Ibid., p. 262.

17. Buber, "Nationalism."

18. Martin Buber, "A Proposed Resolution on the Arab Question," in Mendes-Flohr, *Buber on Jews and Arabs*, p. 61.

19. For a contrasting interpretation, see Bernard Susser, *Existence and Utopia: The Social and Political Thought of Martin Buber* (Rutherford, NJ: Farleigh Dickinson University Press, 1981), p. 167. Buber himself was so disappointed that he refrained from direct political involvement in Congress activity for many years.

20. Mendes-Flohr, *Buber on Jews and Arabs*, pp. 62–63.

21. Ratzabi, *Between Zionism and Judaism*, pp. 22–37.

22. Hattis, *Bi-national Idea*, pp. 38–46.

23. Ibid. For an intellectual history of the radical wing, see Ratzabi, *Between Zionism and Judaism*.

24. Hattis, *Bi-national Idea*, p. 36.

25. Rashid Khalidi, *The Iron Cage: The Story of the Palestinian Struggle for Statehood* (Boston: Beacon, 2007), pp. 35–36.

26. Hattis, *Bi-national Idea*, p. 46. Several years after his tenure ended as high commissioner, Herbert Samuel became a strong proponent of the binational program. Ibid., pp. 157–60.

27. Aharon Cohen, *Israel and the Arab World* (New York: Funk and Wagnalls, 1970), p. 248.

28. Hattis, *Bi-national Idea*, pp. 56, 82, 87–93. "As to the principles of future policy in Palestine and cooperation with the Arabs on binational lines," wrote Weizmann in 1929, "I have never swerved from it." Ibid., p. 87.

29. Cohen, *Israel and the Arab World*, p. 260.

30. Segev, *Life of Ben-Gurion*. At the Fourteenth Zionist Congress in 1925, Ben-Gurion stated, "We must examine the issues before us from one central vantage point . . . Zionism is building a state. . . . Building a state requires first of all, creating a Jewish majority." Ratzabi, *Between Zionism and Judaism*, p. 251.

31. Hattis, *Bi-national Idea*, p. 77; Segev, *One Palestine Complete*, pp. 285–88. Due in part to distinct priorities of private capitalist Jewish investors in Palestine, the Hebrew labor policy was not always followed. Gershon Shafir, "Capitalist Binationalism in Mandatory Palestine," *International Journal of Middle Eastern Studies* 43 (2011): pp. 611–33.

32. Segev, *One Palestine Complete*, pp. 209–210.

33. Ibid., pp. 314–27. To a lesser extent, Jews attacked and killed Arabs. Altogether, 133 Jews and 116 Arabs were killed.

34. Hattis, *Bi-national Idea*, p. 61.

35. Ibid., p. 87. Weizmann did, however, add that he remained in "full agreement with the principles and line of policy" of Brit Shalom.

36. Ibid., pp. 51–52.

37. Ibid., pp. 51–57.

38. Ratzabi, *Between Zionism and Judaism*, pp. 252–56.

39. Hattis, *Bi-national Idea*, p. 57.

40. Mendes-Flohr, *Buber on Jews and Arabs*, pp. 78–91.

41. Martin Buber, *On Zion: The History of an Idea* (London: Horovitz, 1973), p. xix.

42. Ibid., p. xx.

43. Ibid., pp. 147–54.

44. Buber, "Hebrew Humanism," pp. 245–46; Martin Buber, "The Children of Amos," in Mendes-Flohr, *Buber on Jews and Arabs*, p. 257.

45. Buber, *On Zion*, p. 35.

46. Mendes-Flohr, *Buber on Jews and Arabs*, p. 37. Buber expressed this in a letter to Hugo Bergman in 1918, also lamenting that "most leading Zionists . . . are thoroughly unrestrained nationalists."

47. Buber, "Hebrew Humanism," p. 248.

48. Buber, *On Zion*, pp. 123–42.

49. Ibid., pp. 130–33.

50. Buber, "Hebrew Humanism," p. 245.

51. Buber, *On Zion*, pp. 143–47.

52. Ratzabi, *Between Zionism and Judaism*, p. 373. Unlike Buber, Ahad Ha'am gave no independent weight to Judaism's religious component but just appreciated its role in helping shape the Jewish people's unique attributes.

53. Buber, *On Zion*, pp. 144–45.

54. Martin Buber, *Paths in Utopia* (New York: Collier Books, 1949). See especially pp. 46–57. Landauer was a leading exponent of a decentralized socialism, also referred to as libertarian socialism or anarchism.

55. Ibid., p. 55.

56. Buber's impetus for writing *Paths in Utopia* was to dispute the Marxist dismissal of community-based socialism as a narrow, romanticized utopianism.

57. Martin Buber, "Three Theses of a Religious Socialism (1928)," in *Pointing the Way: Collected Essays*, ed. Maurice Friedman (Freeport, NY: Books for Libraries Press, 1957), pp. 112–14. Similarly, Buber maintained that "a Jewish nation cannot exist without religion any more than a Jewish religious community without nationality. Our only salvation is to become Israel again, to become a whole." Buber, "Hebrew Humanism," p. 252.

58. Ratzabi, *Between Zionism and Judaism*, pp. 198–200; Buber, *On Zion*, p. 121.
59. Buber, *Paths in Utopia*, pp. 146–47.
60. Ibid., pp. 142–43.
61. Martin Buber, "National Home and National Policy," in Mendes-Flohr, *Buber on Jews and Arabs*, p. 85.
62. Ibid.
63. He was also disappointed by the absence of a religious spirit, though he generously perceived in them "the half-unconscious after-effects of the Bible's teachings about social justice." Buber, *Paths in Utopia*, p. 142.
64. Buber, "National Home and National Policy," p. 86.
65. Buber, "Nationalism," p. 57.
66. Martin Buber, "We Need the Arabs, They Need Us! An Interview," in Mendes-Flohr, *Buber on Jews and Arabs*, p. 267.
67. Buber, *On Zion*, p. xxi.
68. Buber, "National Home and National Policy," p. 87.
69. Buber, "National Home and National Policy," pp. 86–87; Martin Buber, "Facts and Demands: A Reply to Gideon Freudenberg," in Mendes-Flohr, *Buber on Jews and Arabs*, p. 237.
70. Martin Buber, "Concerning Our Politics," in Mendes-Flohr, *Buber on Jews and Arabs*, p. 139.
71. Hans Kohn, "Zionism Is Not Judaism," in Mendes-Flohr, *Buber on Jews and Arabs*, pp. 95–100. Kohn, a leading figure in Brit Shalom, lamented that only British support and "our own bayonets" would enable a lasting Jewish presence. Such a Jewish Palestine, however, "w[ould] no longer have anything of that Zion for which I once put myself on the line." Ibid., p. 99.
72. Mohandas K. Gandhi, "The Jews," in Mendes-Flohr, *Buber on Jews and Arabs*, pp. 106–111.
73. Martin Buber, "A Letter to Gandhi, Jerusalem 24 February 1939," in Mendes-Flohr, *Buber on Jews and Arabs*, p. 117.
74. Ibid., p. 120.
75. Ibid., pp. 120–21. Buber's frustration with Gandhi's seemingly absolute stance against Jewish settlement led him to underplay the extent to which Jewish settlement had intruded on and displaced Palestinians from their land. Elsewhere, however, when addressing the Zionist community, Buber was more forthright.
76. Mendes-Flohr, *Buber on Jews and Arabs*, p. 6.
77. Avi Shlaim, *The Iron Wall: Israel and the Arab World* (New York: W. W. Norton, 2001), pp. 13–15. Jabotinsky did allow for peaceful relations with the remaining Arab minority and minority rights once the iron wall was firmly established.
78. Hattis, *Bi-national Idea*, p. 57.
79. Buber, "Letter to Gandhi," p. 120.
80. Ibid.
81. Buber, "National Home and National Policy," p. 86.
82. Buber, "Tragic Conflict," p. 187.
83. Ibid.
84. Ibid.
85. Ibid., pp. 198–99.

86. Ibid., p. 199.
87. Ibid.
88. Buber, "National Home and National Policy," p. 88.
89. Martin Buber, "Two Peoples in Palestine," in Mendes-Flohr, *Buber on Jews and Arabs*, pp. 196–97.
90. Ibid., p. 197.
91. Ibid.
92. Buber, "National Home and National Policy," p. 91.
93. Ibid.
94. Buber, "Meaning of Zionism," p. 183.
95. Buber, "National Home and National Policy," p. 87.
96. Buber, "Concerning Our Politics," p. 141.
97. Buber, "National Home and National Policy," pp. 87–91. *Fellahin* refers to peasants, some of whom had become displaced from their land and could now be regarded as incipient proletarians.
98. Ibid., p. 89.
99. Ibid., p. 91.
100. Martin Buber, "The Bi-national Approach to Zionism," in Mendes-Flohr, *Buber on Jews and Arabs*, pp. 207–14.
101. Ibid., p. 211.
102. Ibid., pp. 212–13.
103. Friedman, *Life of Martin Buber*, pp. 208–31.
104. Palestine Royal Commission (Peel Commission), *Mandates Palestine Report* (League of Nations, July 1937), Jewish Virtual Library, http://www.jewishvirtuallibrary.org/text-of-the-peel-commission-report.
105. Kotzin, *Judah L. Magnes*, pp. 247–48.
106. Segev, *One Palestine Complete*, pp. 366–82.
107. Peel Commission, *Palestine Report*.
108. Ibid.
109. Segev, *One Palestine Complete*, pp. 401–4.
110. Mendes-Flohr, *Buber on Jews and Arabs*, pp. 126–27.
111. Martin Buber, "Keep Faith!," in Mendes-Flohr, *Buber on Jews and Arabs*, pp. 128–29.
112. Ibid., p. 130.
113. For Magnes's seventieth birthday, Buber publicly declared, "You have given me a great gift; you have made it possible for me to engage in political action . . . without sacrificing the truth." Kotzin, *Judah L. Magnes*, p. 278.
114. Ibid.
115. Ibid., pp. 220–73.
116. Ibid., pp. 144–50.
117. Ibid., pp. 146–65.
118. Judah Magnes, "There Is No Party I Can Join, June 1934," in *Dissenter in Zion: From the Writings of Judah L. Magnes*, ed. Arthur Goren (Cambridge, MA: Harvard University Press, 1982), p. 305.
119. Judah Magnes, "Eretz Israel and the Galut, May 22, 1923," in Goren, *Dissenter in Zion*, p. 208.

120. Kotzin, *Judah L. Magnes*, p. 236; Judah Magnes, "Letter to Chaim Weizmann, September 7, 1929," in Goren, *Dissenter in Zion*, p. 276.
121. Judah Magnes, "To Dear Friend, May, 1920," in Goren, *Dissenter in Zion*, pp. 183–90.
122. Kotzin, *Judah L. Magnes*, p. 161.
123. Judah Magnes, "Like All the Nations?," *Jewish Daily Bulletin*, January 24, 1930, pp. 2–8, http://www.jta.org/1930/01/24/archive/full-text-of-dr-judah-l-magness-pamphlet-like-all-the-nations.
124. Kotzin, *Judah L. Magnes*, p. 300.
125. Ibid., pp. 299–300.
126. In 1934, he helped Ben-Gurion conduct negotiations. Ibid., pp. 241–52.
127. Ibid., pp. 197–200.
128. Hattis, *Bi-national Idea*, pp. 169–71.
129. Kotzin, *Judah L. Magnes*, p. 277.
130. Hattis, *Bi-national Idea*, p. 212.
131. For more on the capitalist binationalists, see Shafir, "Capitalist Binationalism."
132. At the time of Israel's formation, its political party, Mapam, was the second most popular after Ben-Gurion's Mapai Party. Tom Segev, *1949: The First Israelis* (New York: Free Press, 1986), pp. 268–82.
133. Hattis, *Bi-national Idea*, p. 72.
134. Ibid., p. 73.
135. Ibid., p. 213.
136. Ibid., pp. 256–58.
137. Ibid., p. 259.
138. Ibid., p. 263.
139. Magnes was unsuccessful in recruiting Mizrahi Jews with long roots in Palestine or non-Zionist ultra-orthodox Jews from Agudah Israel. Ibid., pp. 259–60. Among the former were a core of individuals belonging to Kedma Mizrahi (Forward to the East), a group committed to fostering ties between Palestine's Jews and the "nations of the East." Its cofounder argued that Ihud was too quick to declare concessions and lacked adequate knowledge or appreciation of the local Arab community.
140. Friedman, *Life of Martin Buber*, p. 270.
141. Martin Buber, "A Majority or Many? A Postscript to a Speech," in Mendes-Flohr, *Buber on Jews and Arabs*, pp. 165–68.
142. Ibid., p. 166.
143. It also helped that leading figures from a range of Zionist groups belonged to Ihud. Kotzin, *Judah L. Magnes*, p. 286.
144. Hattis, *Bi-national Idea*, pp. 285–86.
145. Ibid., p. 286.
146. Kotzin, *Judah L. Magnes*, pp. 315–16. Magnes and Truman had a pleasant meeting, but the president still reluctantly supported partition. For more on Truman's deliberations, see John B. Judis, *Genesis: Truman, American Jews, and the Origins of the Arab/Israeli Conflict* (New York: Farrar, Straus and Giroux, 2014).
147. Hattis, *Bi-national Idea*, p. 270.
148. Martin Buber, "In the Days of Silence," in Mendes-Flohr, *Buber on Jews and Arabs*, pp. 150–51.

149. Martin Buber, "Dialogue on the Biltmore Program," in Mendes-Flohr, *Buber on Jews and Arabs*, pp. 161–64.
150. Magnes and Buber, *Arab-Jewish Unity*.
151. Ibid., pp. 83–84.
152. *Anglo-American Committee of Inquiry*; Hattis, *Bi-national Idea*, p. 298.
153. *Anglo-American Committee of Inquiry*.
154. The subsequent plan, known as Morrison-Grady, was formulated in 1946 at the British Colonial Office. Hattis, *Bi-national Idea*, pp. 298–301.
155. Hattis, *Bi-national Idea*, pp. 298–301; Kotzin, *Judah L. Magnes*, pp. 304–8; Judis, *Genesis*, pp. 212–52. Judis documents Truman's personal support for the Anglo-American Committee's report.
156. UN General Assembly, Resolution 181 (II), Future Government of Palestine, A/RES/181(II) (November 29, 1947).
157. Hattis, *Bi-national Idea*, p. 317.
158. Buber, "Should the Ichud Accept," p. 245.
159. Ibid., p. 246.
160. Ibid., p. 248.
161. Ibid., p. 250.
162. Ibid., pp. 247–48.
163. Ibid. The leader of Falastin al-Jedida was murdered two weeks after signing the accord.
164. Ibid, p. 251.
165. Ibid.
166. Buber, "Children of Amos," p. 257.
167. Mendes-Flohr, *Buber on Jews and Arabs*, pp. 241–43.
168. Ibid., p. 244.
169. Martin Buber, "Instead of Polemics," in Mendes-Flohr, *Buber on Jews and Arabs*, pp. 269–72.
170. Martin Buber, "Memorandum on the Military Government," in Mendes-Flohr, *Buber on Jews and Arabs*, pp. 286–88.
171. For a comprehensive review, see Shira Robinson, *Citizen Strangers: Palestinians and the Birth of Israel's Liberal Settler State* (Palo Alto, CA: Stanford University Press, 2013). Also useful is Segev, *1949*.
172. Segev, *1949*, pp. 51–52.
173. Mendes-Flohr, *Buber on Jews and Arabs*, pp. 263–64.
174. Martin Buber, "We Must Grant the Arabs Truly Equal Rights," in Mendes-Flohr, *Buber on Jews and Arabs*, pp. 298–99.
175. Ibid., p. 298.
176. Martin Buber, "Israel and the Command of the Spirit," in Mendes-Flohr, *Buber on Jews and Arabs*, p. 293.
177. Buber, "We Need the Arabs," p. 264.
178. Buber, "Command of the Spirit," p. 293.
179. Israel ended martial law in 1966. This was done partly in response to international pressure. However, the government took steps to ensure a continuing subordinate status for the Palestinians. Robinson, *Citizen Strangers*, pp. 188–93.
180. Friedman, *Life of Martin Buber*, pp. 425, 457.

181. Ibid., p. 458. Shortly after Eshkol became prime minister in 1963, Buber commended him for demonstrating a "marked change in tone . . . toward Israel's Arab citizens." Mendes-Flohr, *Buber on Jews and Arabs*, p. 301.

182. The Irgun and other maximalists called for a Jewish state over all of the territory, to extend to Jordan. They allowed for minority rights, but this meant enacting policies that would make Palestinian Arabs the minority. Given the demographics, a Jewish state over all of the Mandate did not gain much international support at the time.

183. In the next chapter, I recount Arendt's devastating critique of minority treaties.

184. Benny Morris, "Revisiting the Palestinian Exodus of 1948," in *The War for Palestine*, ed. Eugene Rogan and Avi Shlaim (Cambridge: Cambridge University Press, 2007), pp. 37–59.

185. Greenstein, *Zionism and Its Discontents*, p. 204.

CHAPTER 3

1. Hannah Arendt, "The Jewish State—Fifty Years After: Where Have Herzl's Politics Led?," in Arendt, *Jewish Writings*, p. 385.
2. Hannah Arendt, "The Jew as Pariah: A Hidden Tradition," in Arendt, *Jewish Writings*, pp. 283–86.
3. Arendt, "Zionism Reconsidered," p. 366. In contrast, Buber and the radical wing of Brit Shalom saw Zionism as enabling Jews to return to their eastern roots, where they could realize their full Jewish identity. Hattis, *Bi-national Idea*, pp. 40–47.
4. Hannah Arendt, "What Remains: The Language Remains—a Conversation with Günter Gaus," in *Hannah Arendt: The Last Interview and Other Conversations* (Brooklyn: Melville House, 2013), p. 18.
5. Elizabeth Young-Bruehl, *Hannah Arendt: For Love of the World* (New Haven, CT: Yale University Press, 1982), pp. 102–7.
6. Arendt, "What Remains," p. 20.
7. Young-Bruehl, *Hannah Arendt*, pp. 152–54.
8. Hannah Arendt, "We Refugees," in Arendt, *Jewish Writings*, p. 265.
9. Arendt, *Origins of Totalitarianism*, p. 5. She illustrates this explanation with a joke from the post–World War I era: "An antisemite claimed that the Jews had caused the war; the reply was: Yes, the Jews and the bicyclists. Why the bicyclists? asks the one. Why the Jews? asks the other."
10. Ibid., p. 7.
11. Arendt, "Zionism Reconsidered," pp. 358–59.
12. Arendt, *Origins of Totalitarianism*, p. 9.
13. Ibid., pp. 15–18.
14. Ibid., pp. 18–21.
15. Ibid., p. 25.
16. Hannah Arendt, "Antisemitism," in Arendt, *Jewish Writings*, p. 78.
17. Arendt, *Origins of Totalitarianism*, p. 23.
18. Ibid., p. 33.
19. Ibid., pp. 229–31.
20. Ibid., p. 231.
21. Ibid., p. 230.

22. Arendt, "Antisemitism," pp. 62–63.
23. Arendt, *Origins of Totalitarianism*, p. 18.
24. Ibid., pp. 227–43.
25. Ibid., p. 227.
26. Ibid., p. 232.
27. Ibid., p. 228.
28. Ibid., p. 229.
29. Ibid., p. 240.
30. Ibid., p. 242.
31. Ibid., p. 22.
32. Ibid., p. 125.
33. Ibid., p. 135.
34. Ibid., p. 124.
35. Ibid., p. 152. The mob consisted of "the refuse of all classes." Ibid., p. 155.
36. Ibid., p. 155.
37. Ibid., p. 128.
38. Ibid., p. 130–34.
39. Ibid., pp. 183–84, 221.
40. Ibid., pp. 156–57, 184.
41. Ibid., p. 153n55.
42. Ibid., p. 126.
43. Ibid., p. 124.
44. Ibid., p. 221.
45. Ibid., pp. 225–26.
46. Hannah Arendt, "A Way toward the Reconciliation of Peoples," in Arendt, *Jewish Writings*, p. 259.
47. Arendt, *Origins of Totalitarianism*, p. 267.
48. They were Poland, Austria, Hungary, Czechoslovakia, Yugoslavia, Finland, Latvia, Lithuania, and Estonia.
49. Ibid., pp. 286–88.
50. Ibid., p. 270.
51. Ibid., p. 275.
52. Ibid., p. 292.
53. Ibid., p. 302.
54. Ibid., p. 289.
55. Arendt, "Jew as Pariah," p. 275 (emphasis in original). Arendt's illustrations of Jewish pariahs included Charlie Chaplin. She defended this selection despite learning that Chaplin was not Jewish because he "epitomized in an artistic form a character born of the Jewish pariah mentality." Ibid., p. 297n1.
56. Arendt invoked the term *double slavery* in "Jew as Pariah," p. 284. The quoted passage is from Hannah Arendt, "Herzl and Lazare," in Arendt, *Jewish Writings*, p. 339.
57. Arendt, "Herzl and Lazare," pp. 339–40.
58. Arendt, "We Refugees," p. 274.
59. Hannah Arendt, "The Minority Question," in Arendt, *Jewish Writings*, p. 129.

60. Arendt, *Origins of Totalitarianism*, p. 120.
61. Hannah Arendt, "Peace or Armistice in the Near East?," in Arendt, *Jewish Writings*, p. 442.
62. Arendt presumably recognized that many supporters of Hebrew University, including Chaim Weizmann, viewed Hebrew University as an institution for building up the state capacity of the Yishuv. But she took hope in Magnes's leadership as well as the presence of other high-profile Humanist Zionists.
63. Arendt, "Peace or Armistice," p. 435.
64. Ibid., p. 442.
65. Ibid., p. 443.
66. The first quotation comes from Hannah Arendt, "To Save the Jewish Homeland," in Arendt, *Jewish Writings*, p. 395; the second part is from Arendt, "Peace or Armistice," p. 443.
67. Arendt, "Zionism Reconsidered," pp. 349, 353.
68. Arendt, "Peace or Armistice," p. 442.
69. Arendt, "Zionism Reconsidered," p. 354.
70. Ibid., p. 344.
71. Arendt, "Peace or Armistice," p. 437.
72. Arendt, "Zionism Reconsidered," p. 367.
73. Ibid., p. 359.
74. Arendt, "Jewish State," p. 385.
75. Ibid., p. 382.
76. Arendt, "Zionism Reconsidered," p. 364.
77. Ibid., p. 362. Arendt added that this tactic had proved unsuccessful for Herzl.
78. Ibid., p. 359.
79. Ibid., p, 362.
80. Ibid., p. 358.
81. Ibid., p. 360.
82. Arendt, "Jewish State," p. 385.
83. Ibid., p. 384.
84. Arendt, "Zionism Reconsidered," pp. 362–63; Rachel Elboim-Dror, "How Herzl Sold Out the Armenians," *Haaretz*, May 1, 2015.
85. Arendt, "Zionism Reconsidered," p. 350.
86. Ibid., p. 363. Arendt softened her indictment by adding the need to "consider how exceptionally difficult the conditions were for the Jews who, in contrast to other peoples, did not even possess the territory from which to start their fight for freedom."
87. Arendt, "Peace or Armistice," pp. 424–25.
88. Ibid., p. 430.
89. Ibid., p. 432.
90. Ibid., pp. 424–25.
91. Arendt, "Zionism Reconsidered," p. 344.
92. Arendt, "Peace or Armistice," p. 434.
93. Arendt's neglect of Mizrahi Zionist outreach is discussed below.
94. Arendt, "Peace or Armistice," pp. 430–31.
95. Ibid., p. 432.

96. Arendt, "Zionism Reconsidered," p. 347.
97. Arendt, "Peace or Armistice," p. 433.
98. Arendt, "Zionism Reconsidered," p. 372.
99. Ibid., p. 345.
100. Arendt, "To Save the Jewish Homeland," p. 396.
101. Ibid., p. 397.
102. Ibid., p. 396.
103. Ibid., p. 394.
104. Arendt, "Zionism Reconsidered," p. 349.
105. Ibid., p. 350.
106. Ibid., p. 364.
107. In two essays in 1943, she faulted Magnes for consigning Jews in Palestine to a precarious "minority status within an Arab empire." Hannah Arendt, "The Crisis of Zionism," in Arendt, *Jewish Writings*, p. 336; Hannah Arendt, "Can the Jewish-Arab Question Be Solved?," in Arendt, *Jewish Writings*, p. 194. But even when criticizing Magnes, she also commended his courage in challenging Zionist orthodoxy. Young-Bruehl, *Hannah Arendt*, p. 226.
108. Young-Bruehl, *Hannah Arendt*, pp. 224–30.
109. Arendt, "To Save the Jewish Homeland," p. 401.
110. Arendt, "Peace or Armistice," p. 444.
111. Arendt, *Origins of Totalitarianism*, p. 290.
112. Lehi was another Revisionist-inspired militia, which broke from the Irgun. It maintained an active militant stance against the British Mandate even during the war with Nazi Germany. It made several unsuccessful attempts to assassinate the British high commissioner. Segev, *One Palestine Complete*, p. 456.
113. Hannah Arendt, "Magnes, the Conscience of the Jewish People," in Arendt, *Jewish Writings*, p. 451 (emphasis in original).
114. Shlaim, *Iron Wall*, pp. 90–93. The attack, led by Ariel Sharon, was part of a series of deliberately disproportionate reprisals to cross-border incursions from Palestinian refugees. The Israeli government originally denied involvement and blamed private Israelis incensed by past Palestinian attacks. This story was widely rejected, leading to a strong UN rebuke.
115. Young-Bruehl, *Hannah Arendt*, p. 291.
116. Moshe Zimmerman, "Hannah Arendt, the Early 'Post-Zionist,'" in Ascheim, *Hannah Arendt in Jerusalem*, p. 182.
117. Ibid., p. 193.
118. Hannah Arendt, "Thoughts on Politics and Revolution: A Commentary," in *Last Interview and Other Conversations*, pp. 102–5; Arendt, *Origins of Totalitarianism*, pp. 497–502.
119. Arendt, *Eichmann in Jerusalem*, pp. 5–10.
120. Arendt did, however, credit the three judges for their principled efforts to prevent the trial from deteriorating into a show trial.
121. Arendt, *Eichmann in Jerusalem*, p. 10.
122. Ibid., p. 19. Hausner led with a reference to Pharaoh and a quotation from Haman.

123. Ibid., p. 8.
124. Ibid., pp. 6–7.
125. Ibid., p. 267.
126. Ibid., p. 10.
127. Hannah Arendt, "A Letter to Gershom Scholem," in Arendt, *Jewish Writings*, p. 468.
128. Arendt, *Eichmann in Jerusalem*, p. 118.
129. Ibid. The internal quotation—with Arendt inserting "community" in brackets—is from a report produced by Rudolf Kastner, head of Hungary's Jewish Council and later an official at Israel's Ministry of Trade and Industry. Kastner was eventually denounced by opponents of the government, which precipitated a political crisis, a libel action, and, ultimately, his assassination by ex-Lehi individuals.
130. Germany, too, noted Arendt, betrayed this distorted moral hierarchy: "There are more than a few people, especially among the cultural elite, who still publicly regret the fact that Germany sent Einstein packing, without realizing that it was a much greater crime to kill little Hans Cohn from around the corner." Ibid., p. 134.
131. Ibid., p. 269.
132. Ibid., pp. 275–76.
133. Ibid., p. 273.
134. Ibid., p. 270.
135. Ibid., p. 294.
136. Ibid., pp. 10–11.
137. She regarded objections of the Jewish victims not being Israeli citizens and the crimes not occurring on Israel's territory as "legalistic in the extreme." Ibid., p. 259.
138. Ibid., p. 273.
139. Elon, "Introduction." The book prodded the ADL to urge all American rabbis to denounce Arendt at the Jewish High Holidays.
140. Young-Bruehl, *Hannah Arendt*, p. 361.
141. Ibid., pp. 455–56.
142. Arendt, "Letter to Scholem," p. 467.
143. Steven Ascheim, "Introduction: Hannah Arendt in Jerusalem," in Ascheim, *Hannah Arendt in Jerusalem*, pp. 3–4.
144. Arendt, "Zionism Reconsidered," p. 371.
145. Ascheim, "Hannah Arendt in Jerusalem," p. 7.

CHAPTER 4

1. Ben-Gurion's diary entry, quoted in Segev, *1949*, pp. 35–36.
2. Smith, *Palestine and the Arab-Israeli Conflict*, p. 223.
3. A/RES/181(II).
4. UN General Assembly, Resolution 194 on final settlement and returning Palestinian refugees, A/RES/194 (December 11, 1948).
5. Khalidi, *Iron Cage*, pp. 135–36.
6. Irene L. Gendzier, *Dying to Forget: Oil, Power, Palestine, and the Foundations of U.S. Policy in the Middle East* (New York: Columbia University Press, 2015), p. 252.

7. Peter Hahn, *Caught in the Middle East: U.S. Policy toward the Arab-Israeli Conflict, 1945–1961* (Chapel Hill: University of North Carolina Press, 2004), p. 87.

8. Gendzier, *Dying to Forget*, pp. 271–73. Jordan provided citizenship to Palestinians, hoping to assimilate them as Jordanians.

9. Mark Ethridge, the U.S. lead delegate at Lausanne, concluded, "If there is to be any assessment of blame for stalemate at Lausanne, Israel must accept primary responsibility." Gendzier, *Dying to Forget*, p. 266.

10. Gendzier, *Dying to Forget*, pp. 266–67; Segev, *1949*, pp. 22–24. Jordan also opposed internationalizing Jerusalem. Israel's one apparent concession on refugees is discussed below.

11. Hahn, *Caught in the Middle East*, p. 87.

12. Segev, *1949*, p. 23. Egypt suggested that this area could serve as the Palestinian state proposed by Resolution 181.

13. Segev, *1949*, pp. 15–17; Zeev Maoz, *Defending the Holy Land: A Critical Analysis of Israel's Security and Foreign Policy* (Ann Arbor: University of Michigan Press, 2009), pp. 393–95.

14. Gendzier, *Dying to Forget*, p. 265.

15. Segev, *1949*, p. 281.

16. Shlaim, *Iron Wall*, p. 162.

17. U.S. pressure eventually prompted Israel to withdraw from the Gaza Strip and Sharm al-Shaykh in the Sinai. Smith, *Palestine and the Arab-Israeli Conflict*, p. 245.

18. Maoz, *Defending the Holy Land*, pp. 77–78. A 1958 National Security Council memorandum opined that given U.S. concern with Pan-Arabism, it would be logical "to support Israel as the only strong pro-West power left in the Near East." Noam Chomsky, *The Fateful Triangle: The United States, Israel and the Palestinians* (Boston, MA: South End, 1983), pp. 20–21.

19. Although there was a Palestinian delegation at Lausanne, its interests were rarely consulted. Gendzier, *Dying to Forget*, p. 266.

20. Shlaim, *Iron Wall*, p. 45.

21. Alexander Bligh, "Israel and the Refugee Problem: From Exodus to Resettlement, 1948–1952," *Middle Eastern Studies* 34, no. 1 (1998): p. 132.

22. Segev, *1949*, pp. 30–34.

23. Ibid.; Shelly Fried, "The Refugee Problem at the Peace Conferences, 1949–2000," *Palestine-Israel Journal* 9, no. 2 (2002), pp. 24–34. The Arab states rejected the proposal as inadequate.

24. Segev, *1949*, pp. 52, 80.

25. Ibid., p. 36.

26. Ibid., p. 52.

27. Ibid., pp. 65–66; Robinson, *Citizen Strangers*, pp. 39–40.

28. Bernard Avishai, *The Hebrew Republic: How Secular Democracy and Global Enterprise Will Bring Israel Peace at Last* (Orlando, FL: Harcourt, 2008), p. 26.

29. Smith, *Palestine and the Arab-Israeli Conflict*, p. 222.

30. Robinson, *Citizen Strangers*, p. 50.

31. Ibid., pp. 98–99.

32. Ibid., p. 108.

33. Smith, *Palestine and the Arab-Israeli Conflict*, pp. 192–200.

34. At Lausanne, the Arab state delegates asked the U.S. member of the PCC to write up the treaty so that it could be seen as UN-imposed. Hahn, *Caught in the Middle East*, p. 87.

35. Khalidi, *Iron Cage*, pp. 189–93; Buber, "Command of the Spirit," p. 293.

36. There did emerge a crisis among Jews in some Middle Eastern and North African states. But this crisis mostly occurred after the war and could likely have been mitigated if Israel had been open to the global consensus on refugees and on borders. I return to the case of the Mizrahim Jews in Chapter 6.

37. Shlaim, *Iron Wall*, p. 78. Initially, Israel heavily relied on the U.S. Jewish community for financial assistance. It also encouraged lobbying of U.S. politicians.

38. Maoz, *Defending the Holy Land*, p. 486.

39. Ibid., p. 482.

40. Shlaim, *Iron Wall*.

41. Maoz, *Defending the Holy Land*, especially pp. 7–16. Most infiltrations involved refugees seeking to reconnect to their old homes, look for relatives, or harvest their old farms. Only a minority were violent, and few of those had the support of the host government. Shlaim, *Iron Wall*, pp. 81–87.

42. Gendzier, *Dying to Forget*, pp. 264–68.

43. Segev, *1949*, p. 35.

44. Ibid., p. 36.

45. Ibid., pp. 40–41.

46. Shlaim, *Iron Wall*, p. 87.

47. At the Knesset in April 1949, however, Ben-Gurion approvingly credited the notorious 1948 Deir Yassin massacre of over a hundred Palestinians for provoking many Palestinians to flee: a "Jewish state without Dir Yassin can exist only by the dictatorship of the minority." Robinson, *Citizen Strangers*, p. 31.

48. Ibid., p. 29.

49. Ibid., p. 30.

50. Segev, *1949*, pp. 35–36.

51. Robinson, *Citizen Strangers*, p. 30.

52. Palestinian residents of East Jerusalem have a distinct status. Many are "permanent residents," who have various civil rights and access to state welfare services but lack voting or other political rights. Gilead Sher, "The Residency Status of East Jerusalem's Palestinians," *INSS Insight*, October 28, 2015.

53. UN Security Council, Resolution 242, "The Situation in the Middle East," S/RES/242 (November 22, 1967). Although the resolution did not specify that Israel withdraw from all the newly conquered territories, the understanding at the time of enactment was for complete withdrawal subject to mutually agreeable minor adjustments. Lord Caradon, "Security Council Resolution 242," in *U.N. Security Council Resolution 242: A Case Study in Diplomatic Ambiguity*, ed. Lord Caradon, Arthur J. Goldberg, Mohamed H. El-Zayyat, and Abba Eban (Washington, DC: Institute for the Study of Diplomacy, 1981), pp. 3–18.

54. UN Security Council, Resolution 237, on protecting the civil populations and prisoners of war, S/RES/237 (June 14, 1967).

55. Shlaim, *Iron Wall*, pp. 285, 290–91.

56. Ibid., pp. 261–313.

57. "Report of the Secretary General under UN Security Council Resolution 331 (1973) of 20 April 1973," S/10929 (May 18, 1973), paras. 80–84.

58. Ahron Bregman, *Cursed Victory: A History of Israel and the Occupied Territories* (New York: Allen Lane, 2014), pp. 6–13. Among the resolutions of rebuke included UN General Assembly, Resolution 252, on reaffirming inadmissibility of acquisition of territory by force, A/RES/252 (May 21, 1968); UN Security Council, Resolution 267, calls on Israel to rescind annexation of East Jerusalem, S/RES/267 (July 3, 1969); and UN Security Council, Resolution 271, on destruction and profanation of holy places in Jerusalem, S/RES/271 (September 15, 1969).

59. Paul Thomas Chamberlin, *The Global Offensive: The United States, the Palestine Liberation Organization, and the Making of the Post-Cold War Order* (New York: Oxford University Press, 2021), p. 86; Chomsky, *Fateful Triangle*, pp. 20–27.

60. Chamberlin, *Global Offensive*, p. 136.

61. Arendt, "Zionism Reconsidered," p. 372.

62. The British UN ambassador and primary author of Resolution 242 later observed that the Palestinians were "not yet organized in their own cause." Caradon, "Security Council Resolution 242," p. 7. For a full account of the events discussed in this section, see Jonathan Graubart and Arturo Jimenez-Bacardi, "David in Goliath's Citadel: Mobilizing the Security Council's Normative Power for Palestine," *European Journal of International Relations* 22, no. 1 (2016): pp. 24–48.

63. Helena Cobban, *The Palestinian Liberation Organization: People, Power and Politics* (Cambridge: Cambridge University Press, 1984), p. 43. Originally, the PLO was subordinate to Egypt's President Nasser.

64. Graubart and Jimenez-Bacardi, "David in Goliath's Citadel," pp. 31–34.

65. Alain Gresh, *The PLO: The Struggle Within—towards an Independent Palestinian State* (London: Zed Books, 1985), p. 179.

66. Sally Morphet, "The Palestinians and the Right to Self Determination," in *Foreign Policy and Human Rights: Issues and Responses*, ed. R. J. Vincent (New York: Cambridge University Press), pp. 93–98.

67. Chamberlin, *Global Offensive*, pp. 93–98. In response, the Palestinian Front for the Liberation of Palestine led a "rejectionist front." Cobban, *Palestinian Liberation Organization*, p. 15.

68. UN General Assembly, Resolution 3236, "The Question of Palestine and the General Assembly," A/RES/3236 (November 22, 1974); UN General Assembly, Resolution 3237, "Observer Status for the Palestine Liberation Organization," A/RES/3237 (November 22, 1974).

69. Regina Sharif, "Latin America and the Arab-Israeli Conflict," *Journal of Palestine Studies* 7 (1977): p. 108; Bichara Khader, "Europe and the Arab-Israeli Conflict, 1973–1983: An Arab Perspective," in *European Foreign Policy-Making and the Arab-Israeli Conflict*, ed. David Allen and Alfred Pipers (The Hague: Martinus Nijjoff, 1984), pp. 168–70.

70. Graubart and Jimenez-Bacardi, "David in Goliath's Citadel," p. 34.

71. S/PV.1879, paras. 47, 53, UN Security Council, 1879th Meeting of Security Council, January 26, 1976.

72. Ibid., paras. 194–208.

73. China and Libya did not vote because they wanted stronger pro-Palestinian wording. Ibid., paras. 59–61.
74. Ibid., para. 116.
75. Ibid., para. 81.
76. UN Security Council, Resolution 446, "Territories Occupied by Israel," S/RES/446 (March 22, 1979).
77. UN Security Council, Resolution 471, "Territories Occupied by Israel," S/RES/471 (June 30, 1980); UN Security Council, Resolution 476, "Territories Occupied by Israel," S/RES/476 (June 30, 1980).
78. UN Security Council, Resolution 465, "Territories Occupied by Israel," S/RES/465 (March 1, 1980); UN Security Council, Resolution 471, "Territories Occupied by Israel," S/RES/471 (June 5, 1980).
79. UN Security Council, Resolution 478, "Territories Occupied by Israel," S/RES/478 (August 20, 1980).
80. Regarding Jerusalem, there was support both for the original idea of internationalizing Jerusalem and for making East Jerusalem the capital of the new state of Palestine.
81. EEC, "Resolutions of the Heads of Government and Ministers of Foreign Affairs of the European Council—Venice Declaration," July 13, 1980; Panayiotis Ifestos, *European Political Cooperation: Towards a Supranational Diplomacy* (Avebury: Aldershot, 1987), p. 460.
82. Ifestos, *European Political Cooperation*, pp. 440–60.
83. Gershon Shafir, *A Half-Century of Occupation: Israel, Palestine, and the World's Most Intractable Conflict* (Oakland: University of California Press, 2017), pp. 102–3. The prior Labor-led government under Rabin had begun the settlement expansion in 1975, but not with the same zeal or geographical scope as Begin's government.
84. Granted, Egypt's acceptance of UN envoy Jarring's proposal in 1971 was not a direct offer to Israel. Yet Israel rejected the proposal because it refused to withdraw to the pre-1967 border with Egypt.
85. Smith, *Palestine and the Arab-Israeli Conflict*, pp. 321–22. Kissinger facilitated two interim accords that included a partial Israeli withdrawal from the Sinai. Shlaim, *Iron Wall*, pp. 334–40.
86. Shlaim, *Iron Wall*, p. 359.
87. William Quandt, *Peace Process: American Diplomacy and the Arab-Israeli Conflict since 1967*, 3rd ed. (Washington, DC: Brookings Institution Press, 2005), pp. 237–42.
88. Seth P. Tillman, *The United States in the Middle East: Interests and Obstacles* (Bloomington: Indiana University Press, 1982), pp. 24–26.
89. Quandt, *Peace Process*, pp. 202–3, 237–38.
90. Ibid., p. 242n28.
91. Graubart and Jimenez-Bacardi, "David in Goliath's Citadel," p. 37.
92. Abba Eban, "Jarring, Lyndon Johnson, Richard Nixon and 242, 1967–1970," in Caradon et al., *U.N. Security Council Resolution 242*, p. 47.
93. Smith, *Palestine and the Arab-Israeli Conflict*, pp. 301–2.
94. Israel might then have been in position to reach a similar accord with Syria, following the latter's acceptance of 242. Ibid., pp. 315, 318.

95. The original Palestinian National Charter in 1964 stated that only "Jews who normally lived in Palestine until the beginning of the Zionist invasion" could remain after Palestine's liberation. Khalidi, *Iron Cage*, p. 189.

96. Although Israel ended martial rule in 1966, it retained a myriad of de jure and de facto discriminations. Robinson, *Citizen Strangers*.

97. Arendt, "To Save the Jewish Homeland," p. 396.

98. Chamberlin, *Global Offensive*, p. 140.

99. Jewish Telegraphic Agency, "Israel Says UN Resolution Will Not Affect Jerusalem's Status as Israel's Capital," August 22, 1980, https://www.jta.org/archive/israel-says-un-resolution-will-not-affect-jerusalems-status-as-capital.

100. Shlaim, *Iron Wall*, p. 311. Israeli officials, including Prime Minister Levi Eshkol, did consider granting partial autonomy to West Bank and Gaza Palestinians but abandoned the idea due to the inability to find credible Palestinian leaders to cooperate in such an initiative and to Israel's fear that such a scheme would legitimize the idea of Palestinian political rights. Ibid., pp. 255–62.

101. Israel Ministry of Foreign Affairs, "Statement to the Knesset by Foreign Minister Allon on UN General Assembly Resolution 3236 on Self-Determination to the Palestinian People," November 22, 1974; Chamberlin, *Global Offensive*, p. 256. Israel's position then was that the only Palestinian claim to a state was in Jordan.

102. UN Security Council, "1899th Meeting of the Security Council," March 25, 1976, S/PV.1899, para. 50.

103. Tom Segev, *The Seventh Million: The Israelis and the Holocaust* (New York: Holt Paperbacks, 1991), p. 399.

104. Jewish Telegraph Agency, "Palestinian Self-Determination Supported by Britain," June 13, 1980, https://www.jta.org/archive/palestinian-self-determination-supported-by-britain.

105. Rashid Khalidi, *Brokers of Deceit: How the U.S. Has Undermined Peace in the Middle East* (Boston: Beacon, 2014), p. 60.

106. Smith, *Palestine and the Arab-Israeli Conflict*, p. 436.

107. United Nations: The Question of Palestine, "Declaration of Principles on Interim Self-Government Arrangements," October 8, 1993, https://www.un.org/unispal/document/auto-insert-180015/.

108. Raja Shehadeh, *From Occupation to Interim Accords: Israel and the Palestinian Territories* (London: Kluwer Law International, 1997), p. 19–27. The accord mentions Resolution 242 but not any specific provision.

109. United Nations: The Question of Palestine, "Israeli-Palestinian Interim Agreement on the West Bank and the Gaza Strip," December 27, 1995, https://www.un.org/unispal/document/auto-insert-185434/.

110. Smith, *Palestine and the Arab-Israeli Conflict*, pp. 447–48.

111. Maoz, *Defending the Holy Land*, pp. 472–73.

112. Ibid., pp. 474–75.

113. Robert Malley and Hussein Agha, "Camp David: The Tragedy of Errors," *New York Review of Books*, August 9, 2001.

114. Ibid.

115. Ibid.

116. Ibid.
117. Khalidi, *Iron Cage*, pp. 179–80; Maoz, *Defending the Holy Land*, p. 471.
118. Smith, *Palestine and the Arab-Israeli Conflict*, p. 495.
119. Ibid., p. 406.
120. Ibid. p. 411.
121. Shehadeh, *From Occupation to Interim Accords*.
122. For example, Daniel Kurtzer, Scott Lasensky, and William Quandt, *The Peace Puzzle: America's Quest for Arab-Israeli Peace* (Ithaca, NY: Cornell University Press, 2012); Khalidi, *Brokers of Deceit*.
123. Kurtzer, Lasensky, and Quandt, *Peace Puzzle*, pp. 419–20. By "political" settlements, Rabin meant those he considered not necessary for Israel's security.
124. David Makovsky, *Making Peace with the PLO: The Rabin Government's Road to the Oslo Accord* (Boulder, CO: Westview, 1995), pp. 62–63.
125. Shehadeh, *From Occupation to Interim Accords*.
126. Quoted in Makovsky, *Making Peace with the PLO*, p. 66 (brackets and ellipses in original).
127. Smith, *Palestine and the Arab-Israeli Conflict*, pp. 448–49.
128. Malley and Agha, "Camp David"; Smith, *Palestine and the Arab-Israeli Conflict*, p. 485.
129. Smith, *Palestine and the Arab-Israeli Conflict*, p. 445.
130. Ibid., p. 451.
131. Ibid., pp. 452–53.

CHAPTER 5

1. Mordechai Bar-On, *In Pursuit of Peace: A History of the Israeli Peace Movements* (Washington, DC: United States Institute of Peace Press, 1996), pp. 14–22; David Hall-Cathala, *The Peace Movement in Israel, 1967–87* (London: Macmillan, 1990), p. 29.
2. Noam Chomsky, *American Power and the New Mandarins* (New York: Pantheon Books, 1969).
3. Noam Chomsky, *Peace in the Middle East? Reflections on Justice and Nationhood* (New York: Vintage Books, 1974), p. 50. Chomsky did not formally join Hashomer Hatzair because of its Leninist views.
4. Ibid., p. 75.
5. Ibid., p. 137.
6. The follow-up essay, "Israel and the Palestinians," is reprinted in Noam Chomsky, *Towards a New Cold War: Essays on the Current Crisis and How We Got There* (New York: Pantheon Books, 1982), pp. 229–64.
7. Chomsky, *Peace in the Middle East*, p. 136.
8. Ibid., pp. 12–13; Chomsky, "Israel and the Palestinians," p. 253. He tempered his criticism of the pre-state Hebrew labor policy by noting the desire of some socialist Zionists to create a Jewish working class rather than exploit indigenous labor.
9. Chomsky, *Peace in the Middle East*, p. 126.
10. Ibid., p. 127.
11. Ibid., p. 255.

12. Ibid., pp. 18–19.
13. Ibid., pp. 20–22.
14. Ibid., p. 62.
15. Ibid., pp. 153–98.
16. Ibid., p. 45n54.
17. Ibid., p. 183.
18. Ibid., pp. 76–77.
19. Chomsky, "Israel and the Palestinians," p. 231.
20. Ibid., p. 263.
21. Chomsky, *Peace in the Middle East*, p. 102; Chomsky, "Israel and the Palestinians," p. 263.
22. Chomsky, *Peace in the Middle East*, p. 38.
23. Ibid., p. 58.
24. Chomsky, "Israel and the Palestinians," p. 263.
25. Ibid., pp. 239–40.
26. Chomsky, *Peace in the Middle East*, pp. 9–10.
27. Chomsky, "Israel and the Palestinians," pp. 261–62.
28. Arendt, "Zionism Reconsidered," p. 351.
29. For example, Michael Walzer, "Noam Chomsky Argues, an Israeli and an Arab Talk," *New York Times Sunday Book Review*, October 6, 1974; Theodore Draper, "War between the States," *New Republic*, October 26, 1974.
30. Edward Said, "Chomsky and the Question of Palestine," *Journal of Palestine Studies* 4, no. 3 (1975): p. 91.
31. Uri Avnery, *Israel without Zionism: A Plan for Peace in the Middle East* (New York: Collier Books, 1971), p. 12.
32. To increase circulation, the journal included gossip columns and luring photos of women. Oren Meyers, "Contextualizing Alternative Zionism: *Haolam Hazeh* and the Birth of Critical Israeli Newsmaking," *Journalism Studies* 9, no. 3 (2008): pp. 374–91.
33. Uri Avnery, *Israel's Vicious Circle: Ten Years of Writing on Israel and Palestine* (London: Pluto, 2008).
34. Avnery, *Israel without Zionism*. Avnery added an epilogue in 1971.
35. Ibid., p. 214.
36. Ibid., pp. 228–29.
37. Ibid., p. 215.
38. Ibid., p. 214.
39. Ibid., pp. 238–39.
40. Ibid., p. 240.
41. Ibid., p. 97.
42. Ibid., p. 100.
43. Ibid., pp. 99, 183.
44. Ibid., p. 69.
45. Uri Avnery, "Zionists All," *Gush Shalom Blog*, January 31, 2015, http://zope.gush-shalom.org/home/en/channels/avnery/1422637382/. For an overview of post-Zionism, see Ephraim Nimni, ed., *The Challenge of Post-Zionism: Alternatives to Fundamentalist Politics in Israel* (London: Zed Books, 2003).
46. Avnery, *Israel without Zionism*, p. 74.

47. Ibid., p. 177.
48. Ibid., pp. 178–79.
49. Ibid., pp. 205–6.
50. Avnery, *Israel's Vicious Circle*, p. 35. Before the 1948 war, he had hoped to create a "new, joint nation."
51. Avnery, *Israel without Zionism*, p. 240.
52. Yeshayahu Leibowitz, "The Territories," reprinted in *Judaism, Human Values, and the Jewish State*, by Yeshayahu Leibowitz (Cambridge, MA: Harvard University Press, 1992), pp. 225–26.
53. Beinart, *Crisis of Zionism*, p. 3.
54. Ibid.
55. Ibid., pp. 16–17; Jerome Slater, "Zionism, the Jewish State, and an Israeli-Palestinian Settlement: An Opinion Piece," *Political Science Quarterly* 127, no. 4 (2011): pp. 607–11.
56. Beinart, *Crisis of Zionism*, p. 14; Gershon Gorenberg, *The Unmaking of Israel* (New York: HarperCollins, 2011), p. 7.
57. Beinart, *Crisis of Zionism*, p. 17; Slater, "Zionism," p. 611.
58. Beinart, *Crisis of Zionism*, p. 19.
59. Ibid., pp. 20–27; Gorenberg, *Unmaking of Israel*, pp. 195–220; David Grossman, *Death as a Way of Life: Israel Ten Years after Oslo* (New York: Farrar, Straus and Giroux, 2004), p. 186.
60. Beinart, *Crisis of Zionism*, p. 33.
61. For a general overview of Peace Now's origins and position in Israel's peace movement, see Bar-On, *In Pursuit of Peace*.
62. Eve Fairbanks, "The Battle to Be Israel's Conscience," *Guardian*, May 12, 2015. With its release of a report finding that Israel as a whole merits classification as an "apartheid regime," B'Tselem may have broken from liberal Zionism. B'Tselem, "Regime of Jewish Supremacy."
63. Haggai Matar, "Why Do So Many Israelis Hate Breaking the Silence?," *+972 Magazine*, December 14, 2015, https://972mag.com/why-do-so-many-israelis-hate-breaking-the-silence/114763/.
64. Ari Shavit, *My Promised Land: The Triumph and Tragedy of Israel* (New York: Spiegel and Grau, 2013).
65. Ibid., p. 131.
66. Gorenberg, *Unmaking of Israel*, p. 54.
67. The 1967 war did, however, produce a new wave of long-term Palestinian refugees.
68. Shavit, *My Promised Land*, p. 209. Such continuity explains why leading Labor Party figures supported the early settlement activity of Gush Emunim.
69. Avishai, *Hebrew Republic*, p. 150. Avishai is referencing the British-appointed grand mufti of Palestine, who fled to Nazi Germany after the Arab revolt and supported the Nazis.
70. Chaim Gans, *A Just Zionism: On the Morality of the Jewish State* (New York: Oxford University Press, 2008).
71. Ibid., pp. 9–11.
72. Given that Zionism was primarily a European Jewish phenomenon, Gans credits the Jewish Bund for asserting an equally compelling case for central-eastern Europe

as the site for Jewish self-determination. But because of the political unlikelihood of attaining sufficient outside support, he regards Palestine as a more viable site. What he seemingly argues, without making it explicit, is that the limited ability of the indigenous population to resist was another justification for choosing Palestine. Ibid., pp. 28–41.

73. Ibid., pp. 43–45. Gans is not clear on whether Jews would have been entitled to exercise cultural autonomy over the resistance of Palestinians. Presumably, this would turn on how Jews were seeking to attain such autonomy and what degree of bloodshed and injustice could be expected.

74. Ibid., pp. 47–49. Gans sympathizes with the pre-Nazi-era Zionist quest for a Jewish state based on the suffering faced by central and eastern European Jews since the 1880s. Nevertheless, he maintains that it was only Nazi rule that justified the displacement and bloodshed.

75. Ibid., p. 50.

76. Ibid., p. 69.

77. Ibid., pp. 76–78. Gans does not, however, categorically dismiss this justification.

78. Ibid., p. 79.

79. Ibid., pp. 94–95.

80. Ibid., pp. 56, 79.

81. Ibid., p. 93.

82. Ibid.

83. Ibid.

84. Ibid., pp. 126–27.

85. Ibid., p. 146.

86. A similar scenario occurred in March 1948 when the United States decided to support a trusteeship. Zionist forces were quick to go on the offensive. Victor Kattan, *From Coexistence to Conquest: International Law and the Origins of the Arab-Israeli Conflict, 1891–1949* (New York: Pluto, 2009), pp. 189–90.

87. See Pappé's opening statement in Uri Avnery and Ilan Pappé, "Two States or One State," Countercurrents.org, June 11, 2007, https://countercurrents.org/pappe110 607.htm.

88. Ilan Pappé, "The Old and New Conversations," in Noam Chomsky and Ilan Pappé, *On Palestine*, ed. Frank Barat (Chicago: Haymarket Books, 2015), p. 27.

89. Ibid.

90. Avnery and Pappé, "Two States or One State."

91. Mark Ellis, *Judaism Does Not Equal Israel* (New York: New Press, 2009), pp. 86–89.

92. Ellis, "Jew vs. Jew," p. 143.

93. Ibid., p. 155.

94. Marc Ellis, *Israel and Palestine out of the Ashes: The Search for Jewish Identity in the Twenty-First Century* (London: Pluto, 2002), pp. 53–54. In *Eichmann in Jerusalem*, Arendt identified a similar Holocaust theology in the way the Israeli government framed its prosecution of Eichmann.

95. Ellis, *Judaism Does Not Equal Israel*, p. xii.

96. Ibid., p. xv.

97. Ibid., p. 211.

98. Butler, *Parting Ways*, pp. 15, 117.

99. Avnery and Pappé, "Two States or One State."

100. Ilan Pappé, "The Futility and Immorality of Partition in Palestine," in Chomsky and Pappé, *On Palestine*, p. 177; Jeff Halper, "The Difficult Passage from a Two-State Solution to Decolonization of Israel-Palestine," *Mondoweiss*, July 17, 2019, https://mondoweiss.net/2019/07/difficult-decolonization-palestine/.

101. Ellis, *Judaism Does Not Equal Israel*, p. 177.

102. Pappé, "Futility and Immorality of Partition," p. 178.

103. Butler, *Parting Ways*, p. 216.

104. Pappé, "Futility and Immorality of Partition," p. 167.

105. Butler, *Parting Ways*, p. 213.

106. Avnery and Pappé, "Two States or One State."

107. Pappé, "Futility and Immorality of Partition," p. 178.

108. Ellis, *Judaism Does Not Equal Israel*, p. 174.

109. Ellis, *Out of the Ashes*, pp. 156–57.

110. Ibid., p. 157 (emphasis in original).

111. Ellis, *Judaism Does Not Equal Israel*, p. 174.

112. Ibid., pp. 184–85.

113. Butler, *Parting Ways*, p. 16.

114. Ellis, *Judaism Does Not Equal Israel*, p. 199.

115. Butler, *Parting Ways*, p. 28.

116. Ibid., p. 217.

117. Moshe Behar, "Competing Marxisms, Cessation of (Settler) Colonialism, and the One-State Solution in Israel-Palestine," in *The Arab and Jewish Questions: Geographies of Engagement in Palestine and Beyond*, ed. Bashir Bashir and Leila Farsakh (New York: Columbia University Press, 2020).

118. Partisans of Israel typically extend the definition of anti-Zionism—and, sometimes, antisemitism—to encompass strong criticisms of Israeli policies. Nevertheless, liberal Zionists, even if embattled, have managed to raise cutting criticisms without being excommunicated in mainstream Zionist circles.

119. Arendt, "To Save the Jewish Homeland," pp. 396–97.

120. Leibowitz, "Territories," pp. 223–28.

121. B'Tselem, "Regime of Jewish Supremacy."

CHAPTER 6

1. Edward W. Said, "The Palestinian Right of Return: An Interview with Ari Shavit," *Raritan* 20, no. 3 (2001): p. 52.

2. Edward W. Said, *The Question of Palestine* (New York: Vintage Books, 1992), p. xliv.

3. Edward W. Said, *Orientalism* (New York: Pantheon Books, 1978).

4. Said, *Question of Palestine*, p. xli.

5. Ibid., p. 8.

6. Chapter 2 of the book is entitled "Zionism from the Standpoint of Its Victims." Said first published a version of this chapter in a self-contained article for the now-defunct journal *Social Text*.

7. Said, *Question of Palestine*, p. 118.
8. Ibid., p. 84.
9. Ibid., pp. 101–2.
10. Ibid., p. 18.
11. Ibid., p. 21.
12. Ibid., pp. 28–29.
13. Ibid., p. 91.
14. Ibid., p. 45.
15. Ibid., p. 38.
16. Ibid., pp. 16–17 (emphasis in original).
17. Ibid., p. 30.
18. Ibid., p. 37.
19. Ibid., pp. 113, 25.
20. Ibid., p. xxxvi.
21. Ibid., p. 124.
22. Ibid., p. 158.
23. Ibid., p. 134.
24. Ibid., p. 178.
25. Ibid., p. 165.
26. Ibid., pp. 139–40.
27. Ibid., pp. 125, 139 (emphasis in original).
28. Ibid., p. 220.
29. Ibid., p. 159.
30. Ibid., p. 125.
31. Ibid., p. 177.
32. Ibid., p. 174.
33. Ibid., p. 122.
34. Ibid., p. 231.
35. Ibid., p. 49.
36. Ibid.
37. Ibid., p. 232.
38. Said, *Question of Palestine*, p. 175. Using similar reasoning, Leila Farsakh characterized the support for a separate Palestinian state as "the only currency the PLO could use in an international system that was constituted of nation-states and of nations' rights to self-determination." Leila Farsakh, "The One-State Solution and the Israeli-Palestinian Conflict: Palestinian Challenges and Prospects," *Middle East Journal* 65, no. 1 (2011): p. 59.
39. Said, *Question of Palestine*, pp. 52–53.
40. Ibid., pp. 175–76.
41. Edward W. Said, *The Politics of Dispossession: The Struggle for Palestinian Self-Determination, 1969–1994* (New York: Pantheon, 1994), p. xix.
42. For a careful articulation of favorable and unfavorable PLO traits, including in its early years, see Khalidi, *Iron Cage*, pp. 164–81.
43. Ibid., p. 194. Interestingly, *Question of Palestine* had been attacked in PLO circles for supporting a two-state resolution. Said, *Politics of Dispossession*, p. xxv.

44. Said, *Politics of Dispossession*, p. xxiii; Edward W. Said, "Where Do We Go from Here?," in Edward W. Said, *End of the Peace Process: Oslo and After* (New York: Vintage Books, 2001), p. 24.
45. Said, *Politics of Dispossession*, p. xxxii.
46. Edward W. Said, "Mandela, Netanyahu, and Arafat," in Said, *End of the Peace Process*, p. 68.
47. Said, *Politics of Dispossession*, p. xviii.
48. Ibid., p. xxi.
49. Ibid., p. xix.
50. Ibid., p. xxxii.
51. Edward W. Said, "The Context of Arafat's American Visit," in Said, *End of the Peace Process*, pp. 152–53.
52. Said, *Politics of Dispossession*, p. xxxiv.
53. Ibid., p. xxxv.
54. Edward W. Said, "Deir Yassin Recalled," in Said, *End of the Peace Process*, p. 158.
55. Edward W. Said, "Where Negotiations Have Led," in Said, *End of the Peace Process*, pp. 18–19.
56. Edward W. Said, "Elections, Institutions, Democracy," in Said, *End of the Peace Process*, pp. 36–37.
57. Edward W. Said, "Reflections on the Role of the Private Sector," in Said, *End of the Peace Process*, pp. 27–31.
58. Edward W. Said, "Responsibility and Accountability," in Said, *End of the Peace Process*, pp. 113–14.
59. Noam Chomsky, "The Responsibility of Intellectuals," reprinted in Chomsky, *American Power*, pp. 323–66.
60. Edward W. Said, "Intellectuals and the Crisis," in Said, *End of the Peace Process*, p. 122.
61. Edward W. Said, "New History, Old Ideas," in Said, *End of the Peace Process*, p. 276.
62. David Barsamian and Edward W. Said, *Culture and Resistance: Conversations with Edward W Said* (Cambridge, MA: South End, 2003), p. 20.
63. Edward W. Said, "The Tragedy Deepens," in Edward W. Said, *From Oslo to Iraq and the Road Map* (New York: Vintage Books, 2004), p. 29.
64. Said, "Tragedy Deepens," p. 30.
65. Edward W. Said, "Archaeology of the Road Map," in Said, *From Oslo to Iraq*, p. 286.
66. Edward W. Said, "Emerging Alternatives in Palestine," in Said, *From Oslo to Iraq*, pp. 145–46.
67. Said, "Archaeology of the Road Map," p. 287.
68. Edward W. Said, "Dignity and Solidarity," in Said, *From Oslo to Iraq*, p. 290.
69. Edward W. Said, "The Screw Turns Again," in Said, *From Oslo to Iraq*, p. 153.
70. Said, "Intellectuals and the Crisis," p. 123.
71. Edward W. Said, "Defiance, Dignity, and the Rule of Dogma," in Said, *From Oslo to Iraq*, p. 72.
72. Said, "Intellectuals and the Crisis," p. 123.

73. Ibid., p. 124.
74. Said, "Defiance, Dignity, and Dogma," p. 75.
75. Said, "Interview with Ari Shavit," p. 37.
76. Edward W. Said, "What Has Israel Done?," in Said, *From Oslo to Iraq*, p. 174.
77. Edward W. Said, "Bases for Coexistence," in Said, *End of the Peace Process*, pp. 207–8.
78. Edward W. Said, "Truth and Reconciliation," in Said, *End of the Peace Process*, p. 319 (emphasis in original).
79. Said, "Bases for Coexistence," p. 209.
80. Ibid., p. 208 (emphasis in original).
81. Edward W. Said, "Fifty Years of Dispossession," in Said, *End of the Peace Process*, pp. 271–72.
82. Edward W. Said, "Uprising against Oslo," in Said, *End of the Peace Process*, p. 112.
83. Said, "Interview with Ari Shavit," p. 44.
84. Said, "Truth and Reconciliation," p. 318.
85. Edward W. Said, "The Arab Condition," in Said, *From Oslo to Iraq*, p. 278.
86. Ibid., pp. 274–75.
87. Edward W. Said, "Making History: Constructing Reality," in Said, *End of the Peace Process*, p. 248.
88. Arendt, "Zionism Reconsidered," p. 372.
89. Said, "Interview with Ari Shavit," p. 46.
90. Ibid., p. 49.
91. Barsamian and Said, *Culture and Resistance*, p. 7.
92. Said, "Truth and Reconciliation," p. 318.
93. Said, "Interview with Ari Shavit," p. 49.
94. Said, "Truth and Reconciliation," p. 318.
95. Barsamian and Said, *Culture and Resistance*, p. 8.
96. Ibid., p. 5.
97. Edward W. Said, "Art, Culture, and Nationalism," in Said, *End of the Peace Process*, pp. 263–65.
98. Said, "Truth and Reconciliation," pp. 318–19.
99. Ella Shohat, "Arab Jews, Diasporas and Multicultural Feminism," in *On the Arab-Jew, Palestine and Other Displacements: Selected Writings* (London: Pluto, 2017), pp. 371–72.
100. Ella Shohat, "Sephardim in Israel: Zionism from the Standpoint of Its Jewish Victims," in *Prophets Outcast: A Century of Dissident Jewish Writing about Zionism and Israel*, ed. Adam Shatz (New York: Nation Books, 2004), pp. 278–322. At the time of the original publication, *Sephardim* was commonly used to encompass Jews from the greater Middle East. The term *Mizrahim* was introduced in the early 1990s by activists to better capture the origin of such Jews and their collective experiences in Israel. Ella Shohat, "The Invention of the Mizrahim," *Journal of Palestine Studies* 29, no. 1 (1999): pp. 13–14.
101. Like Said's chapter "Zionism from the Standpoint of Its Victims," Shohat's essay originally appeared in the journal *Social Text*.
102. Shohat, "Sephardim in Israel," p. 278 (emphasis in original).
103. Ibid., pp. 317–18.

104. Ibid., pp. 282–83.
105. Ibid., p. 286.
106. Ibid., p. 280.
107. Ibid., p. 296. Tom Segev provides dramatic support for Shohat's claim in remarking on Ben-Gurion's close identification of Zionism with Europe's Jews. Ben-Gurion decried Hitler's genocide of Europe's Jews because it "destroyed the substance, the main and essential building force for the state. The state arose and did not find the nation which had waited for it." Segev, *1949*, p. 157.
108. As early as 1942, Ben-Gurion concluded that because of the Holocaust taking place, it was necessary to begin a large-scale recruitment of Mizrahim. Yehouda Shenhav, *The Arab-Jews: A Postcolonial Reading of Nationalism, Religion, and Ethnicity* (Palo Alto, CA: Stanford University Press, 2006), pp. 26–31.
109. Shohat, "Sephardim in Israel," pp. 297–300.
110. For a full account of Israel's absorption of Mizrahim arrivals, see Sami Shalom Chetrit, *Intra-Jewish Conflict in Israel: White Jews, Black Jews* (London: Routledge, 2010), pp. 43–80.
111. Shohat, "Sephardim in Israel," pp. 300–303.
112. Ibid., pp. 306–7.
113. Ibid., p. 304.
114. Shohat, *On the Arab-Jew*, p. 6.
115. Shohat, "Invention of the Mizrahim," p. 11.
116. Shohat, *On the Arab-Jew*, p. 6.
117. Shohat, "Sephardim in Israel," p. 307.
118. Shohat, "Invention of the Mizrahim," p. 11.
119. Shohat, "Sephardim in Israel," pp. 290–91.
120. Ella Shohat, "A Voyage to Toledo: Twenty-Five Years after the 'Jews of the Orient and Palestinians' Meeting," in Shohat, *On the Arab-Jew*, p. 216.
121. Shohat, "Invention of the Mizrahim," p. 8. Said also found the objections to the invitation as "outrageous and unacceptable." Said, "Art, Culture, and Nationalism," p. 263.
122. Shohat, *On the Arab-Jew*, p. 1.
123. For more on the origin of Israel adopting the population exchange view, see Shenhav, *Arab-Jews*, pp. 129–33.
124. Shohat, *On the Arab-Jew*, p. 6.
125. Ibid., pp. 5–6.
126. Ibid., p. 5.
127. Shohat, "Sephardim in Israel," p. 290. For more on Israeli operations in Iraq, see Segev, *1949*, pp. 165–67.
128. Shohat, *On the Arab-Jew*, p. 6.
129. Shohat, "Sephardim in Israel," p. 317.
130. Shohat, "Invention of the Mizrahim," p. 18.
131. For details, see Sami Shalom Chetrit, "Mizrahi Politics in Israel between Integration and Alternative," *Journal of Palestine Studies* 29, no. 4 (2000): pp. 51–65.
132. Shohat, "Sephardim in Israel," p. 309.
133. Ibid., p. 307.
134. Ibid., p. 308.

135. W. E. B. Du Bois, *Black Reconstruction in America, 1860–1880* (New York: Free Press, 1998), p. 256; Shohat, "Sephardim in Israel," p. 309.
136. Shohat, *On the Arab-Jew*, p. 33.
137. Shohat, "Voyage to Toledo," p. 209.
138. Ella Shohat, "The Narrative of the Nation and the Discourse of Modernization: The Case of the Mizrahim," *Critique*, Spring 1997, p. 18.
139. Shohat, "Sephardim in Israel," p. 315.
140. Ibid., pp. 313–16.
141. Chetrit, "Mizrahi Politics in Israel."
142. Shohat, "Voyage to Toledo," p. 220.
143. Said, "Truth and Reconciliation," pp. 318–19. He was especially impressed with Judah Magnes as "a man way ahead of his time." Barsamian and Said, *Culture and Resistance*, p. 8.
144. Farsakh, "One-State Solution," p. 70.
145. Leila Farsakh, "A Common State in Israel-Palestine: Historical Origins and Lingering Challenges," *Ethnopolitics* 15, no. 4 (2016): p. 385.
146. Farsakh, "One-State Solution," p. 70.
147. Ibid., pp. 70–71.
148. "Young Mizrahi Israelis' Open Letter to Arab Peers," *+972 Magazine*, August 1, 2011, https://www.972mag.com/young-mizrahi-israelis-open-letter-to-arab-peers/.
149. Orly Nor, "Meet the Mizrahi Activists Who Support the Joint List," *+972 Magazine*, March 19, 2016, https://www.972mag.com/meet-the-mizrahi-activists-who-support-the-joint-list/.
150. Said, "Truth and Reconciliation," p. 318.
151. Leila Farsakh, "The 'Right to Have Rights': Partition and Palestinian Self-Determination," *Journal of Palestine Studies* 47, no. 1 (2017): p. 64.
152. Behar, "Competing Marxisms," pp. 235–39.
153. Farsakh, "One-State Solution," p. 61.
154. Farsakh, "Right to Have Rights," p. 65.

CONCLUSION

1. Beinart, "Yavne," p. 6.
2. Mouin Rabbani, "Can the Question of Palestine Be Resolved?," *Jadaliyya*, September 13, 2021, https://www.jadaliyya.com/Details/43313.
3. Eldar, "Is Israel Inching Closer?"
4. Butler, *Parting Ways*, pp. 18–19.
5. Ibid., p. 24.
6. Ibid., p. 18.
7. Ibid., p. 19.
8. Greenstein, *Zionism and Its Discontents*, p. 193.
9. Michael Omer-Man, "JVP Just Declared Itself Anti-Zionist and It's Already Shifting the Conversation," *+972 Magazine*, January 30, 2019, https://972mag.com/jvp-anti-zionist-rebecca-vilkomerson-2/139912/.
10. Said, "Interview with Ari Shavit," p. 44.
11. Arendt, "Peace or Armistice," pp. 435–36.

12. Rose, *Question of Zion*, p. 69.
13. Butler, *Parting Ways*, p. 36.
14. Ibid., p. 86.
15. Raz-Krakotzkin, "Binationalism and Jewish Identity," p. 173.
16. Graubart and Jimenez-Bacardi, "David in Goliath's Citadel."
17. Ibid.
18. Rabbani, "Question of Palestine."
19. Nathan Thrall, *The Only Language They Understand: Forcing Compromise in Israel and Palestine* (New York: Metropolitan Books, 2017).
20. Lerman, "End of Liberal Zionism."
21. Beinart, "Yavne," p. 6.
22. Ian S. Lustick, *Paradigm Lost: From Two-State Solution to One-State Reality* (Philadelphia: University of Pennsylvania Press, 2019), pp. 127, 3.
23. Ibid., p. 118.
24. Beinart, "Yavne," p. 7.
25. Ibid., p. 6.
26. Ibid., p. 8.
27. Lustick, *Paradigm Lost*, p. 128.
28. Rabbani, "Question of Palestine," p. 4.
29. Ibid., p. 5.
30. Lustick, *Paradigm Lost*, p. 131.
31. Ibid., p. 137.
32. Ibid., pp. 146–47.
33. Ibid., p. 146.
34. Rabbani, "Question of Palestine," p. 13.
35. Graubart and Jimenez-Bacardi, "David in Goliath's Citadel."
36. For an overview, see "Legal Consequences of the Construction of a Wall in the Occupied Palestinian Territory," International Court of Justice, accessed September 16, 2022, https://www.icj-cij.org/en/case/131.
37. Graubart and Jimenez-Bacardi, "David in Goliath's Citadel," p. 40.
38. Peter Beaumont, "Why Israel Fears the ICC War Crimes Investigation," *Guardian*, March 3, 2021, https://www.theguardian.com/law/2021/mar/03/israeli-officials-start-to-feel-the-impact-of-icc-investigation.
39. "Countries That Recognize Palestine 2022," World Population Review, accessed September 16, 2022, https://worldpopulationreview.com/country-rankings/countries-that-recognize-palestine.
40. Graubart and Jimenez-Bacardi, "David in Goliath's Citadel," p. 40; Rabbani, "Question of Palestine," p. 14.
41. Nathan Thrall, "BDS: How a Controversial Non-violent Movement Has Transformed the Israeli-Palestinian Debate," *Guardian*, August 14, 2018, https://www.theguardian.com/news/2018/aug/14/bds-boycott-divestment-sanctions-movement-transformed-israeli-palestinian-debate; "UN Lists 112 Businesses Linked to Israeli Settlements," BBC World News, February 12, 2020, https://www.bbc.com/news/world-middle-east-51477231.
42. Rabbani, "Question of Palestine," p. 16.
43. Thrall, "BDS," p. 13.

44. Noam Chomsky, "On Israel, Palestine, and BDS," *Nation*, July 21–28, 2014.

45. Greenstein, *Zionism and Its Discontents*, pp. 203–5.

46. Ibid., p. 205.

47. Thrall, "BDS."

48. Rabbani, "Question of Palestine," p. 17.

49. Nathan Thrall, "Israel-Palestine: The Real Reason There's Still No Peace," *Guardian*, May 16, 2017, https://www.theguardian.com/world/2017/may/16/the-real-reason-the-israel-palestine-peace-process-always-fails.

50. Ibid., p. 3.

51. Rabbani, "Question of Palestine," p. 18.

52. Ibid., p. 19.

53. Avnery, *Israel's Vicious Circle*, p. 56. Avnery was chiding one-state advocates.

54. Omar H. Rahman, "The 'State-Plus' Framework: A Confederal Solution for Israel-Palestine" (Brookings Doha Center Analysis Paper No. 29, December 2020); Bernard Avishai and Sam Bahour, "Want Israeli-Palestinian Peace? Try Confederation," *New York Times*, February 12, 2021; Dahlia Scheindlin, "The Confederation Alternative for Israel and Palestine," Century Foundation, February 3, 2020, https://tcf.org/content/report/confederation-alternative-israel-palestine/?agreed=1.

55. "From Conflict to Reconciliation: A New Vision for Palestinian-Israeli Peace," A Land for All, accessed September 16, 2022, https://www.alandforall.org/wp-content/uploads/2021/02/booklet-english.pdf, p. 2.

56. Ibid., pp. 4–6. The plan allows for an initial limit on the overall number of residency rights to avoid "inundation." The overall principle, however, will be to freely grant residency rights.

57. Among these groups are Courage to Refuse, the Israeli Committee against House Demolitions, Ta'ayush, Breaking the Silence, and B'Tselem.

58. Arendt, "To Save the Jewish Homeland," p. 401.

Index

Ahad Ha'am, 20, 29
American Israel Public Affairs Committee (AIPAC), 15, 160
American Jewish establishment, 1, 15–17, 105, 107–108, 118, 124, 148, 160
American Jewry, 40, 79, 114
Amnesty International, 12, 154
Anglo-American Committee (1946), 5, 44, 46, 112
Anti-Defamation League (ADL), 15–16, 160
Antisemitism, 16, 75, 111, 113, 118, 140; International Holocaust Remembrance Alliance definition, 16; politicization, 15–16
Arab nationalism, 46, 109, 137, 139–141, 144
Arab revolt, 36–37, 40
Arafat, Yasser, 88–91, 93, 130–131
Arendt, Hannah, 6–10, 49–74, 76, 82, 87, 95–96, 101–102, 112–117, 119–120, 122–124, 129–130, 132, 135–136, 143, 148, 160–161; Antisemitism, 7, 16, 50–61, 64–69, 71, 140; Capitalism, 54–56; continental imperialism, 55–59; Courting imperialists, 51, 59–64, 118; Eurocentrism, 10, 116, 122–123; European Jewish experience, 49–59, 61–62, 66, 68; Herzl, 49, 58, 60–63, 68–69; Hobson, 55–56; Holocaust, 67–68; Imperialism, 7, 51, 54–59, 61; Internationalism, 69–72; Jewish notables, 52–55, 61–62; Kibbutz, 59–60, 65–66; Lazare, Daniel, 58–59, 68; Magnes, Judah, 59, 65–66; Multinational federation, 50, 59, 65; Nationalism and nation-state, 7, 50–60, 63, 68, 71; Non-Zionist Jews, 65; Palestinians, 62–66, 72; Pan-nationalist movements, 54–59; Solidarity of oppressed, 58–59, 62, 64; Statelessness, 57–58, 65–66; tribal nationalism, 7, 51–54, 56–59, 68–69, 71, 118–119, 139; World War I, 56–57; Zionist attachment, 50, 59–60, 67–70
Ashkenazi Jews, 137–138, 141–144
Avishai, Bernard, 110
Avnery, Uri, 9, 70, 96–97, 102–105, 115, 159; alternative two-state federation, 97, 102–103, 105, 155; replace Jewish nationalism with Hebrew nationalism, 97, 103–104; refugees, 102

Balfour Declaration, 21, 24, 35, 38, 126, 161; Balfour, Arthur, 126

Barak, Ehud, 90–91, 94
Barghouti, Omar, 18, 146
Begin, Menachem, 88
Beinart, Peter, 3, 8, 10–12, 17–22, 97, 106–108, 114, 119, 147–148, 152–153, 155–158; abandons two-state advocacy, 152–153; as conventional liberal Zionist, 106–108
Ben-Gurion, David, 3, 5, 19–21, 26–27, 34, 37, 40, 44–46, 67, 74, 76, 79–80, 138
Benjamin, Walter, 142
Bennet, Naftali, 15
Bernadotte, Folke, 66
Biden, Joseph, 16
Binational program and advocacy, 3–5, 8, 10, 18–22, 27, 39–42, 44, 46, 112, 121, 146, 148, 150, 153, 159–161
Biltmore Program, 20–21, 39
Boehm, Omri, 3, 8, 11–12, 17–22
Boycott, Divestment, Sanctions (BDS), 16, 70, 116, 146, 157, 159–160
Britain, 5, 8, 41; British Mandate of Palestine, 4, 12, 21, 24; favoring Zionists, 21, 113
Brit Shalom, 4, 19, 23, 26–28, 32, 38, 43, 63, 101
B'Tselem, 1, 12, 108, 119, 154
Buber, Martin, 4–11, 22–49, 62, 65, 73–74, 78, 80, 91, 96, 112–114, 116–117, 119–120, 122–123, 128, 136, 143–144, 148, 150; Coexistence with Palestinians, 23, 30–35, 44–45, 119; Community-based socialism, 29–30; Eurocentrism, 10, 116, 122–123; Gandhi, Mohandas, 31–32; Hebrew humanism, 4, 6, 27–30, 44; Herzl, Theodore, 28–29; Importance of dissent, 41; Kibbutzim, 29–30; Opposition to courting imperialists, 35; Palestinian citizens of Israel, 44–45; Palestinian refugees, 23, 44; Political surplus, 6, 32–33, 44, 48; Reckoning with Zionist impact on Palestinians, 6, 31, 33, 35, 48, 119; Regional federation, 23, 45
Butler, Judith, 97, 113–117, 120–121, 148–150

Camp David Summit (2000), 90–92, 105, 151

Carter, Jimmy, 85
Chomsky, Noam, 9, 70, 96–105, 107, 111, 114, 120–121, 129, 132, 135, 157; Attacked by mainstream American Jewish figures, 101–102; Attraction to Zionism, 98; Challenging meaning of "pro-Israel," 99–102, 120; Contradictions of Jewish and democratic, 99–102; Courting U.S.-anchored imperialism, 99–102, 119; Decrying chauvinism and conformity in American Jewish community, 97–100, 119; Discrimination toward Palestinians, 98–99; Israeli militarism, 97; Radicalizing two-state program, 97, 100, 102, 155; Socialist binationalism and internationalism, 97, 100–101, 121
Clinton, Bill, 90–91
Conflict escalation, 79, 90–91, 94

Demolition of Palestinian structures, 13–14
Displaced Jews, 78, 112
Dissenting Zionists pre-state era, 4–5, 23–48, 96, 150
Du Bois, W.E.B., 142

East Jerusalem, 12–13, 47, 74, 77, 81–82, 85, 90, 102–103, 115, 125, 151–152, 156; Judaize area, 12–13
Eban, Abba, 43, 86
Egypt, 70, 76–77, 82–83, 86, 131, 140
Eichmann in Jerusalem, 5, 67–70; crimes against humanity, 68–69; Hausner Gideon, 67
Einstein, Albert, 5
Ellis, Mark, 2, 48, 97, 113–117, 119–121; Coexistence, 116–117; Constantinian Judaism, 2, 17, 114, 117–120; Holocaust theology, 114; Jews of conscience, 114, 120; Reckoning, 116–117; Revolutionary forgiveness, 116, 119; Vision of Jewish liberation, 114–115
European ethno-nationalism, 19–20

Farsakh, Leila, 143–146
First intifada, 91
France, 76–77, 83–84

Galilee, 14–15, 76, 114
Gans, Chaim, 97, 110–113; Jewish right to hegemonic state, 110–111; two-state support, 111; obligation to Palestinians, 110–112
Gaza Strip, 8, 12–13, 47, 74, 84–85, 87, 89, 115, 125, 127, 131, 158; military offensives, 13
Global consensus post-1948, 75–76, 78, 105, 109
Global consensus post-1980, 9–10, 81, 84–85, 87, 89–90, 115, 148, 151, 153, 156, 158–159
Gorenberg, Gershon, 107
Greenblatt, Jonathan, 16
Greenstein, Ran, 47, 157
Gush Emunim, 109, 154

Hamas, 89, 91–92
Haram al-Sharif, 90–91
Hashomer Hatzair, 39–40, 65
Hebrew labor, 27, 63
Hebrew University, 5, 59
Herzl, Theodore, 19
Holocaust, 18–20, 78, 133–134, 138, 141, 144
Humanist Zionists: anti-imperialists, 5, 25–26, 39–40; Eurocentric, 120, 122, 143; Orientalist, 144
Human Rights Watch, 12, 154

Ihud, 4–5, 8, 23, 38–44, 63, 65, 144–145
International Criminal Court investigation, 156
Iraq, 137–138, 140
Irgun, 37, 102
Israel: absentee property law, 77; apartheid, 1, 12, 81, 119; Black Panthers, 143, 145; courting of imperialism, 97, 109, 112, 118; Declaration of Independence, 45, 77, 79; hostility to UN and to international law, 79–80, 82, 87–88; killing of Rabin, 94; land-use system, 77; Law of Return, 78, 135; Martial Law, 42, 45, 77, 80, 87, 109, 125; militarism, 8, 79, 81, 97, 106, 114, 118–119; nationality law, 78; National Religious camp, 93–95, 105, 107, 109, 157; treaty with Egypt, 85–86

Israeli Defense Forces, 13, 79, 106–107
Israeli extremism and intolerance, 14–15, 94–95, 107, 118, 148, 152, 154

Jabotinsky, Ze'ev, 19–22, 27, 32
Jarring, Gunnar, 82, 87
Jaspers, Karl, 70, 72, 123
Jerusalem, 75–76, 79–80, 84, 87, 91–92, 94, 109, 115, 151, 159–160
Jewish Agency, 21
Jewish anti-Zionists, 2–4, 10, 97, 105, 113–120, 148–149
Jewish Currents, 160
Jewish immigrants and immigration, 79–80, 111
Jewish National Fund, 13, 77
Jewish nationalism, 75, 79; tribal nationalism, 74, 80, 87–88, 93–95, 112, 118, 137, 140–144
Jewish Nation-State Law, 1, 15
Jewish-Palestinian coexistence, solidarity, and reconciliation, 97, 115, 117, 144–145, 148, 150, 158–161
Jewish reckoning with Zionism's harms, 97, 109, 112, 115, 120, 148, 150
Jewish self-determination alternative, 7, 47, 117–118, 120–121, 148, 150, 153, 162
Jewish Voice for Peace, 2, 148, 160
Jordan, 75, 77–78, 82–83, 86, 88; King Abdullah, 75, 79

Kibbutzim, 7, 125
King-Crane Commission, 20–21
Knesset, 1, 85; restrictive laws on Palestinian citizens, 14, 48, 80

Labor Party, 85, 88, 90
Labor Zionists, 34
Land for All, 159–160
League of Jewish-Arab Rapprochement (LJAR), 39, 44
Leibowitz, Yeshayahu, 70, 106, 119
Lerman, Antony, 1, 151–152
Liberal Zionists, 2–4, 10, 17–18, 97, 105–113, 115, 152; American liberal Zionists, 107–108; Jewish and democratic state, 2–3, 17, 107–111
Likud, 2, 15, 19, 84, 85, 88, 90, 93, 106, 142
Lustick, Ian, 10, 148, 152–156

Madrid talks, 92–93, 131
Magnes, Judah, 5–6, 23, 35, 37–42, 112, 136, 143; collaboration with Buber, 38–42; death, 42; Hebrew University president, 37; opponent of imperialism and nationalism, 37–38, "radical liberal," 38; well-regarded in U.S., 40
Maoz, Zeev, 79
Meir, Golda, 82, 88
Mizrahim, 9–10, 47–48, 72, 120, 122–123, 136–145; Arab Jew, 139–141, 145; critics of Zionism, 136, 139–140, 143, 145; mass displacement, 140–141, 144; Sephardim, 137–138, 142
Morocco, 138, 140
Morris, Benny, 5

Nakba, 3, 6, 19, 42, 48, 75, 98–99, 109, 111, 113–114, 118, 125–126, 134, 140–141, 144
Nasser, Gamal Abdel, 70, 77, 127
Nazi Germany, 35–36, 62, 81, 112
Negev, 14–15, 76
Netanyahu, Benjamin, 1, 14–15, 90, 93–94
Niebuhr, Reinhard, 126
1929 violence, 27, 31
1948 War, 42
1956 War, 77, 86
1967 War, 9, 46, 70, 81, 86, 107
1973 War, 70, 85
Nixon, Richard, 82
Non-Aligned Movement (NAM), 83–85, 151, 155–156

Occupation, 2, 9, 46, 70, 74, 81, 84, 89, 92, 105, 107–109, 113, 118–119, 126–127, 134, 148, 151, 153–154, 157–159; outside condemnation, 156–157
One-state program and advocacy, 2, 18, 115–116, 146, 152, 156–157
Origins of Totalitarianism, 8–9, 68
Oslo accord and peace process, 10, 88–95, 105, 107, 148, 150–151; Declaration of Principles, 89; permanent status issues, 89; Oslo 2, 89; Areas A, B, and C, 89
Ottoman Empire, 20, 62

Palestinian Authority (PA), 89–90, 94, 131–132, 151

Palestinian Liberation Organization (PLO), 70, 83–89, 91, 93, 100, 105, 127, 129–130, 139–140; Declaration of state, 91, 130; resolutions at UN, 83–88, 151, 155–156
Palestinian National Council, 127, 130
Palestinian National Initiative, 132–133
Palestinians: citizens of Israel, 13–14, 17–18, 44–45, 75, 77–80, 87, 108–109, 136, 145–146, 157–159; observer status at UN, 156, 160; refugees, 2, 6, 42–44, 75–78, 80, 81–83, 86–87, 109, 111, 115, 151, 157, 159–160
Palestinian state, 2, 74, 84–85, 88–90, 105, 107, 109, 115, 129, 131, 151, 154, 156, 159
Pan-Arabism, 76, 83, 85, 127
Pappé, Ilan, 97, 103, 113, 115
Pariahs, 49, 58–59, 72–73, 114, 120, 161
Peace Now, 108, 143
Peel Commission, 19–21, 36–38; compulsory transfer, 36–38
Political surplus, 93, 112

Qibya, 66

Rabbani, Mouin, 147, 151, 154–158, 160
Rabin, Yitzhak, 87–90, 92–94, 105
Raz-Krakotzkin, Amnon, 150
Revisionist Zionism, 19–20, 22, 27, 63, 79
Right of return, 2–3, 113, 131, 135
Rogers Plan, 81–83
Rose, Jacqueline, 4, 148–149

Sadat, Anwar, 85, 130
Said, Edward, 4, 7, 10, 48, 72, 102, 120–121, 122–137, 142–146, 148, 150, 158; Binational advocacy, 135–136; Criticism of Palestinian leaders and society, 123, 129–132; Jewish reckoning, 129, 133–134, 143; Nationalism, 135–136; One-state advocacy, 135–136, 158; Oslo accord and process, 124, 129–131, 134; Outreach to Jews and reconciliation, 123, 125, 128–130, 133–136, 143; Palestinian idea of liberation, 123, 125–128, 130–133, 145; *Question of Palestine*, 124–129, 132, 143;

Settler-colonialism, 125; Shared history, 120, 129, 134, 144, 148, 160; Zionist Orientalism, 123, 125–126, 143–144
Scholem Gershom, 5, 68, 73
Second intifada, 4, 9, 75, 88, 93, 105, 133
Separation barrier, 12–13
Settlements, 2, 12–13, 81, 84–85, 87, 89–90; 92–94, 105, 107–108, 115, 131, 134, 151–154, 158, 160
Settler-colonialism, 113, 117–118, 144, 146
Sharett, Moshe, 80
Sharon, Ariel, 91, 94
Shavit, Ari, 108–109, 123, 135–136, 143
Shohat, Ella, 10, 48, 72, 121, 123, 137–146; Discrimination and disparaging of Mizrahi Jews in Israel, 137–144; Homogenous nationalism, 139–142, 144–145; Mizrahi anti-Arab views, 141–142; Mizrahi-Arab reconciliation, 137, 142–143; Shared Mizrahi-Arab history, 137, 140–142; Zionist Orientalism toward Mizrahim, 137–144; Zionist reckoning, 141, 144
Shumsky, Dmitry, 8, 18–21
Siege mentality, 79, 82, 93, 95, 109, 112, 118
South Africa, 18, 157
Soviet Union, 66, 82–83, 85–86
Sternhell, Zeev, 1, 147–148
Stone, I. F., 99
Syria, 76, 85, 90; Zaim, Husnei, 76
Szold, Henrietta, 5, 39

Thrall, Nathan, 157
Tikkun Magazine, 108
Truman, Harry, 40, 77, 112
Trump, Donald, 1, 16
Twelfth Zionist Congress, 4, 23–26
Two-State program and advocacy, 2, 3, 10, 87, 89, 91–92, 105, 107–108, 111, 115, 117–118, 130, 146–148, 151–152; antiestablishment version, 10, 97, 117, 129, 134, 148, 150–151, 155, 158–160; point-of-no-return opposition, 153–154; weaker post-Oslo version, 10, 115, 151, 153

United Nations, 5–6, 42–43, 74, 78–79, 82–83, 85–86, 91, 156
UN General Assembly Resolution 181 (Partition Plan), 5–6, 41–2, 46, 75–77, 111, 131
UN General Assembly Resolution 194, 75–76, 86
UN Lausanne Conference, 75–76, 78, 87; Israel's belligerency, 76; Palestinian Conciliation Commission, 76; U.S. delegate, 76, 79
UN Security Council Resolution 242, 81, 83–84, 86
UN Special Commission on Palestine, 41
U.S. isolation from global consensus, 83–84, 151
U.S.-Israeli relationship, 9, 74, 76–77, 81–82, 97, 105, 109, 118, 158, 160

Walzer, Michael, 99, 102, 111
Weizmann, Chaim, 26–27, 37, 126
West Bank, 12–13, 47, 74–77, 81–82, 84–85, 87, 89, 102–103, 114–115, 125, 127, 131, 151–152, 154, 156, 158; Areas A, B, and C, 89; Area C, 13, 15; bypass roads and checkpoints, 90, 94, 131, 134; Demolitions, 13, 15

Yishuv, 4, 7, 25, 31, 34, 36–38, 117

Zionism: corrupting impact on Jewish community in U.S. and elsewhere, 15–17, 107, 119; foundational leaders and ideas, 4, 7–8, 12, 17–22, 112, 117–118; imperialist support, 6, 20–21; Mainstream, 8, 18–20, 22, 40; non-statist, 3, 8, 12, 17–21, 65; social justice foundational ideals, 4, 7, 117–118, 120, 148

Jonathan Graubart is Professor of Political Science at San Diego State University. He is on the Academic Advisory Council for both Jewish Voice for Peace and Open Hillel and is the author of *Legalizing Transnational Activism: The Struggle to Gain Social Change from NAFTA's Citizen Petitions*.